haunting legacies

haunting
legacies

VIOLENT HISTORIES AND
TRANSGENERATIONAL TRAUMA

Gabriele Schwab

 Columbia University Press   New York

Columbia University Press
Publishers Since 1893
New York   Chichester, West Sussex
Copyright © 2010 Columbia University Press

Library of Congress Cataloging-in-Publication Data
Schwab, Gabriele.
Haunting legacies : violent histories and transgenerational
trauma / Gabriele Schwab.
p. cm.
Includes bibliographical references and index.
ISBN 978-0-231-15256-3 (cloth : alk. paper) — ISBN 978-0-231-15257-0
(pbk. : alk. paper) — ISBN 978-0-231-52635-7 (e-book)
1. Holocaust, Jewish (1939–1945), in literature. 2. Violence in literature.
3. Psychic trauma in literature. 4. Children of Holocaust survivors—
Psychology. 5. Holocaust, Jewish (1939–1945)—Psychological aspects.
6. World War, 1939–1945—Psychological aspects. 7. Violence—
Psychological aspects. 8. Psychoanalysis and literature. I. Title.

PN56.H55S33 2010
809'.93358405318—dc22
2010007110

∞
Columbia University Press books are printed on permanent and durable
acid-free paper.
This book is printed on paper with recycled content.
Printed in the United States of America

c 10 9 8 7 6 5 4 3 2 1
p 10 9 8 7 6 5 4 3 2 1

References to Internet Web sites (URLs) were accurate at the time of writing. Neither the author nor Columbia University Press is responsible for URLs
that may have expired or changed since the manuscript was prepared.

For Leon

Contents

Preface

In the summer of 2003, I wrote the essay titled "Haunting Legacies: Trauma in Children of Perpetrators." At the time, I did not plan a book, but the topic took over. For several years, I had already felt the urgency to write about my growing up in Germany after WWII. I was in training analysis at the time and in the process of dealing in depth with having grown up in the wake of one of the most atrocious genocides in history. I needed further to explore what it meant to me as a child to live in post-war Germany, especially after finding out about the Holocaust in the early years of high school. After September 11, 2001, and the invasion of Iraq in March of 2003, it became more pressing to deal with violent histories, not only of my home country but also more generally. For the first time I felt like a bystander, a position I had harshly condemned in the German war generation. I needed to face the violence committed by the United States, my country of residence, which had been my home for more than twenty years. It no longer seemed enough to march for peace carrying a sign that read "Not in our Name!" or to wear blue stickers with the names of people recently disappeared under the Bush administration. I realized that in my own case, doing more first meant dealing with the legacy of violence I had inherited. This is why the Holocaust and Germany are at the center of *Haunting Legacies*, but I hope that my interspersed reflections on other violent histories such as colonialism and slavery demonstrate that my main theoretical explorations and arguments are pertinent to violent histories and transgenerational haunting more generally.

Three of my colleagues and close friends had a particularly strong impact on *Haunting Legacies*, and their work provides the material for some of the chapters: Ruth Kluger, Ngũgĩ wa Thiong'o, and Simon J. Ortiz. Ruth Kluger, a child survivor of the Holocaust, began writing her memoir *Weiterleben* (*Still Alive*) in the wake of an episode of heart failure after which her doctors gave her only a few more years to live. While Kluger's memoir, on which I draw in several chapters, deals with living in the wake of the Holocaust, writing also *became* her way of living on in the wake of a medical death sentence. This happened about two decades ago, and Ruth is still alive and as vital as ever. Her book, our many talks, and her joyful energy and resilient spirit have inspired me deeply.

Ngũgĩ wa Thiong'o's work, especially his theoretical essays and his prison diary, strongly shaped my thinking on the mental effects of violent histories. *Decolonizing the Mind* and *Detained: A Writer's Prison Diary*, in particular, were invaluable to my thinking about the psychic life of colonization, imprisonment, and torture. Ngũgĩ's writing and personal life unfailingly convey what matters most: never to give up or lose hope, ever. Ngũgĩ's friendship and intellectual support continue to nourish my work.

Simon J. Ortiz and I met in 2003 at a conference organized by Ngũgĩ wa Thiong'o at the International Center for Writing and Translation. Soon after we began working on *Children of Fire, Children of Water*, a composition of dialogical memory pieces in which we narrate and reflect upon our different violent histories. We juxtapose and interweave stories about growing up under the continued colonization of the Acoma people and in war-torn postwar Germany. Writing down my childhood stories sharpened my theoretical reflections. Simon's unfailing support and encouragement carried me through times when writing became emotionally hard. Often I felt again what I felt as a child, namely, that I was "a girl without words." This new insecurity is linked to the fact that in writing *Haunting Legacies* I could no longer separate the personal from the theoretical. Reflecting my own history in Simon

Ortiz's very different history made me see the familiar in a fresh way. In many ways, *Children of Fire, Children of Water* and *Haunting Legacies* are companion pieces for me.

Working on *Children of Fire, Children of Water* also inspired me to include personal vignettes in *Haunting Legacies* that reflect my subject position and transferential relationship to the material. I could not have anticipated that the time of working on these projects would be one of unusual, if not uncanny, personal turbulence and trauma. I feel that the book was conceived when we buried my mother on September 11, 2001, because it was after my return from Germany to the United States that I began writing about growing up in postwar Germany. I continue to hesitate about disclosing this personal underpinning, but I cannot ignore that some personal experiences during that time became so crucial to the writing itself that it would be a disavowal not to mention them. Writing about my German legacy in the midst of new violent histories and personal trauma was a way of coping and going on.

The past five years have been filled with more violence and trauma than any other period in my life. In 2004, Ngũgĩ wa Thiong'o and Njeeri wa Ngũgĩ, two of my closest friends, were brutally attacked upon their first return to their home country, Kenya, after twenty-two years of Ngũgĩ's exile. In 2004, Jacques Derrida lost his battle with cancer; Renée Hubert followed him in 2005. Both had been my colleagues and friends at the University of California at Irvine for two decades. Last year, my mentor and friend of forty years, Wolfgang Iser, fell in the street and died from the head wound he incurred. Finally, on July 15, 2008, I learned that my colleague Lindon Barrett, with whom I shared a beautiful friendship for eighteen years, was murdered in his home. The trauma of a murder leaves a haunting legacy that I find hard to accept, let alone be at peace with. Lindon's dedication in my copy of *Blackness and Value* reads: "Gaby, here's to our long and rich friendship—intellectual and otherwise. And here's to many more years. Love and Mischief, Lindon." We only had nine more years, but *Haunting Legacies* bears the invisible traces of our exchanges during those years.

I dedicate *Haunting Legacies* to my son, Leon. Only a few weeks after I began writing on this project, Leon experienced a major trauma that took over our family's lives for years. Diagnosed with PTSD and major depression, Leon was briefly hospitalized. The day after I brought him to the hospital, I learned that my brother had died suddenly and unexpectedly of heart failure at age forty-six. The most important insights into trauma came from Leon, who taught me more than he will ever know. From him I also learned about resilience and survival. As I saw him reclaim his life, I understood more deeply than ever before why we need to respond to violent histories with an uncompromising fight for and affirmation of life at every turn. Leon's path to recovery, his quiet persistence and wisdom gained from his experience have shaped this book in so many ways that he has truly become a part of it.

Irvine, September 23, 2009

Acknowledgments

I revised *Haunting Legacies* while I was a fellow at the Institute for Humanities Research at Arizona State University. The institute's generous fellowship was supplemented by the Humanities Dean's Office at the University of California, Irvine, my home institution. My heartfelt thanks go to the colleagues who made my stay at ASU a wonderful experience, particularly director Sally Kitch and assistant director Carol Withers, who made sure that we found a congenial environment for our group. I also thank the members of the group Humanities and Political Conflict. I benefited greatly from our inspiring exchanges and the feedback to my presentations from the project. In addition, I thank several colleagues from ASU who read and made insightful comments on selected chapters: Dirk Hoerder, Ileana Orlich, Claudia Sadowski-Smith, Arieh Saposnik, and Shahla Talebi.

At UCI, my first thanks go to Travis Tanner, my research assistant, who commented lucidly on the entire manuscript and worked tirelessly and with unparalleled patience on compiling the final version for the press. I also thank my friends and colleagues who gave me invaluable feedback on specific chapters: Ackbar Abbas, Alex and Mieke Gelley, David Goldberg, Annette Schlichter, Ngũgĩ wa Thiong'o, and Ruth

Kluger. My graduate students all deserve thanks for their feedback during seminars and discussions. Special thanks go to Julia Elyachar, the most scrupulous editor I have ever had. Her commitment to my work means more to me than she can know. I also thank the members of the New Center for Psychoanalysis and the UC Psychoanalytic Consortium who have engaged with my work: Esther Dreifuss-Kattan, Bettina Soestwohner, Sharon Zalusky, Liz Constable, Naomi Janowitz, Afsaneh Alishobani, Peter Loewenberg, and Jeff Praeger.

Among the many colleagues and friends from different universities in the United States and other countries who supported my work in various ways, I must mention those who have read my manuscript (or parts of it) and supported me with lucid feedback: Larry Bogad, Philomena Essed, Donna Haraway, Marianne Hirsch, Andreas Huyssen, E. Ann Kaplan, Michael Levine, Gayatri Spivak, Kathleen Woodward, and my former students who remain faithful and supportive readers: Gregg Lambert, Naomi Mandel, and Natalie Eppelsheimer. I am moved by the engaged and meaningful support of many colleagues at Hebrew University who have sent me detailed and pointed responses over the years: Zephyra Porat, Ruth Ginsburg, Baruch Hochman, Shlomith Rimon-Kenan, and Mikhail Govrin. I thank my Chinese colleagues and friends involved in the translation of selected chapters for a book of my work in critical theory: Jiajun Tao, my translator; Wang Fengzhen, my publisher; and Sola Liu, who wrote an introduction that goes right to the heart of my most central concerns. From the Postcolonial Institute at Melbourne, I profoundly thank director Phillip Darby and John Cash, with whom I have collaborated for many years. The challenging and supportive feedback from my colleagues in Germany made the idea of giving up impossible: Irene Albers, Aleida and Jan Assman, Vittoria Borso, Reinhold Goerling, Ulla Haselstein, Renate Lachmann, and Florian Sedlmeier. I want to express my gratitude to the many people who helped with the production of the book for Columbia University Press. As always, my first thanks go to my editor, Jennifer Crewe, for her continued support of many years. I also thank Afua Adusei-Gontarz and Michael Haskell for their invaluable assistance in seeing the manuscript through its final stages to publication.

Last, but not least, I thank my family and those I consider my extended elective family for their encouragement and dedication to my work and for providing a holding environment when I needed it: first and foremost my sons, Manuel Schwab, one of my sharpest readers, and Leon Schwab, to whom I dedicate this book. Simon Ortiz, Martin Schwab, Yael Hirschhorn, and Njeeri wa Ngũgĩ sustained me through challenging times, each in his or her own particular way. Robert Cummings, my analyst, could not have known what he triggered when he first asked me about my goal in analysis. I thank him for accompanying me on this unforeseeable journey at the intersections of life and writing.

Three chapters of *Haunting Legacies* were previously published and appear here in revised or expanded form. Chapter 2, "Writing Against Memory and Forgetting," appeared in *Literature and Medicine* 25, no. 1 (2006): 95–121. Chapter 3, "Haunting Legacies: Trauma in Children of Perpetrators," appeared in *Postcolonial Studies* 7, no. 2 (2004): 177–95. Chapter 5, "Replacement Children: The Transgenerational Transmission of Traumatic Loss," appeared in a shorter version in *American Imago* vol. 66, no. 3 (2009): 277–310. I thank the journals for granting me permission to reprint the essays.

haunting legacies

chapter**one**

Introduction

Where there is no grave, we are condemned to go on mourning.
—Ruth Kluger, *Still Alive*

It is the children's or descendants' lot to objectify these buried tombs
through diverse species of ghosts. What comes back to haunt are the
tombs of others.
—Nicolas Abraham, *The Shell and the Kernel*

Our innocence had been replaced by fear and we had become
monsters. There was nothing we could do about it.
—Ishmael Beah, *A Long Way Gone*

The epigraphs borrowed from Ruth Kluger, Nicolas Abraham, and
Ishmael Beah raise the question of how both victims and perpetrators
pass on the ineradicable legacies of violent histories through generations. The transmission of violent legacies by far exceeds the passing
on of historical knowledge or even of stories with thick descriptions of
personal involvement. What I call "haunting legacies" are things hard
to recount or even to remember, the results of a violence that holds an
unrelenting grip on memory yet is deemed unspeakable. The psychic
core of violent histories includes what has been repressed or buried in
unreachable psychic recesses. The legacies of violence not only haunt the
actual victims but also are passed on through the generations. Nicolas
Abraham envisions a *crypt* in which people bury unspeakable events or
unbearable, if not disavowed, losses or injuries incurred during violent
histories. It is as if in this psychic tomb they harbor an undead ghost.
According to Abraham, under normal circumstances a person mourns
a loss by *introjecting* the lost person or object. Introjection facilitates
integration into the psychic fabric. By contrast, a person who refuses to
mourn *incorporates* the lost object by disavowing the loss, thus keeping
the object "alive" inside. Incorporation is a defensive operation based

on a denial of loss. In a fusion of boundaries, the ego comes to identify and merge with the lost object. As Diana Fuss argues in *Identification Papers*, the person who refuses to mourn becomes like the living dead.[1]

Designed to circumvent mourning, a crypt buries a lost person or object or even a disavowed part of oneself or one's history, while keeping it psychically alive. "Where there is no grave, we are condemned to go on mourning,"[2] says Ruth Kluger. But what happens when we build a grave within ourselves? While we can foreclose mourning by burying the dead in our psyche, those dead will return as ghosts. Violent histories have a haunting quality even before their legacy is passed on to the next generation. In his memoirs of his time as a child soldier in Sierra Leone, *A Long Way Gone*, Ishmael Beah describes being assaulted by intrusive memories and thoughts as if they were hostile alien forces coming from outside: "I spent most of my time fighting myself mentally in order to avoid thinking about what I had seen or wondering where my life was going, where my family and friends were. . . . I became restless and was afraid to sleep for fear that my suppressed thoughts would appear in my dreams."[3]

Traumatic memories come in flashbacks or nightmares. They come in the memories of the body and its somatic enactments. Traumatic memories entrap us in the prison house of repetition compulsion. To the extent that we are successful in banning thoughts and memories, we become a body in pain, leading a somatic existence severed from consciously or affectively lived history. Trauma disrupts relationality or is, as Bion calls it, an attack on "the capacity for linking," and ultimately an attack on thought itself.[4] Beah tries to stop or drown out thought itself to keep psychic pain away, but the pain only migrates into the body, into splitting headaches, as his head becomes almost literally a tomb for the staging of a theater of dead voices: "I did not want to show my friends the pain I felt from my headache. In my mind's eye I would see sparks of flame, flashes of scenes I had witnessed, and the agonizing voices of children and women would come alive in my head. I cried quietly as my head beat like the clapper of a bell."[5]

How do we deal with a haunting past while simultaneously acting in the present, with its own ongoing violence? Is the politics of mourning advocated by psychoanalysis adequate after catastrophic events? And is mourning, indeed, as psychoanalysis and trauma theory would have it, a precondition for moving beyond violence and avoiding repetition?

Haunting Legacies is concerned with what happens to psychic life in the wake of unbearable violence and focuses on irresolvable, impossible, or refused mourning of losses that occurred under catastrophic circumstances. Warfare and genocide, as well as more individual violent acts such as torture and rape, are liminal experiences that bring us to the abyss of human abjection. These violent acts cause soul murder and social death. No other species tortures or wages war. No other species pursues soul murder for the sake of pleasure. Torture and rape, the two most prominent forms of soul murder, eradicate psychic time because time cannot heal the victim's suffering in the same way time heals other wounds. Similarly, the trauma experienced after catastrophic losses, such as the violent death of a loved one, annihilates a shared sense of time and forecloses proper mourning. Victims fall into a melancholia that embraces death-in-life. Where there is no grave, one cannot mourn properly; one remains forever tied to a loss that never becomes real. Violent histories generate psychic deformations passed on from generation to generation across the divide of victims and perpetrators. No one can completely escape the ravages of war or the dehumanizing effects of atrocities, not even those perpetrators who seem to have escaped unscathed or those who frantically rebuild their lives, their cities, and their nations. The damages of violent histories can hibernate in the unconscious, only to be transmitted to the next generation like an undetected disease.

Haunting Legacies explores the psychic life of violent histories as translated into and recreated in literary texts, memoirs, and creative nonfiction. Occasionally, I draw on my own memories of growing up in West Germany after World War II under French occupation as a framework or trigger for my theoretical reflections.[6] I use these memories as markers of my own positionality within the project. Theoretically, I use psychoanalysis and trauma theory as well as other critical, cultural and social theories and philosophies that work toward understanding fascism, colonialism, war, and genocide—or even more specific and widespread forms of violence such as torture, rape, and humiliation. I draw on critics who think the psychological, the political, and the social together, including a wide range of critical theories by Hannah Arendt, Giorgio Agamben, Nicolas Abraham and Maria Torok, Frantz Fanon, Alexander and Margarete Mitscherlich, Jacques Derrida, Judith Butler, Achille Mbembe, and Ngũgĩ wa Thiong'o—to name just a few. I treat these theories as heuristic tools and literature as empirical data gleaned from the creative reworking and translation of experiences. Fictional and autobiographical texts thus gain primacy as tools to challenge theories and push toward their refinement, if not revision.

Among the theories that most influenced this project are Nicolas Abraham and Maria Torok's theories of psychic haunting, transgenerational trauma, and the crypt. In this context, I also draw on Jacques Derrida's elaboration of Abraham and Torok in "Fors," where he develops a concept of cryptonymy, that is, a traumatic designification of language to ward off intolerable pain. The creation of cryptic enclaves in language marks the traces of refused mourning. They appear, so to speak, as the linguistic scars of trauma and are not unlike the tombs in psychic life that bury the lost person or object but refuse to acknowledge the death. Live burials of sorts, these crypts in the psyche and in language contain the secrets of violent histories, the losses, violations, and atrocities that must be denied. "Doubtless the Self *does* identify . . . but in an 'imaginary, occult' way, with the lost object, with its 'life beyond the grave,'"[7] writes Derrida. The traces this endocryptic identification leaves in language can only be deciphered, de-crypted in a symptomatic reading, mindful of a secret in language. For Derrida, cryptographic writing is fractured writing that always "marks an effect of impossible or refused mourning."[8]

Language, Derrida asserts, inhabits the crypt in the form of words buried alive, that is, defunct words relieved of their communicative function.[9] Traumatic silences and gaps in language are, if not mutilations and distortions of the signifying process, ambivalent attempts to conceal. But indirectly, they express trauma otherwise shrouded in secrecy or relegated to the unconscious. Cryptographic writing can bear the traces of the transgenerational memory of something never experienced firsthand by the one carrying the secret. It is the children or descendants, Abraham insists, who will be haunted by what is buried in this tomb, even if they do not know of its existence or contents and even if the history that produced the ghost is shrouded in silence. Often the tomb is a familial one, organized around family secrets shared by parents and perhaps grandparents but fearfully guarded from the children. It is through the unconscious transmission of disavowed familial dynamics that one generation affects another generation's unconscious.

4

This unconscious transmission is what Abraham defines as the dynamic of transgenerational haunting.

In *Haunting Legacies*, I approach violent histories from the perspective of diverse practices of transgenerational writing, including literature, memoirs, and testimonies. By drawing on both autobiographical and fictional modes of writing about violent histories, I hope to open up a double perspective on haunted writing. Memoirs often bear the traces, gaps, and lacunae of trauma like raw scars; fiction, poetry, and film can create a more protected space to explore the effects of violence from within multiple voices embedded in imagined daily lives. Since I am concerned with transgenerational haunting, I place second-generation narratives about the Holocaust at the center. In this respect, the book is part of my own process of coming to terms with being born in West Germany in the wake of the Holocaust. German American writer Sabine Reichel emphatically states: "I . . . hated Germany. I hated being German."[10] Reichel's statement could have been my own. Most of my life, I hated being German. When I tried to bring up the topic of the Holocaust at home, my parents called me a "*Nestbeschmutzer*," a term referring to a bird that soils its own nest. The first time I tried to write about my experiences of growing up in postwar Germany was in high school after I learned about the Holocaust. The urge to pursue this project has been on my mind ever since, but like most Germans of my generation, I was for a long time too scared and in other ways not yet ready to face the challenge. For decades, I couldn't bring myself to come near the topic. It was too close to a home that was not home. Of course, this avoidance was also an involuntary participation in Germany's silencing of the Holocaust, and as such an unwitting collusion with the parental generation. I can now see the kind of public and personal silencing I experienced, and the censoring of my own voice, as a form of magical thinking in which, rather than conjuring and believing in a wishful reality, one attempts to make something unbearable simply go away.

It is no coincidence that the origins of this book coincide with the beginning of my training in psychoanalysis. In the first session of my training analysis, my analyst asked me: "If you were to name one prominent goal you want to reach in this analysis, what would it be?" Without hesitation I answered: "Writing a book about what it meant to grow up in Germany after the war." I utterly surprised myself with my own answer. For all practical purposes, I had given up this project a long time ago when I found myself incapable of living up to the challenge. It was certainly not foremost on my mind, at least not consciously so. But I could not ignore my spontaneous answer and had to take this step in my own long process of coming to terms with my legacy. As I write about memoirs and literature, I am also following the traces of the violent history passed down to me in vicarious ways.

Obviously, for the descendants of both victims and perpetrators there is no innocent way to approach the personal legacies of violence. There is no way to escape the traps of writing about violent histories, especially since we live in a culture that routinely commodifies representations of violence. Critics have exposed the fallacies of a wound culture or an involuntary attachment to injurious states as well as the fallacies of seemingly exculpating narratives of perpetration.[11] At the same time, we know that silence is not an option. Perhaps the only way to avoid the fixation on past violence and injuries is to bring their traces into the present. Focusing on traumatic history often seems to release us from the present. We can ignore the violent histories that unfold before our very eyes when we are fixated on the past. I therefore decided not to focus exclusively on German history, but rather also to reflect on my engagement with this legacy through other histories of violence that reach into the present. I have lived in the United States for twenty-five years now. I had always wanted to leave Germany, but only in the 1980s when I took an academic position in the United States did I realize this wish. Now I am deeply immersed in this country's cultural life, including the contradictions and the violence that I witness on a daily basis. I sometimes think that I was born in the most violent country of that time, and ran away only to arrive in one of the most violent countries today. With the invasion of Iraq, I began to understand what it meant to feel like a bystander to a senseless war. Writing about histories of violence counters some of the helplessness I have experienced in the face of the violence committed by my new home country, the wars it has waged and continues to wage, and the global destruction of our planet for which it is responsible in disproportionate ways. Writing helps, but it is not enough. Writing is but a gentle nudge for those who struggle with the experience of living in today's violent world.

As a literary critic who works with an interdisciplinary framework at the intersections of literary studies, anthropology, and psychoanalysis, I ground my analysis of transgenerational haunting in specific readings. I have selected texts that illustrate both the psychic life and the transgenerational duration of violent histories as well as the translation of trauma into communal and political conflict. Literature is central to my project because it is through literature (and artistic works more generally) that one can tap into experiences that were never fully known but have nonetheless left their traces. In their foreword to *Testimony: Crises of Witnessing in Literature, Psychoanalysis, and History*, Shoshana Felman and Dori Laub highlight that "art inscribes (artistically bears witness to) *what we do not yet know of our lived historical relation to events of our times.*"[12] It is such unthought knowledge that I am trying to trace at both a personal and a cultural level.

In this respect, the understanding of literature as a transformational object further expands upon my theory of literature and reading first developed in *Subjects Without Selves* (1994) and *The Mirror and the Killer-Queen* (1996). In these works I conceptualize literature's role in a continual process of transforming and redefining the boundaries of subjectivity and culture, including the boundaries between conscious and unconscious experience and knowledge. Focusing on memory and cryptographic writing, *Haunting Legacies* takes this general theory in a new direction. Cryptographic writing functions as a transformational object by breaking through the walls of silence or the sealed boundaries of a crypt. In this process, cryptographic writing accesses experiences that have been unconsciously registered without ever becoming fully conscious. In this sense, we can say that the crypt harbors not only the ghosts of lost objects, but also the "unthought knowledge" of disavowed traumatic losses.

I borrow the term "unthought knowledge" from Christopher Bollas. In *The Shadow of the Object*, Bollas argues that, in contrast to repressed unconscious knowledge, "unthought knowledge" constitutes a dimension of the unconscious that emerges from experiences that have been lived but never fully known.[13] While Bollas refers to experiences in infancy before the acquisition of language, the concept of "unthought knowledge" is also relevant for the inscription of traumatic experiences that are, as trauma theorists argue, registered but not fully lived in a conscious and remembered way. Much of the transgenerational transmission of trauma, I argue with respect to cryptographic writing, operates at the level of such unthought knowledge. That is why, in order to make trauma accessible, a form needs to be found that translates into language or symbolic expression an experience that is only unconsciously registered and left as a mere trace on the affective and corporeal levels. Literature and the arts can become transformational objects in the sense that they endow this knowledge with a symbolic form of expression and thereby not only change its status but also make it indirectly accessible to others.[14] It is in this sense that I understand what Felman and Laub call "artistically bearing witness."

In certain respects, this project follows the pathbreaking work of Cathy Caruth, Dominick LaCapra, Shoshana Felman, and Dori Laub on trauma in the United States and the work of Renate Lachmann as well as Aleida and Jan Assmann's work on memory culture (*Gedächtniskultur*) in Germany.[15] Caruth with *Unclaimed Experience: Trauma, Narrative, and History* and LaCapra with *Writing History, Writing Trauma* have used different routes to introduce the highly influential debate about trauma in literary studies and the humanities more generally. In a similar vein, the work of Aleida Assmann on trauma, collective memory, and "memory culture" and her collaborative work with Jan Assmann on memory culture have reopened the debates in literary and historical studies in Germany on the trauma of World War II.[16] *Haunting Legacies* builds on and expands this body of work by emphasizing and theorizing the crucial role of the unconscious and of transference not only in the experience and writing of violent histories but also in the transmission of their legacies to future generations.

In this context, Dominick LaCapra's and Eric L. Santner's reflections on transference are crucial. In "Representing the Holocaust" LaCapra writes:

The Holocaust presents the historian with transference in the most traumatic form conceivable—but in a form that will vary with the difference in subject position of the analyst. Whether the historian or analyst is a survivor, a relative of survivors, a former Nazi, a former collaborator, a relative of former Nazis or collaborators, a younger Jew or German distanced from more immediate contact with survival, participation, or collaboration, or a relative 'outsider' to these problems will make a difference even in the meaning of statements that may be formally identical. Certain statements or even entire orientations may be appropriate for someone in a given subject position but not in others.[17]

LaCapra's insistence on the need to reflect one's subject position in writings about the Holocaust comes from the acknowledgment that these writings are inevitably marked by transference. According to LaCapra, traumatic transference puts an inordinate amount of pressure on language: "How language is used is thus critical for the way in which transferential relation is negotiated. It is also decisive in determining the manner in which subject-positions are defined and redefined."[18] I argue that transference is crucial not only in analyzing and writing violent histories but also in reading them. In addition, as I will argue in more detail later, transference is crucial in the formation of a syncretistic memory that operates at the intersections of different violent histories. The different subject positions LaCapra outlines from victim and perpetrator to their descendants also affect the reading process and the specific ways in which the writing of violent histories is received. The recognition of transference is, for LaCapra, a precondition of "working-through" personal involvement in the past that counteracts a "projective reprocessing":

> Working-through requires the recognition that we are involved in transferential relations to the past in ways that vary according to the subject positions we find ourselves in, rework, and invent. It also involves the attempt to counteract the projective reprocessing of the past through which we deny certain of its features and act out our own desires for self-confirming or identity-forming meaning.[19]

I lay open my own transferential relationship to the Holocaust by including personal vignettes that reflect on what it meant to grow up in postwar Germany. I show how some of these events shaped my understanding of the Holocaust, my readings of Holocaust memoirs and my lifelong preoccupation with violent histories. Moreover, in the chapter "Identity Trouble," I reflect on my "own desires for self-confirming or identity-forming meaning" by looking back at the history of negative identity formation shared by many Germans of my generation. I thus confront the Holocaust not as a historian, and not even exclusively as a literary critic. Rather, I rely so heavily on literary texts and memoirs because they were central to mediating my own precarious knowledge about the Holocaust and, indeed, to shaping my own subject position toward it. Those texts penetrated through the German silence and supplemented the traces of a hidden history that I received from my relatives and teachers. If I choose an approach marked by personal experience, it is not because I want to claim an "authority of experience"[20] but rather in the spirit of the distinction LaCapra introduces between "accurate reconstruction of the past and committed exchange with it."[21]

Writing about one's own involvement in and transferential relationship to a history of genocide—even if it is from the distance of a second generation—complicates the processes of mourning that accompany such writing. "It is arguable that certain ritualized aspects of language may be essential to processes of mourning that are bound up with working-through transference,"[22] writes LaCapra. However, if transference itself is traumatic, as LaCapra argues, it is also bound to mobilize defenses. In "History Beyond the Pleasure Principle," Eric L. Santner analyzes the link between an inability or refusal to mourn and a form of writing that he calls "narrative fetishism":

> By narrative fetishism I mean the construction and deployment of a narrative consciously or unconsciously designed to expunge the traces of the trauma or loss that called that narrative into being in the first place. The use of narrative as fetish may be contrasted with that rather different mode of symbolic behavior that Freud called *Trauerarbeit* or the "work of mourning." Both narrative fetishism and mourning are responses to loss, to a past that refuses to go away due to its traumatic impact.[23]

Linking narrative fetishism to a failed attempt at the psychic mastery of trauma, Santner emphasizes the importance of the work of mourning for the postwar German generation: "I am concerned here with the project and *dilemma* of elaborating a post-Holocaust German national and cultural identity. Germans are faced with the paradoxical task of having to constitute their 'Germanness' in the awareness of the horrors generated by a previous production of national and cultural identity."[24] Like LaCapra, Santner insists on the importance of forms of writing violent histories that reach beyond positivist accounts of historical facts. Moreover, he reminds us that one can acknowledge the historical facts of the Holocaust and yet continue to disavow its existential and experiential impact.[25] This is a crucial point regarding the infamous silencing of the Holocaust in postwar Germany. The facts were not hidden. Most Germans of my generation learned about the Holocaust in their early teens in high school. My classmates and I learned about it one day when, without preparation, our history teacher showed the film *Night and Fog* in a class on German history. We received factual knowledge of the historical events. And yet, I would later realize, the silence had not been broken. Silencing in Germany at that time was not a withholding of facts; it was caused by the absence of any kind of emotional engagement at both the personal and collective levels. To break this kind of silence, Santner, LaCapra, and others insist, mourning is crucial to avoid both the distancing effects of a positivist historicism and the illusory psychic mastery gained by narrative fetishism.

Haunting, trauma, and mourning are also conceptual cornerstones in my theoretical framework. "To take seriously Nazism and the 'Final Solution' as massive trauma means to shift one's theoretical, ethical, and political attention to the psychic and social sites where individual and group identities are constituted, destroyed, and reconstructed,"[26] writes Santner. In *Haunting Legacies*, I am trying to trace these social and psychic sites in various forms of writing that emerge from the Holocaust and other violent histories. In my selections, I privilege writings that go to the heart of violent histories and place their readers in an emotionally involved transferential relationship. I am interested in the collective process instigated by texts that penetrate the "psychic skin"[27] of readers in order to enlist them in the collective work not only of mourning but also of "reparation," however limited it must remain in the face of catastrophic atrocities.

Santner's perspective on mourning also allows one to put a different spin on what Alexander and Margarete Mitscherlich diagnosed as the "inability to mourn" and the concomitant psychic immobility, if not paralysis, in postwar Germany.[28] The authors link this inability to mourn predominately to the loss of the *Führer*, that is, a leader whom the German people cannot mourn because of the intense defense against feelings of guilt, shame, and fear. In consequence, the authors argue, Germans tended to de-realize the Nazi past and fall into a melancholic depletion of self. Alexander and Margarete Mitscherlich argue that recognizing the inordinate guilt, shame, and fear caused by the Holocaust would have been impossible in the immediate aftermath of the war. They attribute the German pathological inability to mourn to the fact that even later there was no adequate work of mourning for the masses of fellow human beings that were murdered by Germans. To address this inability, a committed exchange with Germany's legacy must be grounded in the "collective responsibility" of Germans as Karl Jaspers first defined it.[29] Such collective responsibility also includes the task "to keep alive the memory of the suffering of those murdered at the hands of the Germans" that Habermas invokes in "Concerning the Public Use of History."[30]

Die Unfähigkeit zu trauern, the German original of *The Inability to Mourn*, was first published in 1967, roughly twenty years after the Nuremberg trials. Alexander Mitscherlich had been the head of the German Medical Commission to the American Tribunal at Nuremberg, and *The Inability to Mourn* is undoubtedly marked by this experience. The English translation appeared in 1975, and in his preface Robert Jay Lifton speaks about the book's timeliness for the post-Vietnam and post-Nixon United States. After September 11, 2001, the book became timelier than ever. It opens up new ways to think about the Iraq War, homeland security, and the dismantling of social justice and violation of human rights in the United States during the Bush administrations.

In the preface to the American edition, the Mitscherlichs insist that thirty years after the end of World War II, the true human and political significance of the murder of millions of Jews, Poles, Russians, Slovenes, gypsies, homosexuals, and the mentally ill, as well as communists and people of political dissent, is in Germany still perceived only reluctantly or not at all. The authors insist that working though the losses is a prerequisite to experiencing guilt and remorse. Speaking of the loss of segments of one's life or of national history from memory and of blanks in the autobiography or history, they ask: "why is it that . . . terrorism, the atrocities of war, and the eradication of freedom fail, from one generation to the next, to exercise any visible deterrent effect on those peoples who have the power to determine the course of history?"[31]

It took several more decades of frozen memories and narrative fetishism in Germany before more meaningful work of mourning began. As I argued earlier, the infamous German silence after the Holocaust was less a silence emerging from the lack of words or revelation of facts than an emotional silence. And while there seems to be something almost obscene in discourses that look at the effects of the war and the Holocaust on Germans in terms of trauma, ignoring that we are dealing with a defensive traumatic silence is itself a defensive posture. Remaining frozen in guilt not only sustains a culture of silence but also induces defenses that prevent working through the past. Understood in this way, mourning is not a melancholic attachment to injury but, on the contrary, prepares the ground for a future-oriented integration of the past.

During the past decades and under the impact of Holocaust studies, theories of trauma and mourning have evolved in relation to studies of transgenerational trauma. Using a series of family photographs, Marianne Hirsch's *Family Frames: Photography, Narrative, and Postmemory* approaches the transgenerational legacy of the Holocaust through the optical unconscious of photography.[32] Hirsch explores the residues of trauma in the stories of loss and longing that family pictures leave out, but nonetheless reveal in a signifying ellipsis. Hirsch locates her project historically in "the period following WWII, the Holocaust, and the Gulag, the moment of decolonization and the Cold War, of widespread engagements in civil rights and feminist struggles."[33] She argues that these intersecting histories have given rise to new aesthetic questions and forms. I would add that they also facilitated new forms of memory and commemoration as well as new trajectories of transference that mark the establishment of links between them.

Hirsch sees Art Spiegelman's *Maus* as a paradigmatic and generative text for this change in aesthetics that happens at "the intersections of private and public history."[34] War presupposes the intersection of private and public histories. The processing of trauma and transgenerational haunting, even after collective histories of war or genocide, is always mediated through intensely private individual histories. Family legacies of transgenerational haunting often operate though family secrets and other forms of silencing. Such silences and secrets inevitably affect aesthetic forms and modes of production and representation in second-generation narratives about the legacies of violent histories.

Both *Family Frames* and *Haunting Legacies* raise the vexed question of transgenerational memory: How do children of parents who lived through violent histories "remember" events they did not experience themselves? Hirsch coins the term "postmemory" to designate the vicarious transmission of such memory. While those who actually live through the violence are often left with gaps, holes, or distortions of memory, the second generation receives traumatic memories differently: "Postmemory—often obsessive and relentless—need not be absent or evacuated: it is as full and as empty, certainly as constructed, as memory itself."[35] While victims of trauma live with the scars of memory so to speak—gaps, amnesia, distortion, revision, or even fugue states or intrusive flashbacks—the recipients of transgenerational trauma live with a "postmemory" that comes to them secondhand. Like the memory of the parental generation, it is fragmentary and shot through with holes and gaps, but in different ways. These children need to patch a history together they have never lived by using whatever props they can find—photographs and stories or letters but also, I would add, silences, grief, rage, despair, or sudden unexplainable shifts in moods handed down to them by those who bring them up.

It is almost as if these children become the recipients not only of their parents' lived memories but also of their somatic memories. Children of a traumatized parental generation, I argue, become avid readers of silences and memory traces hidden in a face that is frozen in grief, a forced smile that does not feel quite right, an apparently unmotivated flare-up of rage, or chronic depression. Like photography, traumatized bodies reveal their own optical unconscious. It is this unconscious that second-generation children absorb. Without being fully aware of it, they become skilled readers of the optical unconscious revealed in their parents' body language. I would add that, beyond the optical unconscious, children read their parents' unconscious more generally in the embodied language of affects. The second generation thus receives violent histories not only through the actual memories or stories of parents (postmemory) but also through the traces of affect, particularly affect that remains unintegrated and inassimilable.

While Hirsch reads Spiegelman's *Maus* as a gendered collaborative narrative of father and son that relegates the mother to a "double dying,"[36] my own reading of *Maus* emphasizes the "impossible psychological birth" of Art, who is not only the recipient of his father's traumatic narrative but also his "replacement child" destined to make up for the loss of his firstborn son, Richieu, who died during the war. I dedicate an entire chapter to narratives of replacement children. The parental fantasy of a replacement child is a symptomatic instance of a transgenerational transmission of the trauma that follows the loss of a child during a war or genocide. Fantasies of a replacement child and their unconscious enactment betray a form of failed mourning that operates through a logic of substitution. They constitute an (always failing) attempt to erase and rewrite history under new premises by denying loss and foreclosing pain. I analyze these narratives of replacement children as symptomatic of not only the transgenerational transmission of the effects of violent histories but also of new formations of subjectivity and forms of writing created as an effect of impossible mourning.

The figure of the replacement child also points to another symptom of traumatic legacies, namely, a particular form of haunting that generates the phenomenon of "death-in-life." In *Against the Unspeakable: Complicity, the Holocaust, and Slavery in America*, Naomi Mandel reads the figure of Art in *Maus* as a "speaking corpse." Referring to the passage in which Art accuses his mother of having killed him with her suicide, she concludes that "the stories of the living do not stand for the absent stories of the dead; they *are* the stories of the dead."[37] In a complicated dialectics of identification, substitution, and complicity, those who survive and bear testimony to the Holocaust often occupy, Mandel argues, the figural position of a speaking corpse. This puts a new spin on Art's role as a replacement child. In conflating his living child, Art, with his dead child, Richieu, Art's father, Vladek, symbolically condemns Art to a position of "death-in-life." In his reading of *Maus*, Michael G. Levine argues, "While Art is symbolically killed by his father's slip of the tongue, Richieu is revived as the addressee of his father's last words. This role reversal suggests that Vladek's testimony will have been addressed not merely to the living and the dead, but to the living *as* the dead."[38]

Is "death in life" only an individual form of foreclosed mourning and grief, or can it also afflict entire communities or countries? According to Freud, "death-in-life" is a condition of melancholia that afflicts those with an inability to mourn. Geoffrey Hartman compares this condition with a "struggle with the Angel of Death, who threatens to vacate the entire achievement of a generation in which fathers and mothers started almost from scratch, like the patriarchs. It is as if they, the survivors, belonged to the dead after all."[39] Tropes such as "death-in-life" or the "speaking corpse" can therefore also be read as figurations of a traumatic foreclosure of mourning or a communal, if not national inability to mourn such as the one that Alexander and Margarete Mitscherlich have diagnosed in postwar Germany. Among the debilitating effects of foreclosed mourning they name a pervasive paralysis and deadening of intellectual, mental and emotional life. Art or literature may mobilize this symptomatic condition of a traumatic legacy, and it is this very mobilization that can, almost paradoxically, become the basis for reawakening psychic life. Shoshana Felman succinctly grasps this function of the language of art in contrast to legal language in *The Juridical Unconscious*: "Art is a language of infinity and of the irreducibility of fragments, a language of embodiment, of incarnation, and of embodied incantation or endless rhythmic *repetition*. Because it is by definition a discipline of limits, law distances the Holocaust; art brings it closer."[40]

At this point I should briefly address the other side of a critical divide, namely, the controversial debates about trauma and trauma studies. In *The Holocaust of Texts*, Amy Hungerford takes the passage in which Art accuses his father of killing his mother twice as a target of her critique of personification in Holocaust narratives:

> We see personification at work, for example, in the final panel of Art Spiegelman's graphic novel, *Maus I*, where the protagonist, Art, calls his father a "murderer" for burning the diaries of his dead wife, as if the destruction of Anja's record of her experiences at Auschwitz were somehow equivalent to the kinds of destruction that took place at Auschwitz. . . . Although the equation between the destruction of representations (the diaries) and the destruction of persons (the Jews) may seem at best hyperbolic, the equation in fact plays a role not only in the imaginative representations of the Holocaust from the late 1980s and 1990s but also in contemporary critiques of the very imaginative representation of the Holocaust.[41]

For Hungerford, personification amounts to "the fantasy that we can really have another's experience, that we can become someone else."[42] This critique misses the fact that symbolic equivocations belong to the most basic operations of language and a signifying ordering of human reality. *Prosopopoeia* is a basic rhetorical figure of speech that uses anthropomorphic language to describe an inanimate object.[43] Only the most primordial forms of identifying with someone else's experience emerge from a fantasy of becoming the other. More commonly, empathy is a form of intersubjective relationality—a gift of emotional connection to the other.

Hungerford also decries, "it has become more important to 'remember' the Holocaust than simply to learn about it."[44] "Simply learning about it," however, can happen in the coldness of a pseudo-objective distance that reduces the Holocaust to a scholarly object. Pitting such scholarly studies against emotionally engaged and personally inflected engagements, including emotionally embedded literary or artistic narratives such as Spiegelman's, is not only reductive but also politically questionable. Inadvertently, Hungerford's position feeds into the type of emotional silencing of the Holocaust that has been practiced in Germany despite an abundance of available factual materials.

An ethical stance that wants to purge personification from Holocaust representations lends itself to a scholarly attitude that categorically severs the ties between people and their cultures, histories, and languages, as well as symbolic objects and practices. I see this as a categorical violence that fails to acknowledge any kind of violence—symbolic or otherwise—that is not directed against material bodies. Targeting the personification inherent in the fight against the "death of languages," Hungerford, for example, asks: "Why is it better to have Yup'ik or Eyak spoken in the world than not to have it spoken? . . . If we believe that language is the same thing as a person, of course we do not want it to die."[45] Only if one thinks that languages can be understood in isolation from the people who speak them and from their form of life and culture can the disappearance of a language appear as a quasi-neutral historical event, judged by a reductive cost-benefit ethics and placed within a larger narrative of the progress of civilization that is itself not problematized.

Hungerford's critique of personification in Holocaust representations leads her to address issues of preservation and ecology: "Is not the desire for this kind of preservation itself—or for the preservation of wilderness or spotted owls—the product, in some sense, of the fact that we have electricity, running water, and the rest? Would we renounce our own acquisition and enjoyment of such things in order to preserve cultural or natural diversity?"[46] Ecology is indeed pertinent in evaluating the scholarly ethics Hungerford sets up against trauma and Holocaust studies. While Hungerford propagates a rigid categorical and rhetorical separation of language and personhood (and ultimately of body and mind), a Batesonian "ecology of mind," by contrast, sees people and their bodies and minds as well as their language, culture, and natural environment as so deeply interconnected that they must be thought together both theoretically and categorically.

What then is at stake when Art calls his father a murderer for burning the diaries of his dead wife? Art does not, as Hungerford claims, naively act as if "the destruction of Anja's record of her experience at Auschwitz were somehow equivalent to the kind of destruction that took place at Auschwitz."[47] Apart from advocating a purism that believes in the ability to eliminate transference in the use of language and representation, Hungerford's literalism misses the relational function of language as a symbolic system. Art reacts to a deadly transference on his father's part. By destroying his wife's diaries, the father wants symbolically to erase the past by eliminating its material (symbolic) traces. For Art, this is a form of killing. Trauma theory speaks of "soul murder." Of course, the discourse of soul murder relies on personification, but not in the naïve sense of a literal equation. Speaking of "soul murder" refers to the fact that one may "kill" what is most essential to a person while leaving his or her body alive. For Art, the destruction of the diaries is a symbolic soul murder. Psychoanalysis and trauma theories insist that such acts have material consequences for both those who perform and those who witness them.

Art also accuses his mother of having killed *him* with her suicide. How are we to read this personification? Hungerford states: "The material difference between texts and persons comes down to embodiment, and . . . the capacity for pain and the fact of mortality."[48] While this basic difference seems hardly contestable, it does not follow that pain and even mortality cannot be expressed and transmitted through representations. Personifying representations may best approximate the pain and fear in facing the vulnerability of embodied lives. Restricting the discourse of "killing" to the killing of actual material bodies would, for example, prohibit one from addressing some of the most devastating injuries inflicted on survivors, those that have been called "soul murder." How to address those injuries without acknowledging that something has been killed? We recall Naomi Mandel's astute observation that those who survive and bear testimony to the Holocaust often occupy the figural position of a "speaking corpse." Such a position can only be figural in the sense that a "speaking corpse" is a personification of death. But this personified death reaches far beyond the material death of the body. The figure of the "speaking corpse" is interesting precisely because it is able to address the paradoxical psychic condition of "death-in-life" that we can trace in so many Holocaust memoirs and representations. Writers use the figure of the "speaking corpse" not because they imagine experiencing the Holocaust but because something of the quality of "death-in-life" has been transmitted to them in a complex transference from those who were actual witnesses and survivors. And if, as Freud asserts, "death-in-life" is a condition of melancholia, artistic representations and theories that insist on remembering and the work of mourning perform important work against cultural melancholia.

Work against cultural melancholia is complicated. The danger of emphasizing memory and mourning lies in using trauma as the foundation of identity. Such attachment to injury is problematic, especially in a "wound culture" oversaturated with stories and studies of trauma. An excessive emphasis on mourning may indeed contribute to an identitarian definition of cultural belonging by tying identity to victimization. Moreover, as we know, narratives of trauma as well as suffering and victimization are eminently exploitable. In *Trauma: A Genealogy*, Ruth Leys argues with Walter Benn Michaels that the concept of transgenerational trauma "makes the Holocaust available as a continuing source of identitarian sustenance."[49]

Other theorists echo this concern. Gary Weissman, for example, expresses unease with the institutionalization of Holocaust memory when he refers to "the encroaching sense that the Holocaust seems unreal or pseudo-real in American culture."[50] In particular, he cautions that the concepts of trauma, memory, and witnessing tend to blur the boundaries between victims and those who witness the trauma secondhand. Since "most Americans, including Jews, know of the Holocaust not from listening directly to survivors but from watching television, seeing Hollywood movies, and reading popular books," Holocaust studies satisfy a deeply rooted "fantasy of witnessing" and are increasingly compromised by their eminent marketability.[51] Weissman wonders with Elie Wiesel "whether a saturation point has been reached, whether mention of the Holocaust produces only apathy,"[52] and predicts a similar apathy in future generations: "If the legacy of slavery offers any indication of how future generations will regard the Holocaust, it points to a different fate: not denial but disassociation."[53]

Weissman's argument challenges the pertinence of transgenerational trauma. If, as he claims, future generations tend increasingly to "disassociate" from the traumatic histories of their parents, how should we understand such disassociation? It might be helpful to place "disassociation" in the context of "dissociation," that is, a defensive strategy to ward off the overwhelming impact of massive trauma. Dissociation is an extreme form of psychic splitting that helps to sustain one's daily life under catastrophic circumstances. In her groundbreaking work *Life and Words*, the anthropologist Veena Das describes this form of splitting after the massacres during the Partition of India.[54] The women were left with the daunting task of continuing to feed their children and take care of their families, regardless of how deeply they were affected by the violent events. On the surface it seemed that they ignored the violence and just resumed their lives. But the trauma resurfaced at times of communal gatherings in the form of storytelling. In those stories, pain and grief reemerged and found their place. Storytelling became a crucial practice of processing, working through, and integration. For everyday life to go on, Das suggests, the processing of violence must happen in contained spaces and practices. The lack of such spaces plunges a culture into debilitating paralysis. While Das insists that under catastrophic circumstances this form of psychic splitting may be the only option, she also emphasizes the need to return to and process the incurred losses in contained practices of mourning. The transitional space of narrative, and especially memoir and literature, may facilitate such a practice in the service of healing and reparation.[55]

Psychic splitting is relevant for the formation of traumatic memories. Weissman refers to Charlotte Delbo's distinction between two types of Holocaust memory. "Deep memory" contains sensory memory traces of the time of being in Auschwitz; "common memory" is linked to recollected events from that time. Sensory memory functions for Delbo like an "impermeable skin that isolates it [the time in Auschwitz] from my present self." The two memory states are split off from each other so that, Delbo writes, "everything that happened to that other, the Auschwitz one, now has no bearing on me . . . doesn't interfere with my life."[56] Psychic splitting is generally designed to prevent trauma from interfering with one's life. However, it is an effective mechanism only if supplemented (as in the case described by Veena Das) by practices of working through and integration. For Delbo, nightmares that return her to her state of being in Auschwitz regularly break through the "impermeable" skin. While the splitting helps her lead a quotidian life without constant overwhelming intrusions of past trauma, Delbo also needs to talk and write about these experiences as a form of integration.

Forms of splitting can also occur across generations, and I understand the "disassociation" Weissman describes in this way. It may be true, as Weissman suggests, that many African American people today no longer define their identities through the traumatic legacy of slavery. If we look at their daily lives, many may appear to be "disassociated" from this distant history. However, we also witness a continued working-through of its legacy, including in new forms of rewriting the history of slavery. Toni Morrison's *Beloved*, to which I will return in a later chapter, is only one example.[57]

Peter Novick's *The Holocaust in American Life* criticizes a different form of disassociation. Novick states that the Holocaust has become so prominent in American life because it serves the need for a consensual symbol. It functions, according to Novick, "as virtually the only common denominator of American Jewish identity"[58] at a time when a particularist ethos that stresses differences and divisions has threatened that identity in the late twentieth century.[59] Deploring the growth of a victim culture and the Jewish claim to "superior victimization," Novick takes issue with the paradigm of exceptionalism: "The assertion that the Holocaust is unique—like the claim that it is singularly incomprehensible or unrepresentable—is, in practice, deeply offensive. What else can all of this possibly mean except 'your catastrophe, unlike ours, is ordinary.'"[60] In the sharpest possible terms, Novick concludes that the discourse of exceptionalism, with its assertion that "whatever the United States has done to blacks, Native Americans, Vietnamese, and others pales in comparison to the Holocaust," ultimately "leads to the shirking of those responsibilities that *do* belong to Americans as they confront their past, their present, and their future."[61]

Novick's critique puts an important spin on Santner's notion of "narrative fetishism" as a narrative designed to expunge the traces of the trauma or loss that called that narrative into being in the first place. Novick's claim implies that in American culture the discourse of the Jewish Holocaust may unconsciously displace onto the history of Jews the traces of trauma or loss left by U.S. histories of violence performed onto other peoples. For Novick this is a fetishization by displacement that ultimately serves similar defensive purposes as the narrative fetishiza-tion Santner identifies.[62] Other scholars have similarly claimed that the Holocaust has been misused as a "screen memory" in the American imaginary. Such screen memories, according to critics including Huys-sen, Hansen, Weissman, and Rothberg, allow Americans to confront racism and genocide in a displaced setting comfortably removed from the violent histories of American involvement in slavery, the genocide of the Americas' indigenous peoples, and the many wars of the twentieth and twenty-first centuries. Both Huyssen and Rothberg emphasize the intrinsic ambivalence of screen memories. While Huyssen points out that remembering the Holocaust in new constellations of genocide and massacres can produce both cultural memory and forgetting,[63] Rothberg highlights the double function inherent in screen memories: "they serve both as a barrier between consciousness and the unconscious, and as a site of projection for unconscious fantasies, fears, and desires, which can then be decoded."[64] In my own project, I address screen memories in relation to transgenerational haunting. I radicalize Abraham's notion of the crypt by envisioning it as a collective burial ground. Abraham argues that "what comes back to haunt us is the tombs of others."[65] Screen memories can become yet another burial ground because they function like a crypt that contains many graves of those who cannot be mourned. By covering one's violent history with the memory of another, screen memories can assume both a transgenerational and a transhistorical dimension that needs to be decoded.

Holocaust and trauma studies have tended to focus on the trauma and related screen memories of victims and victimized peoples. By con-trast, *Haunting Legacies* emphasizes the entwined legacies of the descen-dants of victims and perpetrators. Looking at histories of perpetrators can reveal yet another aspect of screen memories. It is well known that narratives of perpetrators often displace perpetration onto victimhood. This is shockingly clear in Claude Lanzmann's *Shoah*, where perpetra-tors almost invariably portray themselves as victims. The majority of Germans, in fact, focused on stories that cast them as war victims. These are exculpating narratives in which the memory or knowledge of an un-speakable guilt (even if only by association) is covered up by memories of one's own victimization. Screen memories operate according to a logic of psychic splitting: they split perpetration and victimhood with-out acknowledging the existence of more complex scenarios in which people can be both victim and perpetrator or others in which victims themselves can become perpetrators.

Screen memories can also perform psychic splitting by focusing on histories of violence elsewhere in order to split them off from one's own violent histories. This spatiotemporal—historical and geographic— splitting conjures a past or remote violent history in order to either cover up or else work through another affectively closer history that would be more problematic to deal with. A different type of splitting is at work in the current focus in German literature and public discourse on Allied air raids and destruction of German cities, the famine, and the mass rape of women. These discourses juxtapose the positions of perpetrator and victim instead of acknowledging that Germans became victims *because* they were perpetrators or at least belonged to a perpetrator nation.

The use of screen memories, however, is only one of many manifestations of psychic splitting. Let me briefly return to the screening of *Night and Fog* as an example of another form of splitting. It was absolutely impossible for us children to "experience" what it was like to be in Auschwitz. But nonetheless, seeing these images and knowing it was our people who had committed these murders was a profoundly disturbing and terrifying experience. What did we do? We fell into complete silence. We didn't talk to one another about what we had seen. After class, we packed our schoolbooks and went home just like any other day. We resumed our daily lives. On the surface it looked as if nothing had changed, while in fact nothing was ever going to be the same. At the surface, one could have assumed that we were completely disassociated from the events we had seen on the screen, but for many of us this film changed how we thought about human beings and the world we inhabited. It reshaped many of us as who we were and became. One of my classmates would eventually write the book *Die Tiengener Juden* (The Jews of Tiengen) about the fate of the Jewish people in our hometown, to which I will return in chapter 3, "Haunting Legacies: Trauma in Children of Perpetrators." We would most likely not have been affected in the same profound way if we had merely been presented with historical facts. The film did more because it engages viewers at an affective level and thus creates a powerful ground for transference.

Experiences like these can only be fully understood if one looks at the intertwined histories of both victims and perpetrators. Killing of the mind and killing of the psyche have a dynamic in violent histories that

affects victims and perpetrators alike—albeit in different and complementary ways. But in contrast to the plethora of studies of the trauma of
Holocaust victims, analyses of the long-term effects of violent histories
on perpetrators and perpetrating nations are rare. Angelika Bammer's
work on identity and displacement in the postwar German generation
is a notable exception. Her pathbreaking book *Displacements: Cultural
Identities in Question* explores the impact of guilt and shame on the
troubled identity formation of Germans growing up in the postwar
years.[66] By contrast, analyses of violent histories from the perspective
of a system that damages both victims and perpetrators have barely
begun. In *Second-Generation Holocaust Literature: Legacies of Survival
and Perpetration*, Erin McGlothlin writes, "One might ask why there
have been very few attempts to look at the literature of both groups
[second-generation victims and perpetrators] in conjunction with one
another."[67] One way is through the concept of phantom pain. Com-
paring the transgenerational trauma inherited by children of perpetrators with phantom pain, McGlothlin writes: "The offspring of perpetrators inherit the history of their parents' unacknowledged crimes, a
legacy of violence and violation whose effects are felt as a stain upon
their souls."[68]

If the Holocaust is, as Santner argues, the "primal scene of socialization" for second-generation Germans, then this "stain on the soul"
becomes the mark of a negative identity formation. Santer writes: "Legacies—or perhaps more accurately: the ghosts, the revenant objects—of
the Nazi period are transmitted to the second and third generations at
the site of the primal scene of socialization, that is, within the context
of a certain psychopathology of the postwar family."[69] Following Dan
Diner's assertion of a "negative symbiosis"[70] between second-generation
Jews and Germans and Eva Hoffman's sense of "contrapunctual" second-
generation groups,[71] McGlothlin argues that children of victims and perpetrators are conjoined in a "communality of opposites."[72] Critics such
as McGlothlin, Santner, Diner, and others insist that the Holocaust is
transmitted as a transgenerational trauma to the second generation of
both victims and perpetrators. The latter inherit their parental generation's guilt, especially if, as Sigrid Weigel argues, the parents deny and
reject that guilt.[73] Because this guilt is abstract and inherited from a
genocide experienced only secondhand, McGlothlin argues that the German second generation "finds itself in a sort of epistemological state of

exile, left stranded on the other side of a history it does not know by an event it did not experience, cut off from the essential knowledge of what happened to their parents or what their parents did."[74]

To come out of this epistemological state of exile, the second generation must perform the labor of putting this mourning of Holocaust victims into language. "Narrative becomes the space where the anonymous deaths are marked and mourned, taking 'the place of graves for those who have no graves.'"[75] Marianne Hirsch pushes this thought even further: "Perhaps it is *only* in subsequent generations that trauma can be witnessed and worked through, by those who were not there to live it but who received its effects, belatedly, though the narratives, actions and symptoms of the previous generation."[76] The long silence in West Germany after the Holocaust suggests that this is also the case on the side of perpetrators. Mourning the victims is a task the descendants of both victims and perpetrators must take over. While they tend to perform this task in isolation from each other, building bridges across the divide between victims and perpetrators reaches a step further. Dan Bar-On's work with groups of second-generation Jews and Germans as well as Israeli Jews and Palestinians pursues the goal of facilitating encounters between victims and perpetrators. This task cannot be completed in one generation. As Vamik Volkan observes, the task of working through the divide between the descendants of victims and perpetrators is rarely completed by the second generation: "If the next generation cannot effectively fulfill their shared tasks—and this is usually the case—they will pass these tasks on to the third generation, and so on."[77]

I locate *Haunting Legacies* in the genealogy of critics, clinicians, and writers concerned with transgenerational haunting in the histories of both victims and perpetrators, in no small part because of my commitment to a psychoanalytically informed study. This commitment frames my approach and defines my key premises. Central among them is the claim that trauma presents an attack on memory and the recovering of memory and concomitant processes of mourning in response to catastrophic loss and injury are a precondition for reparation and healing, however limited the healing may be. But in contrast to theorists such as Cathy Caruth, for example, who insist on the "unrepresentability" of traumatic experience, I emphasize the often delayed urge toward a recovery of memory and representation, not in a literal sense but in the sense of the creative and integrative writing of trauma that comes with working through an event. The delay in this memory work may indeed take one or more generations. Yet the literature about violent histories that has affected me most and that I address in *Haunting Legacies* testifies to the transformational effect of creative rewritings. I also find the delayed urge toward recovering and reworking traumatic memories supported by my socialization in postwar Germany and by my work as a psychoanalyst with victims of trauma, including the trauma of survivors of war.

I hope to contribute to debates in Holocaust studies as well as studies of colonialism, slavery, and torture through my textual material and my focus on the transgenerational haunting of descendants of both victims and perpetrators. Why is this focus controversial and, indeed, upsetting to some? The deepest concern with work that looks at victims and perpetrators together or systematically explores their interactions after the end of violent encounters seems to be the fear of blurring the line between victims and perpetrators.[78] The very notion of presenting legacies of perpetration, including the transgenerational memory of children of perpetrators, in terms of an overall concept of traumatic haunting would from this perspective be highly problematic. To talk about a "trauma" of the German postwar generation—or a trauma of descendants of other perpetrators—can be seen to construct them, too, as victims, comparable to their parents' victims. Yet is it not plausible that the children of perpetrators would be haunted by the crimes committed by the generation of their parents? Is it not plausible that the transference or deposition of shameful somatic memory into their bodies haunts them? This acknowledgment of the effects of transgenerational haunting in no way exculpates or absolves these descendants of perpetrators from assuming responsibility for their legacy. On the contrary, such a systemic perspective suggests that people have no choice but to be responsive to and take responsibility for the history they inherit, no matter on which side of the divide they were born. It is in this sense that the controversial term *Kollektivschuld*, that is, a transgenerational transmission of guilt and shame, can be used in productive ways.

In a similar vein, I also wish to foreground the political underpinnings of a concept of transgenerational haunting by highlighting the effects of trauma as a "colonization of psychic space."[79] This perspective places engagement with the Holocaust in the context of confronting violent histories more generally. Theories of the "decolonization" of the mind and of psychic space help to expand the scope of what "de-Nazification" could and should have meant in postwar Germany by insisting on the inextricable intertwining of the psychic and the political in processes of decolonization and de-Nazification.[80] Decolonization of the mind and of psychic space is a political necessity for both victims and perpetrators. It is psychic work we cannot afford to ignore in the struggle for social justice and a less violent world.

This points to one of the ways in which *Haunting Legacies* is not exclusively about Germany. Going against the tendency to think about the Holocaust in terms of German Jewish exceptionalism, my reflections about transgenerational hauntings and the legacies of violent histories in both victims and perpetrator include examples of transgenerational legacies from other periods, histories, and cultures. This comparative approach is grounded in my own experiential and political history. Michael Rothberg's *Multidirectional Memory: Remembering the Holocaust in the Age of Decolonization*, in which he calls for a theory able to account for the productive intercultural dynamic of memory, is also a source of inspiration. Rothberg's interest in "transfers that take place between diverse places and times during the act of remembrance" resonates with my interest in exploring the transference that occurs at intersecting sites of historical memories of violence.[81]

Rothberg emphasizes histories in which cultural memories of the Holocaust intersect with memories of other histories of violence, insisting that even in its inception "the emergence of collective memory of the Nazi genocide in the 1950s and 1960s takes place in a punctual dialogue with ongoing processes of decolonization and civil rights struggles and their modes of coming to terms with colonialism, slavery, and racism."[82] Against discourses of competitive victimhood, Rothberg's focus on multidirectonal memory envisions new alliances and collectivities in today's global struggles. While Rothberg focuses on the histories of victims, my inclusion of histories of perpetration presents a profound challenge to the coalitional politics of multidirectional memory.

Transgenerational memories and narratives of perpetrator nations can help create the conditions for the descendants of perpetrators to become allies in the struggle against violence and oppression. The shock of recognizing the atrocities committed by one's own people may prepare the ground for potential alliances with the victims. For example, while the knowledge of what we had learned as children when we saw *Night and Fog* remained encapsulated in our psychic lives, it was at the same time precisely such unprocessed toxic knowledge that sensitized many of us to other forms of violence, oppression, and atrocities.

The encapsulated affective knowledge of the Holocaust was re-awakened collectively many years later during the student revolution of the sixties and seventies. It is highly significant that these political struggles took up the issue of fascism and the Holocaust within the larger and more global civil rights struggles at the time. In many respects it was easier to focus on the protest against the Shah and his repressive regime, the Vietnam War, the worldwide movements of decolonization, the solidarity committees with Angela Davis and Leonard Peltier, or, later, the Chilean refugees than to address the haunting legacies of the Holocaust directly. It is not that we ignored the Holocaust or even failed to accuse the parental generation of participation or complicity but rather that the focus of the debates and struggles was in the present. The ethics of "never again" largely skipped the "work of memory," or what the Germans call *Vergangenheitsbewältigung*, that is, the coming to terms with the past (how could one ever?). At least in this sense we displaced the confrontation with our country's history onto other sites of political struggle and used them as "screen memories." It is the reverse dynamic but the same logic of some uses of the Holocaust in the United States as a screen memory for the genocide of indigenous peoples or the violence of slavery.

However, to read such displacement according to a simple logic of cover-up or substitution ignores the complexities and fundamental ambivalence of memory work. In the case of the German postwar generation, for example, the shocking unprocessed knowledge about the Holocaust created a disposition for, as Rothberg phrases it, a "nonappropriative hospitality to histories of the other."[83] It also predisposed many in the postwar generation against new forms of racism, war, and social injustice. Even if facilitated by screen memories, the engagement with other histories of violence—in Germany, the United States, or elsewhere—should not be reduced to a cover-up (which doesn't preclude its being that also). In order to grasp the complexities, contradictions, and paradoxes of traumatic if not toxic memories, one needs to reach beyond a mere either-or logic. Even an engagement that comes out of the displaced energies of the memory of another violent history, including a transgenerational memory of past violence, can be entirely genuine and valid. In postwar Germany, the engagement with other violent histories, screen memory or not, allowed an indirect and therefore psychically more manageable confrontation with issues of war, human violence, atrocities, and genocide.

Memory work can thus perform a double function: the "displaced memory work" facilitated by collective screen memories can address the traces of past injuries and bring them into the present in order to fight against violence in the here and now. At the same time, addressing actual violence in the past is crucial to the work of mourning, without which a negative fixation on past trauma remains active. Among other things, I see the turn of the German debates toward personal narratives that address the psychic legacies of the Holocaust and the air raids also as a delayed—perhaps necessarily delayed—work of mourning.

While Rothberg calls for a conceptual model of multidirectional memory able to grasp the dynamic transfers between diverse places and times of remembrance,[84] I argue that we also need a model for understanding the psychic processes of *transference* that facilitate such transfer. This puts a new spin on psychoanalytic theories of transference and their political relevance. A model of intercultural transference between different violent histories expands the narrower psychoanalytic notion of interpersonal transference. I am indeed arguing that histories of violence can be put in a dialogical relationship with one another, thus creating a transferential dynamic for those who participate in, witness, or inherit those histories transgenerationally. Epistemologically, the notion of transference between discourses and narratives rests upon the acknowledgement that <u>discourses have embedded agencies</u>. Those embedded agencies can be the facilitators of transference. In turn, those who engage in these discourses do so on the basis of their own historical memories. In this process, they use intersecting discursive memories as the basis of their own transference. If the term "collective memory" is meaningful, it cannot be in the sense of a common identical memory in the service of identity politics. Collective memory rather emerges as an evolving and internally diverse process that unfolds when histories intersect and different participants or agents read them in conflicting ways, especially when they come from different sides of the divide between victims and perpetrators.

In light of such a transferential model of memory, one might even expand Rothberg's notion of "multidirectional memory." It is not so much that our memories go in or come from many directions but rather that they are always already composites of dynamically interrelated and conflicted histories. We may think of syncretistic or condensed memories, that is, remembrances composed when people experience and participate in intersecting historical legacies, movements, and presences. Huyssen speaks of complexes of palimpsestic memories, including palimpsests of transnational memories or, as Appadurai calls them, "transnational memoryscapes."[85] The global trend since the nineties to enlist memory work for identity politics, according to Huyssen, obscures the fact that conflicting fields of memory are not only linked or intertwined but also constitutive of one another. They come to form transnational palimpsests of memory.[86] Often these memories are, I argue, condensed or syncretistic memories that operate according to a logic of the unconscious with displacements, substitutions, fusions, and condensations. Much of how we process violent histories is bound to operate on an unconscious level not only because traumatic amnesia may block the conscious memory of violence but also because, as Freud asserts, pain leaves the deepest memory traces in the unconscious. Beyond loss, devastation, and injury, the pain from violent histories includes shame and guilt, which, in turn, mobilize powerful defense mechanisms. This is true for victims as well as for perpetrators and their descendants.

As Huyssen states, conflicting fields of memory are mutually constitutive because of the transferential relation between them at both an individual and collective level. Rothberg points out that "the comparative critic must first constitute the archive [of multidirectional memory] by forging links between dispersed documents."[87] The cultural transference between different sites of memory, however, can be used to generate not only an archive of multidirectional and composite memories but also a political practice of transversal encounters across the Manichean divide between victims and perpetrators. Dan Bar-On and others who work in groups with victims and perpetrators and collect the narratives of their encounters engage in such political practice. They work against the politics of splitting that segregates violent histories at the cost of perpetuating violence.

It is my hope that by writing about the legacy of my country of origin in light of other violent legacies, I will invite further multidirectional engagement of memory that uses the space of transfer and transference for both working through the past and engaging in struggles against war, violence, and new forms of racism and genocidal politics. While some argue that the work of mourning is an indulgence in light of the urgency of political struggle, I insist that the work of mourning cannot be reduced to its psychic and affective dimensions. Psychic and political struggles must go hand-in-hand lest political action be haunted by an unprocessed past. A true politics of mourning must acknowledge that violent histories today are related to the vulnerabilities of increasing global interdependency.

Judith Butler's *Frames of War* addresses this intertwining of the psychic and the political and the conditions under which mourning can be translated into political action. She argues that "an ontology of discrete identity cannot yield the kinds of analytic vocabularies we need for thinking about global interdependency and the interlocking networks of power and position in contemporary life."[88] Similarly, thinking about discrete violent histories tied to national or ethnic and racial identities cannot account for the increasingly global interdependency of violence, war, and genocidal or environmentally destructive politics. A theory of multidirectional, composite, and transferential memory is more attuned than an identitarian memory politics to such global interdependency. As Butler asserts, "a struggle must be waged against those forces that seek to regulate affect in differential ways."[89] Butler's stance is pertinent for a politics of mourning since it acknowledges that the vulnerability to violence "cuts across identity categories" and that our very survival depends on "recognizing how we are bound up with others."[90] Moreover, a theory that acknowledges the rhizomatic connections of memory is more able to account for the fact that we live at the intersections of so many histories of violence that the trauma we experience may well be compared to a "cumulative trauma." The intersections of violent histories generate a structure of condensed experience in which the encounter with new violent histories operates via the recall of earlier histories—not only cognitively but affectively and experientially as well.

A concept of multidirectional memory based on a structure of condensed experiences of violence may finally also address Butler's question of "how we might respond effectively to suffering at a distance."[91] It is often through the detour of displaced yet related memories of violence that social injustice can be addressed on a more encompassing scale, and it is the transference between different collective histories and memories that may facilitate a particular responsiveness to suffering at a distance and to the fact that all lost lives are grievable. Yet such responsiveness hinges on our ability to, in Butler's words, "reconceive life itself as a set of largely unwilled interdependencies, even systemic relations."[92]

Outline

I have organized *Haunting Legacies* to reflect the intersectionality and interdependency of different violent histories. The five chapters following this introduction approach the overarching topic of transgenerational haunting from different historical, cultural, and literary angles and theoretical perspectives. In all the chapters, I elaborate my theoretical and conceptual framework in tandem with textual analysis and interpretation. In particular, I analyze how literary texts and memoirs break through silences and trauma's attack on language to reintegrate conflicted histories into a communal and political space. I juxtapose the narratives of different violent histories not only to highlight their interdependencies and systemic relations; I also attempt to create a discursive transference among those narratives that may mobilize, enforce, or even generate the multidimensional or composite memories of readers.

Chapter 2, "Writing Against Memory and Forgetting," analyzes the attack on mind, psyche, and memory caused by traumatic experiences or knowledge. My readings of testimonies and stories, predominately about the Holocaust but also about colonialism and slavery, highlight the effects of transgenerational haunting. Traumatic experiences are often sealed off from communal communication and exchange; related conflicts thus remain hidden and unresolved. In such cases, the mourning, working-through, and redress necessary for communal healing remain incomplete if not blocked entirely. This psychopolitical dynamic enhances the danger of historical repetition. Hannah Arendt, for example, links the atrocities of the camps to an unresolved legacy of colonial histories of violence. She argues that the collective or communal silencing of violent histories leads to the involuntary repetition of cycles of violence.[93] In a similar vein, Alexander and Margarete Mitscherlich describe the German people's inability to mourn after World War II as a source of political conflict and paralysis hidden under the surface of frantic reconstruction (*Wiederaufbau*).

"Writing Against Memory and Forgetting" focuses on selected Holocaust memoirs, including Ruth Kluger's *Still Alive (Weiterleben)*, W. G. Sebald's *Austerlitz*, Georges Perec's *W, or The Memory of Childhood*, and Marguerite Duras's *The War (La Douleur)*. For comparative purposes I include references to texts that evoke earlier traumatic histories of colonialism and slavery in the United States, including Toni Morrison's *Beloved*, Simon Ortiz's *from Sand Creek*, and William Heyen's *Crazy Horse in Stillness*. Through the perspective gained from these conjoined readings, I expand on theories of transgenerational haunting, traumatic secrecy, and cryptonymy by showing how the literature in question uses writing—and by extension reading—as a "transformational object" that facilitates the creative reworking, integration, and healing of trauma.[94]

I look at the linguistic traces in these literary and autobiographical texts left by traumatic disturbances of the symbolic order such as ruptures, gaps, designifications, and mutilated or invented words. Finally, I view these writings of trauma as attempts to work toward psychic integration and a concomitant reparation of the symbolic. Literary writings of traumatic history often resort to experimental uses of language in order to approximate trauma through the tracing of its effects and inscription in mind, body, and language. In Georges Perec's novel *W*, to use just one example, the letter *W* was used in his childhood to create fantasies that enabled him to cover up the loss of his parents. The letter originally stood for a designification, but Perec creatively reworks it in his memoir in a way that performs a resignification. Using the cryptonymic letter *W* as a transformational object in order to *w*rite the memory of the void left by his parents' death, Perec is able finally to assert life.

I end this chapter with a reading of Samuel Beckett's cryptic voices, suggesting that Beckett can be read as one of the most radical writers of the crypt. Beckett's writings unfold in a paradoxical transitional space between life and death, tying the crypt to a psychic void and to gaps in language. Language in Beckett is haunted by the silence of the tomb. Some of his characters are explicitly figured as "speaking corpses" whose voices emerge from within a horror of the void that comes from facing death in life. Perhaps this is why *writing* trauma matters, if only by murmurs and stammers, or tortured attempts at approximation.

It counters the work of death and breathes life back into the silences haunted by dead words.

"Haunting Legacies: Trauma in Children of Perpetrators" (chapter 3) deals with the legacy of second-generation children of perpetrators or perpetrator nations, with a particular emphasis on postwar West Germany. The silencing of past atrocities is the most common way in which traumatic legacies are transmitted to the next generation. Among the legacies unwittingly inherited by future generations, I argue, is the task of breaking the silence in order to take responsibility for the violence committed by the parental generation. I move from a notion of "collective guilt" to a notion of "collective responsibility."[95] Taking up the work of collective responsibility entails facilitating psychic redress and reparation across the divides of victims and perpetrators, as well as across the boundaries of peoples and nations that have endured violent histories. Such work is the necessary groundwork for addressing the residual psychic and political damage that inevitably remains a legacy of violent histories.

I begin this chapter with an analysis of the psychosocial dynamics of growing up in postwar Germany under foreign occupation that includes relevant readings of historical and literary texts. Finally, I include two personal narratives, titled "The Phantom Brother" and "The Phantom Town." In "The Phantom Brother" I provide a concrete example of the transgenerational transmission of trauma by tracing the psychic effect on my life of a brother who was killed as an infant during the war. In "The Phantom Town," I analyze the discovery of a book about the history of Jews in Tiengen, the town where I grew up as a child. I symptomatically read the shock of recognition when I discovered, like in an archeological excavation of a city's buried history, the erased traces of Jewish life in my hometown. This is when I realized that, despite my many attempts to learn more about the Holocaust than the sparse knowledge offered to us at school, I had never thought for a moment that the persecution and deportation of Jews during the Nazi era could have included the small medieval town where I grew up. My own unwitting complicity in not asking about the history that was right there in front of me is a typical unconscious mechanism of children born after violent histories. Silencing the past by not wanting to see is one of many such futile attempts to numb the inheritance of pain, guilt, and shame of the second generation.

More generally, the chapter addresses the complicated dynamic between knowing and not knowing, belonging and not wanting to belong that marked the psychic life of many German postwar children. Silence does not need to be complete to operate as a shaping and censoring force. As I argued earlier, in Germany after the war there was an open politics of acknowledgment of war crimes, including the Nuremberg trials and the process of "de-Nazification" as well as the monumentalization of victimhood and official politics of reparation. But these acts did not include a psychosocial politics that addressed the responsibility, complicity, guilt, shame, and psychosocial deformation of the culture at large. Ultimately, the official politics did not break through the politics of silencing, denial, and disavowal. The latter politics became a haunting legacy for postwar children, a legacy that marked the formation of psychic space and the affective politics that shaped public discourse and private lives with unacknowledged if not unconscious feelings of guilt and shame.

In "Identity Trouble: Guilt, Shame, and Idealization" (chapter 4) I further expand on my analysis of the legacy of violence and its transgenerational impact. I assess the psychic deformation and identity trouble of the generation that inherits the legacy of violent histories by drawing on psychoanalytically inflected theories of social psychology. Here I include Frantz Fanon's theory of decolonization, Kelly Oliver's concept of the "colonization of psychic space," Ashis Nandy's notion of "intimate enemies" and the dynamic he calls "isomorphic oppression," and Dan Bar-On's work with mixed groups of victims and perpetrators. I also analyze the "politics of emotions," as theorized by Sara Ahmed, in political constructions of what anthropologists define as guilt-versus shame-cultures.

I call chapter 4 "Identity Trouble," because violent histories deeply affect notions of identity and belonging in both victims and perpetrators. While "identity" is widely recognized as a troubled concept in the wake of identity politics, I believe that descendants of victims as well as descendants of perpetrators struggle with more specific and often debilitating issues of identity formation. Frantz Fanon's famous statement "I am a white man" exemplifies internalization of the colonizer's value system and raises the problem of projective identification not only as a phenomenon of individual pathology but also as a potentially pathological form of transcultural relationality. When Scott Momaday says, for example, "I don't know how to be a Kiowa Indian," he refers to the identity trouble of a colonized person whose people coexist in subaltern positions with the colonizers in their own stolen land. Centuries of ongoing colonization have so thoroughly imposed the culture of the colonizer on indigenous peoples that their own culture has often been at least temporarily buried. The cultural devastation is such that it is hard to know "how to be a Kiowa Indian" in today's day and age.

But Momaday also stands for cultural revival. His novel *House Made of Dawn* is said to have initiated the so-called Native American Renaissance. At the same time, cultural revival does not preclude and is indeed often propelled by the experience of identity trouble. Cultural revival often comes with an increased awareness of colonization's continued effects. This is a form of identity trouble that affects Kiowa and other indigenous people on both a personal and cultural level. It also continues to haunt the descendants of former slaves, even at a time when the United States has elected its first black president. As Barack Obama says in *Dreams from My Father*, "I was trying to raise myself as a black man in America, and beyond the given of my appearance, no one around me seemed to know exactly what that meant."[96]

In "Identity Trouble," I also reflect on how a history of perpetration can instill identity trouble in children of perpetrators, including a pervasive self-hatred and concomitant sense of not wanting to belong. Sabine Reichel's laconic statement, "I . . . hated Germany. I hated being German," is not an isolated personal reaction but a widely shared sentiment among second-generation Germans, one that is prominent in those Germans who left their country. In this context, I also rethink Alexander and Margarete Mitscherlich's notion of an inability to mourn, as well as Abraham and Torok's notion of failed mourning and transgenerational haunting, including its Derridean reworking in "Fors." With Dan Bar-On, I argue that mourning violent histories cannot come to a resolution unless one develops collective practices of mourning that cross the divide between victims and perpetrators.

"Replacement Children: The Transgenerational Transmission of Traumatic Loss" (chapter 5) focuses on the figure of the so-called replacement child as a specific manifestation of transgenerational trauma. Psychologists have identified the wish for a replacement child as a widespread response to the traumatic loss of a child, especially during or after violent histories such as the Holocaust or other genocidal wars. Children born after such wars may feel the burden to replace more than merely the child or children their parents lost during the war. They grow up with the sense that their generation must replace the entire generation that was destined for genocide. I analyze this phenomenon and its political ramifications in two Holocaust memoirs, Art Spiegelman's *Maus* and Philippe Grimbert's *Secret*.

Political cartoonist Art Spiegelman is perhaps one of the best known replacement children. Born after the shoah to Jewish parents, he grew up with the sense that he was competing with his "ghost-brother," Richieu. *Maus*, the critically acclaimed experimental memoir written as a comic book, is dedicated to Richieu and to Spiegelman's daughter, Nadja. The autobiographical character Art displays the prominent symptoms of a replacement child. Haunted by a brother who was killed before Art's birth, Art struggles with parents who refuse to accept their firstborn's death. The replacement child confronts the bitter irony that the ideal child is a dead child. In his parents' fantasies, the dead son Richieu would have fulfilled all their dreams while Art, their living child, fails them. One cannot compete with a dead child, and yet one cannot avoid the ghostly competition handed down with parental fantasies. This tacit competition with a dead sibling is a classical syndrome of replacement children. It is also a prevalent form in which parental trauma is transmitted to the next generation and often to generations to come.

In *Secret*, Philippe Grimbert paradigmatically illustrates the phenomenon of "transgenerational haunting."[97] As a child, Grimbert is haunted by the ghost of his brother who died at Auschwitz, even though his parents had kept the existence of this brother a family secret. Only after the secret is revealed can Grimbert begin the work of mourning and of coming into his own, a process for which writing trauma forms the basis. In the context of these readings, I also analyze the uncanny resemblance the psychological dynamic of replacement children bears to the logic of supplementarity that Derrida introduces in *Of Grammatology*. Art's parents, for example, keep Richieu *alive* in a nostalgic, almost hallucinatory presence that denies his actual death. Under these conditions, Art can only move into the position of a supplement to the *real*, originary child. Like other replacement children, he comes to feel like a sign that must replace the absence of the thing itself.

I continue the chapter with a reading of two Maori novels that deal with the issue of replacement children in a different fashion, Witi Ithimaera's *Whale Rider* and Patricia Grace's *Baby No-Eyes*. *Whale Rider* deals with a girl who is haunted by the impossible legacy of replacing the twin brother who died in childbirth and who was supposed to have taken over the patrilineal tribal leadership. This novel reveals the frequent intersection of identity trouble with gender trouble in replacement children, especially in partriarchal cultures. *Baby No-Eyes*, another Maori novel, reflects the phenomenon of replacement children in the context of biocolonialism, which is directed at the genetic inheritance of indigenous people. The ghost of a sister who died in a car accident and whose eyes were stolen for genetic research haunts Tawera, the main character. Incorporating the ghost as a character with her own voice, Patricia Grace uses this experimental device of a "speaking corpse" to give agency to the ghosts of the past over and beyond their effects on the living.

Finally, I conclude with reflections on such political figures as Gandhi and Amy Biehl, whose parents "adopted" the murderer of their daughter as a deliberate act in a larger anti-Apartheid struggle. These reflections open the issues of mourning and forgiveness, as well as redress and reparation. In this context, I explore how the work of mourning is impeded in a culture that is accustomed to and values replacements and substitutions more generally.

Chapter 6, "Deadly Intimacy: The Politics and Psychic Life of Torture," analyzes torture as an illegitimate and politically dysfunctional response to political conflict. Torture induces psychic death, and the violation of humane ethics in torture reaches the very heart of human vulnerability. Its effects are enhanced by the fact that it happens within a custodial relationship. Extreme terror and pain generate a malignant intimacy between the torturer and his victim. Ashis Nandy's metaphor of "intimate enemies," which he uses to describe the dialectics of oppression, precisely captures the psychic relationship between a torturer and his victim. My textual material in the chapter on torture ranges from Ngũgĩ wa Thiong'o's and Leonard Peltier's prison writings to Ruth Kluger's Holocaust memoir, *Still Alive*, and Ariel Dorfman's *Death and the Maiden*, a play about the military dictatorship in Chile. In addition, I include reflections on Liliana Cavani's controversial film, *The Nightporter*.

I read these works in the context of current debates on torture in the wake of Abu Ghraib and Guantánamo Bay. My general argument is that, in the long term, torture destroys not only the victim but also the perpetrator, if only because in order to kill his victim's self, the torturer must also kill his own soul. Once torture is sanctioned, it cannot be confined. It kills the self, family, community, and country. In essence, it attacks not only the victim's but also the perpetrator's hold on life. At the same time, many have survived torture and become reintegrated in their social, professional, and family lives. Writing torture is one of the ways in which some have reclaimed their lives. These writings defy the torturer's attack on language, memory, psyche, and the communal world.

I end the chapter on torture with a brief reflection on war children and the specific forms of torture inflicted upon them. My thoughts are inspired by the current wave of memoirs of child soldiers and their commodification in a global media culture, especially Ishmael Beah's *A Long Way Gone*. Within the overarching topic of transgenerational trauma, war children play a central role because they are forced to carry not only the psychic legacy but also the concrete material and political legacy of violent histories. Child soldiers, for example, are coerced to put their bodies and lives on the line for wars handed down to them from the parental generation. Torture—often performed as an "initiation torture" during which the child is forced to kill a friend or a relative—is an all too frequent element in the recruitment and training of child soldiers. The very act of torture, in other words, consists in turning the child victim into a perpetrator. Forcing a child to become a perpetrator by killing a friend or a member of the family is perhaps the most abject form of torture imaginable. What are the traumatic legacies that have been passed on to these children and what are the legacies they will carry through their lives and pass on to their own children? And what can we do to stop these histories of violence and survive as individual human beings, as a people and as a species?

It seems appropriate to end this book on violent histories and transgenerational trauma with a reflection on the torture inflicted on children in our global world. The estimated number of child soldiers around the world is approximately 300,000.[98] Children are icons in the cultural imaginary because they herald a future to come. If the moral standing and indeed the very humanity of a culture can be measured by how it treats its children, today's world does not fare well. The wars and other forms of violence that haunt the globe have changed the face of child-hood. In the introduction to *Small Wars: The Cultural Politics of Child-hood*, Nancy Scheper-Hughes and Carolyn Sargent write:

> The perennial losers, however, in the aggressive restaging of the new world order were certain categories of "superfluous" people, among them peripheral peasants, indigenous peoples, and poor children. The dependent and "supernumerary" child of the poor and marginalized populations of the world has emerged as one of late capitalism's residual categories—its quintessential nonproductive, "parasitical," Other.[99]

My emphasis of *Haunting Legacies* is on the transgenerational transmission of trauma. In the case of child soldiers and poor children deemed superfluous and parasitical, we see violence and trauma inflicted on children firsthand. This malignant rupture of human caring at the heart of a global world must concern everybody. The destiny of trau-matized children around the world is a signpost pointing to the future of our globe. What kind of trauma will these children pass on to their children if they even survive this violence? What will we reap from the seeds of catastrophic loneliness we have sown in them? Who will be the new victims of these victims if we cannot break the cycle of violence? Who will take responsibility for this theft of childhood?

chaptertwo

Writing Against Memory and Forgetting

Holes and gaps are so central in narrative fiction because the
materials the text provides for the reconstruction of a world (or a
story) are insufficient for saturation.
—Shlomith Rimmon-Kenan, *Narrative Fiction: Contemporary Poetics*

Stories are told to register a truth that cannot be found in the simple
telling of facts.
—Sue Grand, *The Reproduction of Evil*

For to end yet again skull alone in the dark the void no neck no face
just the box last place of all in the dark the void.
—Samuel Beckett, *For the End Yet Again*

We tell or write stories in order to defer death. In his story "The End,"
Samuel Beckett approximates the end from the distant memory of a possible life story: "The memory came faint and cold of the story I might
have told, a story in the likeness of my life, I mean without the courage
to end or the strength to go on."[1] Stories in "the likeness of . . . life"
reside in a transitional space between memory and forgetting. They arise
from faint memories, memories not to be trusted. Life writings often
emerge from a traumatic core, occupying a space between two parallel
universes: daily life and trauma. In real life, it is dangerous for these
universes to touch. In writing, they must converge. Otherwise, writing
remains cut off, the words stranded in the silence they try to cover,
orbiting trauma like satellites. Writing from within the core of trauma
is a constant struggle between the colonizing power of words and the
revolt of what is being rejected, silenced. Trauma kills the pulsing of
desire, the embodied self. Trauma attacks and sometimes kills language.
In order for trauma to heal, body and self must be reborn, and words
need to be disentangled from the dead bodies they are trying to hide. In
A Child Is Being Killed: On Primary Narcissism and the Death Drive,

Serge Leclaire writes: "The subject is born and reborn solely from the constant disentanglement of body and words, from a perpetually repeatable crossing of the grid of signifiers, from the ghostly, hallucinated reunion with the lost but immediately present object, right there, so very close to us."[2]

There is no life without trauma. There is no history without trauma. Some lives will forever be overshadowed by violent histories, including colonial invasions, slavery, totalitarianism, dictatorships, wars, and genocide. Some murders, including soul murders, are committed by people using sanctioned disciplinary regimes that enforce subjugation and oppression. These may include kidnapping, lynching, torture, mutilation, captivity, disappearances, police brutality, and rape. Collective trauma is passed down to individuals in multifarious and refracted ways. Some lives are hit with catastrophic trauma over and over again; then trauma, with its concomitant strategies of survival, becomes a chronic condition. Defenses and denial become second nature; traumatic repetition becomes second nature. Trauma as a mode of being violently halts the flow of time, fractures the self, and punctures memory and language. And then there are those afflicted by what Freud called "*Schicksalsneurose*," that is, a "fate neurosis," who seem to be living under a bad spell, haunted by a curse that often precedes their lives, an ancestral curse perhaps, hidden and intangible, relegated to secrecy and silence.[3]

When I was a child I loved to talk to old people. I sought them out because I felt an insatiable curiosity about their life stories. Looking back, I realize that old people tell stories about trauma. Yet, in these stories, trauma is often curiously contained. Words seal over violent ruptures and wounds. Voice has settled into quiet detachment. Occasionally, a few tears emerge, like traces leading away from an old wound. Mostly, however, the stories have grown over the open wound like a second skin.

Perhaps my sense of life narratives is colored by my growing up with war stories told night after night by adults around the dinner table. These stories were not addressed to me, not meant for me. They were stories told in my presence as if I was not there, stories that left me stranded in a muted space outside.

I remember the traumatic core of these stories. Their broken images and fragmented scenes remain inside me like ruins of memory: bombs falling from the sky, howling sirens, burning houses, people huddled in damp cellars, people running and screaming, people buried under ruins. And then there is an image that assaults me at times out of the blue. My mother put it inside me the day she took me to see the street where our old family house that was bombed to the ground had stood. "Right down the street there used to be a playground," my mother said. "One day they bombed the playground. There were children's bodies everywhere, torn arms and limbs and the severed head of a little boy." I was six or perhaps seven when my mother told me this, and the image merged with another story told myriad times throughout my life, the story of the infant brother I never knew, poisoned by the smoke of burning houses and dying a slow and painful death.

As a child I thus became the silent witness to these war stories, the one not allowed to ask questions or interrupt the flow of words. Yet I became much more. I became an empty vessel to hold a deeper terror that remained untold, a silence covered by words, a history condemned to secrecy, a deadly guilt and mute shame handed down as shards of splintered affect. It took me almost half a century to understand that the purpose of those stories was not to remember but to forget. They were supposed to cover up, to mute the pain and guilt and shame, to fill the void of terror. Yet, even as a child, I picked up on something amiss in these stories. That, more than anything else, left me confused. It was as if the words themselves were emptied of the very feelings invoked in me when I was confronted with the facts of horror. It was not that the stories were devoid of emotions but rather that words and emotions did not quite fit together; words echoed falsely. Children have a sense of this discrepancy but do not understand it. Today, I am convinced that I picked up on something untold, silenced, violently cut out. At the time, I was just confused and mortified by a silent terror that lay under the surface of what was told. It upset my trust in words, I think, as well as my sense of attunement. It complicated how I related to those I was supposed to trust, my parents and my grandmother. Words could be split into what they said and what they did not say. It was as if they carried a secret that cast me out. I had a vague sense of something deadly, of words filled with skeletons. My own words were stolen, and I became withdrawn and taciturn, a girl without words, as I used to think of myself.

In my mind, war stories were the stuff of the real world, a terrifying place. They contrasted sharply with the stories I loved, the fairy tales my grandmother read to me when we were alone at home. Fairy tales were scary, too, but beautifully alive; they contained and transformed the fear. Looking back, I think they helped me process the onslaught of raw emotions, the fears, terrors, and loneliness of a child exposed too early to stories of trauma, including stories told to cover up trauma. Even though my grandmother's voice was sad and distant when she read aloud, I hungered for those stories and wanted to hear them again and again. My grandmother always pulled her chair up to the window and put me on her lap, where I sat listening and forgetting about the outside world. The string of words connected me to my grandmother; they were the connective tissue of my childhood days.

Words that were lifted out of books were different. These stories held mysteries, secrets that only the adults could reveal. As far back as I can remember, books and the letters they held fascinated me. My parents had a bookshelf in the living room, and years before I learned to read I would sit in front of the shelf, taking out book after book, holding them, touching them, opening and smelling them. I would gaze at the letters, trying to figure out how they could hold the stories I heard. "There are writers," my mother explained. "They write the stories down for others to read." I wanted to be a writer. I wanted to write down the stories that came to mind when I held the books and pretended to read. When nobody was around, I secretly fulfilled my dream. In between the lines of my parents' books I inserted squiggly lines and dots and signs, a child's hieroglyphs. A few years ago, browsing through my parents' old books, I came across my scribbles again. Lines after lines filled the empty spaces, crawling all over the margins like worms on a page—bookworms. They reminded me of the squiggly lines the Indians from the Amazon rainforest presented to Claude Levi-Strauss, the anthropologist who prided himself for having given them the gift of writing. I now realize that the squiggly lines of my child writing were apt depictions of my sense that words held secrets that longed to be deciphered. I had spontaneously invented my own cryptographic writing; only it never had a code. It had some sort of referent, however, because when I took a book out and found my writings from the day before I remembered the story I wanted it to tell. The thought that I was the only one able to read my books never occurred to me. Writing was lonely from the very beginning. Writing was also the fulfillment of the wish to inhabit a space of secret desire.

Today I am trying to grasp these tacit spaces of storytelling and writing. I am trying to understand the silent witnessing of the child exposed to stories not meant for her ears. I am trying to trace the long-term effects on language and psyche. I am looking at stories as carriers of transgenerational trauma. In their pathbreaking work on mourning and melancholia, *The Shell and the Kernel*, Nicolas Abraham and Maria Torok develop a theory of cryptonymy that traces different ways and forms of hiding in language. "Cryptonymy" refers to operations in language that emerge as manifestations of a psychic crypt, often in form of fragmentations, distortions, gaps, or ellipses. Abraham and Torok write about the crypt as an effect of failed mourning: it is a burial place inside the self for a love object that is lost but kept inside the self like a living corpse. The crypt is a melancholic, funereal architectonic in inner space, built after traumatic loss. Traumatic loss, Abraham and Torok assert, needs to be silenced and cut off from the world. The crypt contains the secrets and silences formed in trauma. Accordingly, the secret conceals a trauma whose very occurrence and devastating emotional consequences become entombed and consigned to internal silence by the sufferers. Freud argues in "Mourning and Melancholia" that the melancholic attachment to lost objects is not confined to the loss of loved ones but can include the loss of a place or a community or even the loss of ideals. It can also include the loss of self after a trauma such as rape, torture, or severe forms of rejection and humiliation. A crypt could thus, for example, be built as a tomb for one's lost self. In this narcissistic form of encryptment, the old self is treated like a <u>lost love object</u>. Trauma shatters the self, yet trauma usually also blocks mourning. Melancholia may take over and encrypt the old self while the newly traumatized self is repudiated as contaminated. If the lost object is the self, melancholia resembles an act of self-cannibalization: the encrypted self eats away at the traumatized surviving self from inside, trying to kill it off by severing its ties to the world outside. Often it is the body that becomes the site of narration, enacting in corporeal cryptography the conflict between the encrypted lost self and the traumatized self. In telling this story, the body can speak as a cannibal from inside, devouring food or ejecting it violently. It can speak as the old self, requiring to be touched like the child who is still whole, seeking a healing touch that can put the body back together. The body can abandon itself and speak the trauma of disrupted care; it can hurt itself to speak the pain; it can waste away to speak the wish to die.

There can be collective crypts, communal crypts, and even national crypts. Alexander and Margarete Mitscherlich were the first to theorize the inability to mourn experienced by the German people after World War II.[4] The frantic *Wiederaufbau*, the rebuilding of Germany after the war, was a manic defense that covered an equally desperate construction in the national psyche, the secret erection of a crypt in which the Germans buried what they had lost yet denied having lost: their sense of themselves as a human people. Many of them also encrypted their own losses—the children, husbands, brothers, and sisters killed in the war. Could it be that some of them encrypted the lost Jewish German people? Could it be that perpetrators encrypt their own humanity? Or—the scariest thought of all—could it be that some of them encrypted the lost (idealization of the) *Führer*? And what about the Jewish people? How many of them encrypted their lost homes in Germany and their lost attachment to German culture, even to friends among the German people? Under what conditions does it make sense to speak of a collective crypt? And how would it manifest itself in speech and writing, in stories and narration?

People have always silenced violent histories. Some histories, collective and personal, are so violent we would not be able to live our daily lives if we did not at least temporarily silence them. A certain amount of splitting is conducive to survival. Too much silence, however, becomes haunting. Abraham and Torok link the formation of the crypt with silencing, secrecy, and the phantomatic return of the past. While the secret is intrapsychic and indicates an internal psychic splitting, it can be collectively deployed and shared by a people or a nation. The collective or communal silencing of violent histories leads to a transgenerational transmission of trauma and the specter of an involuntary repetition of cycles of violence. We know this from history, literature, and trauma studies. In *The Origins of Totalitarianism*, for example, Hannah Arendt, writes about the "phantom world of the dark continent."[5] Referring to the adventurers, gamblers, and criminals that came as luck hunters to South Africa during the gold rush, Arendt describes them as "an inevitable residue of the capitalist system and even the representatives of an economy that relentlessly produced a superfluity of men and capital" (189). "They were not individuals like the old adventurers," she continues, drawing on Conrad's *Heart of Darkness*, "they were the shadows of events with which they had nothing to do" (189). They found the full realization of their "phantomlike-existence" in the destruction of native life: "Native life lent these ghostlike events a seeming guarantee against all consequences because anyhow it looked to these men like a 'mere play of shadows. A play of shadows, the dominant race could walk through unaffected and disregarded in the pursuit of incomprehensible aims and needs'" (190). When European men massacred the indigenous people, Arendt argues, they did so without allowing themselves to become aware of the fact that they had committed murder. Like Conrad's character Kurtz, many of these adventurers went insane. They had buried and silenced their guilt; they had buried and silenced their humanity. But their deeds came back to haunt them in a vicious cycle of repetition. Arendt identifies two main political devices for imperialist rule: race and bureaucracy: "Race . . . was an escape into an irresponsibility where nothing human could any longer exist, and bureaucracy was the result of a responsibility that no man can bear for his fellow-man and no people for another people" (207). The genocide of indigenous peoples under colonial and imperial rule was silenced in a defensive discourse of progressing civilization, but it returned with a vengeance. Race and bureaucracy were the two main devices used under fascism during the haunting return to the heart of Europe of the violence against other human beings developed under colonial and imperial rule. The ghosts of colonial and imperial violence propelled the Jewish Holocaust, Arendt shows.

In a similar vein, in *Discourse on Colonialism*, Aimé Césaire writes about the rise of Nazism in Europe as a "terrific boomerang effect."[6] He argues that before the people in Europe became the victims of Nazism, they were its accomplices, that "they tolerated that Nazism before it was inflicted on them, that they absolved it, shut their eyes to it, legitimized it, because, until then, it has been applied only to non-European peoples" (36). Césaire continues: "Yes, it would be worthwhile to study clinically, in detail, the steps taken by Hitler and Hitlerism and to reveal to the very distinguished, very humanistic, very Christian bourgeois of the twentieth century that without being aware of it, he has a Hitler inside him, that Hitler *inhabits* him, that Hitler is his *demon*" (36, Césaire's italics). This is as close as we can come to an argument that, until they face the ghosts of their own history and take responsibility for all the histories of violence committed under their rule, Europeans encrypt the ghost of Hitler in their psychic life. Césaire's statement also contains an argument about what Ashis Nandy calls "isomorphic oppression," that is, about the fact that histories of violence create psychic deformations not only in the victims but also in the perpetrators.[7] No one colonizes innocently, Césaire asserts, and no one colonizes with impunity, either. One of the psychic deformations of the perpetrator is that he turns himself into the very thing that he projects onto and tries to destroy in the other: "The colonizer, who in order to ease his conscience gets into the habit of seeing the other man as *an animal*, accustoms himself to treating him like an animal, and tends objectively to transform *himself* into an animal. It is this result, this boomerang effect of colonization that I wanted to point out" (41, Césaire's italics).[8] What Césaire calls the "boomerang effect" emerges from a dialectics of isomorphic oppression that as a rule remains largely unacknowledged and relegated to the cultural unconscious. Together with the ghost effect that emerges from the silencing of traumatic memories, this boomerang effect increases the danger of a repetition and ghostly return of violent histories. What do we have to offset such a vicious circle of violent returns? Many victims emphasize testimony, witnessing, mourning, and reparation. Many theories, including psychoanalysis, concur with this assumption.

Let me therefore turn to the telling and writing of traumatic histories and their relationship to mourning and reparation. What is silenced and what can be said about histories of violence and trauma? To counter silence, the victims of history have produced an abundance of literature of witnessing, testimonials, and memoirs. At the same time, we have a whole body of theories that claim trauma's unrepresentability. There are forms of violence—the Holocaust, genocide, torture, and rape—that are considered beyond representation. Yet they also call for speech, testimony, and witnessing. This is an irresolvable paradox at the core of traumatic writing. How, then, do we both write and resist representation? We know that traumatic amnesia can also generate other prohibitions on thought and emotion that are fundamentally opposed to narrative and storytelling. And yet we know that telling and witnessing are necessary for healing trauma. We need a theory of traumatic narrative that deals with the paradox of telling what cannot be told or what has been silenced.

Returning to Abraham and Torok's theory of the crypt and cryptographic speech, we may begin to outline a framework for looking at traumatic narrative. Their basic premise is that unless trauma is worked through and integrated, it will be passed on to the next generation. If this happens, the next generation will inherit the psychic substance of the previous generation and display symptoms that do not emerge from their own individual experience but from a parent's, relative's, or community's psychic conflicts, traumata, or secrets. This process is experienced as if an individual were haunted by the ghosts, that is, the unfinished business, of a previous generation. People tend to bury violent or shameful histories. They create psychic crypts meant to stay sealed off from the self, interior tombs haunted by the ghosts of the past. Crypts engender silence. However, untold or unspeakable secrets, unfelt or denied pain, concealed shame, covered-up crimes, or violent histories continue to affect and disrupt the lives of those involved in them and often their descendants as well. Silencing these violent and shameful histories casts them outside the continuity of psychic life but, unintegrated and unassimilated, they eat away at this continuity from within. Lives become shadow lives, simulacra of a hollowed-out normality. In this way, the buried ghosts of the past come to haunt language from within, always threatening to destroy its communicative and expressive function.

Attacks on language are the material manifestations of attacks on memory, and yet it is language that preserves traces of the destroyed memory: this is the paradox of writings from the crypt. A passage from W. G. Sebald's *Austerlitz* describes the eponymous character's attack on memory and his subsequent loss of language in vivid terms:

> I realized then, he said, how little practice I had in using my memory, and conversely how hard I must always have tried to recollect as little as possible, avoiding everything which related in any way to my unknown past. Inconceivable as it seems to me today, I knew nothing about the conquest of Europe by the Germans and the slave state they set up, and nothing about the persecution I had escaped. . . . I was always refining my defensive reactions, creating a kind of quarantine or immune system which, as I maintained my existence on a smaller and smaller space, protected me from anything that could be connected in any way, however distant, with my own early history. Moreover, I

had constantly been preoccupied by that accumulation of knowledge which I had pursued for decades, and which served as a substitute or compensatory memory. . . . Yet, this self-censorship of the mind, the constant suppression of the memories surfacing in me, Austerlitz continued, demanded ever greater efforts and finally, and unavoidably, led to the almost total paralysis of my linguistic faculties, the destruction of all my notes and sketches . . . up to the point of my nervous breakdown in the summer of 1992.[9]

Meant to silence his early traumatic history, Austerlitz's attack on memory not only leads to a loss of language but also to a shrinking and contraction of his world. Needing to cut off whatever belongs to or could remind him of this trauma turns him into a being outside historical space and time, a being belonging nowhere, not even to himself. Thus quarantined from the world, he remains immune to traumatic impingements and mnemonic intrusions, a state that ultimately translates into immunity to being. It is a form of death in life. Instead of a lively connection to the world, he finds a gaping hole; instead of stories that carry his memories, he finds a void that he frantically tries to fill with "substitute or compensatory memory." The latter emerges from a mere accumulation of cold knowledge that remains abstract and aloof and leaves his self stranded in empty speech. Narratives composed under traumatic self-censorship impose an inhibition on subjective focalization, systematically attempting to expunge traces of psychic life in favor of objective description.[10] And yet, to the extent that the narrative deals with traumatic history, we may assume that traces of trauma assert themselves in hidden form. This "self-censorship of [the] mind," as Austerlitz calls it, attacks the function of speech to the point of an "almost total paralysis of [his] linguistic faculties." The actual destruction of all of Austerlitz's notes and sketches allegorically enacts the destruction not only of memory but of its displaced and compensatory traces as well. One can see the ambivalence in this act. Destroying the defenses of compensatory memory traces is an act of despair, a futile attempt to halt the attacks on memory and history and life. Sometimes breaking down is an attempt to heal. Sometimes the breakdown of language forces us to listen to the silence, to acknowledge the gap, to inhabit it and rebuild the world from inside out. It is not long after his nervous breakdown that Austerlitz comes across the exhibition hall of the Trade Fair precinct where his people had been herded together by the Nazis. He comes across "identity papers stamped EVACUATED or GHETTOIZED," which is, the reader realizes, what he has done with his memories of trauma: he has evacuated and ghettoized them.[11] This is how the effects of trauma continue to repeat the traumatic event and fulfill the perpetrator's task long after the fact, indeed long after the facts have been "forgotten." In attacking his memories, Austerlitz assumes the identity stamped on the papers: along with his memories, his self has become evacuated and ghettoized as well.

The attack on memory that Austerlitz experiences is not confined to his individual memory but comprises the collective transgenerational memory of his people. Memories are passed on from generation to generation, most immediately through stories told or written, but more subliminally through a parent's moods or modes of being that create a particular economy and aesthetics of care. Formed during the earliest phases of life, the latter are often remembered not as thoughts or words or stories but existentially as moods or even somatically in the form of embodied psychic life.[12] Often it is through the transgenerational transmission of body memories and forms of somatic psychic life that trauma is unconsciously received and remembered. In one of his poems in *from Sand Creek*, Simon J. Ortiz uses a stunning image of a traumatic disruption of cellular memory:

> They crossed country
> that would lay
> beyond memory.
> Their cells
> would no longer bother
> to remember.
> Memory
> was not to be trusted.[13]

Traces of psychic life can be transmitted from person to person and from generation to generation. This process may unfold through individual as well as collective histories, and it becomes particularly significant in the presence of unhealed wounds, unbearable secrets, or unspeakable violence. The descendants of violent histories—be they children of victims or perpetrators—are the carriers of a collective psychology comprising several generations. Abraham and Torok use a tropology of haunting—composed of tropes such as ghosts, phantoms, and revenants—to invoke the existence of a transindividual psychic life. In *The Shell and the Kernel*, they state, "Only certain categories of the dead return to torment the living: those who were denied the rite of burial or died an unnatural, abnormal death, were criminals or outcasts, or suffered injustice in their lifetime."[14] The dead pass on their unresolved conflicts to their descendants. This foreign presence finds its way into speech and writing, a process Abraham and Torok liken to ventriloquism. An individual or a generation can unwittingly speak the unconscious of a previous individual or generation in a cryptic speech marked by an unspeakable secret. Thus, we can see the consequence of secret family, communal, or national histories and how silenced or secretive histories haunt and inscribe themselves in cryptic forms into the stories that are told. This is what Toni Morrison allegorizes in her novel *Beloved* with the return of the murdered child as a ghost. Morrison's reiterated incantation at the end of the novel—"It was not a story to pass on"—marks *Beloved* as the story of a crypt that is at the same time personal, communal, and national.[15]

A poem by William Heyen titled "December 29, 1890" expresses particular insight into the dynamic of communal and national haunting:

The Sioux massacred
at Wounded Knee wear magic
white ghost shirts whose force fields
were not/can not be solved by white bullets.[16]

During the massacre at Wounded Knee, the medicine man Yellow Bird danced a few ghost dance steps and chanted a holy song that was meant to prevent the soldiers' bullets from penetrating the sacred garments of his people. "The bullets will not go toward you," he chanted in Sioux. "The prairie is large and the bullets will not go toward you."[17] While Yellow Bird could not protect his people by literally deflecting the bullets, Heyen suggests another reading of the sacred chant. The force field of the Sioux's ghost shirts reaches beyond the confines of material history and indicates something indestructible: the history of Wounded Knee cannot be silenced, and it will come to haunt those who fired the bullets. Yet how much and what of the history of Wounded Knee can be told? What if memory can no longer be trusted? What do we know about the dread of those who perished and those who survived and passed this dread on from generation to generation? In *from Sand Creek*, Ortiz writes about the Cheyenne and Arapaho people massacred at Sand Creek on November 29, 1864. He includes a poem about the settlers who came in the name of Manifest Destiny and left death and ghost towns in the wake of their conquest:

Frontiers ended for them
and a dread settled upon them
and became remorseless
    nameless
    namelessness.[18]

Often, nameless dread is translated into an attack on memory and language: the settlers buried their memories in order to escape the nameless dread instilled by their own violence. And yet the settlers share this nameless dread with the surviving Cheyenne and Arapaho, as histories of violence damage both victims and perpetrators—isomorphic oppression. Nameless dread leads perpetrators in their futile attempt to silence history, but it can also silence the victims of trauma, foreclosing their testimonies even to the point of literal muteness—as we know from children who stop speaking, sometimes for years, after an exposure to trauma. Finally, nameless dread can attack the communicative function of language and employ ingenious devices to hide its meaning under undecipherable traces of trauma. Abraham and Torok's theory of cryptonymy can thus be read as a theory of the readability of trauma's secret spaces. The crypt becomes traceable, visible, or readable not only in cryptic or hieroglyphic verbs—such as in the Wolf Man's "fetish words"—but in other gaps in or deformations of language: incoherencies, discontinuities, disruptions, and the disintegration of meaning or grammar or semantic and rhetorical coherence.[19] In order to find the crypt in language, we need to read speech and writing as a "system of expressive traces."[20] Dysfunctions in expressiveness may then be read as symptoms and symptomatic silences or traces pointing to a secret that is paradoxically both kept and revealed in language. It is not so much the content of the secret or the story that is revealed but rather the imprint it has left, perhaps over generations, on affect and its expression in speech or writing. Nicolas Rand speaks of "the blocked expression of a memory trace which cannot tell the submerged history of its own (traumatic) origins."[21] He highlights the fact that while contemporary theories of reading from phenomenology, structuralism, poststructuralism, and deconstruction focus on the emergence or failures of meaning, Abraham and Torok focus on the possibility of reinstating meaning after its traumatic collapse.[22] Trauma causes what Nicolas Rand calls a "psychic aphasia" that disturbs and obfuscates meaning and aims at the destruction of the expressive power of language.[23] In the case of the Wolf Man's cryptonymy, for example, we find the erasure or concealment of a significant link within a chain of words. And yet, Abraham and Torok argue, the link is preserved in a crypt within language. This is why they supplement Freud's theory of dynamic repression of censored emotions, which is based on a desire to get rid of the emotions, with a "preservative repression" that preserves the emotion but seals it off and encrypts it in order to hide the traces of an obliterated event.[24] It is the ghostly emergence of such traces in language that indicates the preservative economy of the crypt. "The phantom represents the interpersonal and transgenerational consequences of silence," Rand writes in his editor's note to the chapter "Secrets and Posterity."[25] Language itself becomes haunted, and haunted language uses a gap inside speech to point to silenced history. Haunted language refers to what is unspeakable though ellipsis, indirection and detour, or fragmentation and deformation. A whole range of rhetorical figures may be mobilized to perform the work of crypts in language: metaphor, metonymy, homophony, homonymy, puns, semantic ambiguities, malapropisms, anagrams, and rebus and similar figures that all combine concealment and revelation. This is not to say that the use of these rhetorical figures is always in the service of a crypt but rather that they lend themselves for linguistic encryptment because of their ability to conceal yet retain a revealing trace.

As a rule, haunted language has vacated the emotions, the pain and terror, pertaining to the silenced history. As a result, it has become empty speech, either coldly detached and abstract or filled with a false emotional ring. Haunted language can also just dissipate in mindless chatter, releasing a cascade of words meant to fill the gaps and silences. In "Notes on the Phantom," Abraham speaks of words that have "stripped speech of its libidinal grounding." In extreme cases, secreted "phantom words" can become the carriers of another's story.[26] Abraham tells the story of a son who has become the carrier of his mother's phantom. After the grandmother denounced the mother's lover, he was sent to a labor camp to "break rocks" (*casser les cailloux)* and later died in a gas chamber. The grandmother's act became an unspeakable family secret. The son, who never knew the story, is obsessed throughout his life not only with issues of "forced labor" but also with "breaking rocks." He becomes "a lover of geology, he 'breaks rocks,' catches butterflies, and proceeds to kill them in a can of cyanide."[27] While the effects of such "phantom words" are relatively rare and notoriously difficult to detect, the phantom effects of haunted language may take many forms and can, as Abraham asserts, become established as social practices. Abraham likens the "staging of a word"—whether as metaphor, alloseme, or cryptonym—to an "attempt at exorcism, an attempt, that is, to relieve the unconscious by placing the effects of the phantom in the social realm."[28] We could see cryptonymic writing more generally as an attempt to force the ghosts of violent histories into the open and work toward social recognition and reparation.

Violent histories can be silenced and relegated to secrecy in spite of a circulation of stories and narratives. Hiding in language exists even when stories are told; the traces of such hiding are to be found at the surface of language. To read language for these traces is, in a sense, to read against the grain of overt narratives. It is consistent with what rhetorical and deconstructive readings have done in different ways. Cryptonymic reading, or "decrypting," Rand states in his editor's notes to "New Perspectives in Metapsychology," "seeks to reveal the processes that inhibit the emergence of signification."[29] Stories and narratives about violent histories can relate to this secret substance in two ways. They can leave the secret intact and cover it up defensively, thus cementing incorporation and encryptment. Or they can work toward integration, introjection, and even reparation. According to Abraham and Torok, the distinction between introjection and incorporation marks the two basic principles of psychic functioning. This very distinction, I argue, operates within language and provides a tool to assess the status of narratives and stories in relation to trauma and traumatic histories. But we must not assume that narratives simply mirror the psychic processes of introjection and incorporation; the relationship is less referential than generative and transformational. Rather than describing the process of mourning and introjection, telling the story of trauma may actually *be* a form of introjection in the sense of Abraham and Torok's definition of introjection as the substance of psychic life and perpetual self-creation. We could then say that introjection is an autopoetic process in which loss is taken in, transformed, and translated into the emergence of something new. Introjection is, in other words, a transformational process that furthers continual self-fashioning. By contrast, incorporation is linked to blockage, stasis, and even paralysis. Incorporation follows the psychic tendencies toward isolation of painful realities by removing them from a free flow of ideas, emotions, and modes of relating and creating. Incorporation thus severs the processes of vital exchange between self and world and forecloses transformation and emergence. Abraham and Torok link incorporation to cryptonymy, that is, the manifestation of a psychic crypt in language. Yet, again, cryptonymy should not be understood in referential terms. While cryptonymy is linked to various forms of hiding in language, we must remember that it also bears the traces of the secret it tries to hide. Following the logic and dynamic of dream language, cryptonymy belongs to the paradoxical formations of speech and writing that simultaneously hide and reveal. As much as it is a manifestation of the crypt, cryptonymy also offers secret pathways into the crypt that hold the promise of its transformation and social recognition. Moreover, narratives can also describe the process of traumatic encryptment and its impact on psychic and social life, thus bringing a different social recognition to histories of violence not by revealing the silenced violent act but by giving testimony to its lingering toxic effects and its transmission to those forced to suffer the silence.

Traumatic writing and cryptonymy unfold in a transitional space between psychic and social life and mediate the continual processes of exchange between the two. Traumatic writing testifies to both the individual and the collective manifestation of trauma: the crypt and the phantom. If the crypt is a secret psychic configuration arising from an individual's own life experiences, the phantom represents the interpersonal and transgenerational consequence of the silence imposed by the crypt. The phantom, according to Abraham and Torok, emerges as an effect of the unwitting reception of someone else's secret. The phantom, in other words, presupposes the transindividual circulation of silenced traumatic psychic memory traces. Abraham and Torok discuss the survival of memory traces derived from the experience of earlier generations and the unwitting transmission of secrets by one generation to another, be it a shameful family history or a shameful communal or national history. The falsification or disregard of the past or the destruction and silencing of collective memories, they insist, is the breeding ground for the phantomatic return of shameful secrets on the level of individuals, families, communities, and possibly even nations.

As we know all too well, silence is never complete. There can be a silencing of the past that is covered up by empty speech, coldly distancing information, or a clutter of defensive storytelling. There was, for example, plenty of concrete data and information circulated in Germany after World War II as well as war stories that left the shameful secrets intact. The information and the stories remained emotionally disconnected, displaced, or disavowed; they left a gap or a crypt in the narrative that eclipsed or sealed the secret inside. The crucial question then is: How can one write a narrative about what cannot be spoken and yet avoid creating a crypt in language? This question marks the distinction between a narrative that merely informs and one that performs an act of witnessing. Another distinction is that between a crypto-narrative, that is, a narrative that encrypts the secret, and a narrative about the experience of a crypt. There are instances of genuine witnessing in which the secret is not revealed. Let's take a childhood trauma as an example: A child can reveal her secret to a parent, who then becomes a carrier of the child's secret. The parent can tell or write a story that protects the child's secret while allowing listeners and readers to witness the effects of the trauma and the "family secret" on the child and her entire family. Such a narrative would convey an experience of the crypt while protecting the secret. In other cases, family secrets remain hidden under an official history that legislates their erasure. In *Remembering Generations: Race and Family in Contemporary African American Fiction*, Ashraf Rushdy explores slavery as the "family secret of America."[30] Rushdy maintains that the family secrets of mixed genealogies stemming from the rape of female slaves, silenced by official history, are a national secret. The traumatic effects and the family secrets generated by slavery and colonization continue to be part of a national crypt, albeit always vulnerable to irruption—as we have seen in the forced rewriting of America's racial history after the recent disclosure of Thomas Jefferson's family secret. It took generations for this crypt of the unspeakable racial genealogy of the nation to be opened and for Sally Hemings, the slave woman who was the mother of several of Jefferson's children, and her descendants to be acknowledged as carriers of this family secret. Assuming almost allegorical dimensions, the Jefferson-Hemings genealogy reveals the dynamic of the family secrets and haunting legacies of racism that mark the crypt of the American nation. Like the story of Margret Garner, the runaway slave woman who inspired Toni Morrison's *Beloved*, this was "not a story to pass on."

Since, as Dominick LaCapra argues, trauma causes disturbances in the symbolic order, we may view certain literary representations of trauma as attempts to work toward a reparation of the symbolic.[31] Literary writings of traumatic history often resort to experimental forms in order to approximate trauma through the tracing of traumatic effects and their inscription in mind, body, and language. Georges Perec's work is a case in point. Perec is obsessed with letters that, I suggest, function like a cryptonym. In *La Disparition*, translated as *A Void*, a three-hundred-page novel, Perec works with the formal constraint of including only words without the letter *e*. Using the absence of the letter *e* and composing his novel around lacunae and ellipses, Perec translates an existential void into an alphabetical and formal gap. In his article "Reading Georges Perec," Warren Motte writes: "The absence of a sign is always the sign of an absence, and the absence of the E in *A Void* announces a broader, cannily coded discourse of loss, catastrophe, and mourning. Perec cannot say the words *père, mère, parents, famille* in his novel, nor can he write the name *Georges Perec*."[32] The erasure of the proper name and the void in the self that is caused by an unnamable loss are encrypted in an absent letter covered by three hundred pages of a crypto-narrative. And, as if Perec were to perform a return of the repressed, he composes another narrative, *Les Revenentes*, in which *e* is the only vowel he uses. As the title suggests, this is a ghostly return, albeit one that leaves the crypt intact while producing yet another mirror image of a traumatic absence.

Finally, in *W, or The Memory of Childhood*, Perec, a child survivor whose parents perished during the war, composes a hybrid text in which elliptical autobiographical memory pieces alternate with the story of a fantasy world, *W*, a society ruled by oppression and death. Perec composed the original story of *W* during his teen years, a tale reminiscent of a child's imaginary vision of the Nazi concentration camps. Again, we find an obsession with a letter. For the narrator, the imaginary ethnography of *W* and the letter *W* become placeholders for the traumatic knowledge of the Holocaust and the murder of his mother. Together, the memory pieces and the story of *W* are attempts to approximate a void or a crypt that cannot be properly remembered and experienced. Motte argues that, as these narratives alternate, "often one is saying what the other cannot."[33]

W, or The Memory of Childhood opens with a dedication that enacts a new return of the absent letter while remembering its "disappearance": "for E."[34] In the memoir sections, Perec performs a meta-discourse on writing from within the trauma of disappearance and loss that runs parallel to the assembled fragments of his sparse childhood memories. "It is not—as for years I claimed it was—the effect of an unending oscillation between an as-yet undiscovered language of sincerity and the subterfuges of a writing concerned exclusively with shoring up its own defenses: it is bound up with the matter of writing and the written matter, with the task of writing as well as with the task of remembering" (42). The crypt in Perec is not the effect of a defensive silencing but an erasure that inevitably inscribes itself into the materiality of traumatic writing, as it approximates the void of memory left after the early "disappearance" of his parents. "Written matter" serves as a stand-in, tracing the effects this loss has on memory and life. Perec is well aware of claims that writing about the Holocaust means facing the paradox of *saying the unsayable.* For him, this paradox is intimately tied to the need to write from within the unconscious and for the preservation of a memory under attack.[35] Propelled by the unconscious, attacks on memory can only be countered by speaking from within and against the void. This is why he challenges the common use of the trope of unrepresentability and cryptic language: "The unsayable is not buried inside writing, it is what prompted it in the first place" (42). Insisting that writing does not hide what cannot be said but is generated by it, Perec moves beyond a narrow representational perspective of trauma toward a notion that emphasizes the responsive, interactive, and transformational quality of writing. Propelled by the crypt or the void, writing becomes the material trace and sign of an existential void: "I know that what I say is blank, is neutral, is a sign, once and for all, of a once-and-for-all annihilation." Annihilation is translated into words, lines, and the gaps between lines. Annihilation is transformed into written matter: "That is what I am saying, that is what I am writing, and that's all there is in the words I trace and in the lines the words make and in the blanks that the gaps between the lines create" (42).

Perec's insistence on wresting unconscious materials and memory traces from the materiality of language is crucial to understanding his unique use of cryptonymy. He asserts that interpreting the unconscious is not a matter of hunting down Freudian slips, and it is almost as if he attempts to rewrite the unconscious with cryptic alphabetical and permutational games. Playing with letters, scraps of memories, and childhood fantasies, he teases out new pieces from an unconscious chain of signification, sometimes inadvertently producing new memories. This writerly practice relies on the emergence of the unconscious from a free play within material constraints. Perec presents us with an emergentist and transformational rather than representational notion of the unconscious. In the same stroke, Perec also distances himself implicitly from Beckett, declaring that he is not writing in order to say that there is nothing to say. An act of mourning and assertion of life in one, writing, for Perec, is the ultimate existential trace:

> All I shall ever find in my very reiteration is the final refraction of a voice that is absent from writing, the scandal of their silence and mine . . . I write because we lived together, because I was one amongst them, a shadow amongst their shadows, a body close to their bodies. I write because they left in me their indelible mark, whose trace is writing. Their memory is dead in writing; writing is the memory of their death and the assertion of my life.
> (42)

How does one write from within an absence of memory, from within a loss that is less remembered as a story or an image or a thought than as a mood, an existential void, or a sense of annihilation? Writing is performed in the shadow of a lost object. Writing is the shadow of an absent voice. Writing assembles an ungrounded body's fragmented speech.

Perec's childhood writings from age eleven through fifteen, he tells us, filled whole exercise books with human figures unrelated to the ground, machines of war, engines of death, disengaged wheels rotating in the void, detached wings of planes, and arms disconnected from torsos. Images of fragmented bodies and machines supplement memories that are "scraps of life snatched from the void" (68). Words do not cohere, do not form a line, let alone a sustained narrative. Like the objects Perec describes or draws, his texts shatter and come apart. We are reminded of Jacques Derrida's description of the effect of the crypt and cryptonymy: "And then I can feel, on the tip of my tongue, the angular cut of a shattered word."[36] It takes decades for Perec to transform the shattered word into a letter able to bear the unspeakable pain of the void, a letter able to carry the lack of memory and its "fantasy treatment" in a story. Both the memoir and the story of W are linked to but cannot express pain: "More like supports than like straightjackets, these *marks* of *suspension* indicated pains that could not be named" (80, Perec's italics). Unnamable pains crystallize into memories and screen memories, that is, childhood memories that are unusually sharp but whose content appears insignificant. Like the symptom, the screen memory is a compromise formation that defends against and replaces a painful memory.[37] Together, pain and memory mark an absence at the core of being that needs to find symbolic expression in order to assume psychic reality. "Fantasy treatments" are attempts to create a world to fill the absence and to liken that world to mnemonic traces from before trauma. They are creative transformational objects to heal the traumatic splitting of the self.

Sometimes memory uses similar creative pathways to fashion cryptic images or objects that link the split-off pre- and post-traumatic worlds. Memory, for Perec, is not narrative or scene but follows the materiality of language as a mobile tool of inscription: "My memory is not the memory of a scene, but a memory of the word, only the memory of a letter that has turned into a word" (77). The letter is *double v* or *w.* In his childhood games of sequential permutations, Perec manipulates the letter until it becomes first a swastika and then a Star of David. Finally, he uses it to develop the fantastic tale of the imaginary island W. One particular memory underlies the formation of the letter and the link it establishes between memoir and fantasy: the memory of a medal Perec received as a child. He remembers the teacher pinning the medal to his smock and later ripping it off after a false accusation. Perec analyzes this scene as a likely screen memory: "I wonder if this memory does not in fact conceal its precise opposite: not the memory of a medal torn off, but the memory of a star pinned on" (54). Like dream language, cryptic memories and memories from the crypt often work with a system of reversals. Later we find this very association of the medal with the star further elaborated in the fantasy of the island W, where men in grey tracksuits wear "an outsize W emblazoned on the back" (67).

The complicated transformations that underlie this chain of fantasy treatments are crucial: absence of memory and psychic void engender a chain of permutations on the memory trace of a bodily inscription. The latter is already an inversion of an event that is lost to memory but known as historical information: the pinning on of the Star of David. The absent traumatic memory is thus replaced by a screen memory: the deep imprint left by the medal on the body. It is this imprint that leads Perec to speculate about an unconscious inversion in which the memory of the ripping off of the medal covers the memory of a pinning on of the Star of David. Finally, this memory finds a new permutation in the fantasy of the W emblazoned on the backs of the male inhabitants of W. Memory becomes encrypted in a letter. We find not only an insistence of the letter in the unconscious, as the psychoanalyst Jacques Lacan calls it, but also the transformational force of the letter. Encrypting death, it is used to assert life. Standing in for the absence of memory, it becomes the carrier of memory.

Memories of letters constitute a trace of something that was never present to an experience mediated by thought. Christopher Bollas calls such an experience "the unthought known," that is, a memory that cannot be thought but is felt as a mood, a void, or a shattering of language and thought.[38] "How would one be able to contain, within the opposition between words and things, the trace this 'word' constitutes of an event which has never been present?" asks Jacques Derrida in his analysis of the Wolf Man's "*Verbarium.*"[39] For Perec, the death of his mother was never present: she disappeared; she never had a proper burial. Her disappearance left a void that swallowed his memories. W is the memory of a letter and a fantasy. It stands for a designification of the world and performs a resignification. This is how Perec grounds his text, finally able to do what he could not do as a child: hold writing together, hold thought together. Writing the memory of the void left by his parents' death, Perec asserts (his) life.

Marguerite Duras's *La Douleur*, translated as *The War*, presents another form of writing from within trauma. In a short preamble, Duras reflects on this piece, which she found in a diary, decades after the end of World War II. She had no recollection of writing it. "How could I have written this thing I still can't put a name to, and that appalls me when I read it?" she writes, only to state a little later, "*The War* is one of the most important things in my life. It can't really be called 'writing.' I found myself looking at pages regularly filled with small, calm, extraordinarily even handwriting. I found myself confronted with a tremendous chaos of thought and feeling that I couldn't bring myself to tamper with, and beside which literature was something of which I felt ashamed."[40] I have always been intrigued and slightly troubled by this preface to *La Douleur*, especially by the last sentence. What is this piece if it is not literature, and why does literature appear as shameful in comparison with it? Reading Duras's assessment of what she wrote decades earlier, we feel a deep ambivalence yet also attraction: she is appalled by "this thing," yet it is "one of the most important things in [her] life." Since she never tells us, we can only guess what might appall her. Most likely it has to do with the raw quality of writing trauma, the self-exposure it requires, and the willful relinquishing of restraint and defense. Looking at raw horror, terror, or violence cannot but appall, but we also know of its inevitable attraction. And it is this attraction that often becomes most appalling and haunting at the same time. Shame itself is ambivalent, and one can detect a trace of shame when Duras confesses to being appalled by *La Douleur*. But then she turns around and claims pride, elevating "this thing" above anything literature could ever be to the point of turning literature itself into an object of shame.

In a sense Duras's piece is the opposite of writing from the crypt, the opposite of hiding within language, and it is because of this that the exposure can paradoxically cause unmitigated shame and pride at the same time. And yet, despite of Duras' disclaimer, it is writing, after all. We are not exposed to raw trauma but rather to what can be recaptured from it belatedly in the deferred action of writing. As Duras suggests when she points to the "pages regularly filled with small, calm, extraordinarily even handwriting," the very act of writing is always already a form of containment. These neatly inscribed pages contain the narrative voice of a woman who consumes herself in a hysterical identification with images of a corpse—the corpse of her husband—in a ditch in a concentration camp. Even here we find a curious, willfully staged inversion of the crypt. Duras forces us to witness not the denial but the anticipation of the death of a loved one. Rather than burying a lost love object alive in a crypt inside the self, Duras hysterically stages her own burial next to her husband's imagined corpse. Hysterical identification appears here as an alternative version of the crypt. In both cases we receive an impression of someone buried alive, but in the formation of a crypt, the life burial denies the death, whereas in Duras's case the life burial anticipates the death and thereby denies the life. The two examples illustrate two opposite forms of death in life. In both, writing contains this death, albeit in different ways: in the case of the crypt, writing tries to hide the death; Duras exposes the death. Her writing can be seen as a psychic equivalent of a photographic overexposure: "In a ditch, face down, legs drawn up, arms outstretched, he's dying. Dead. Beyond the skeletons of Buchenwald, his. It's hot all over Europe. The advancing Allied armies march past him. He's been dead for three weeks. Yes, that's what happened" (7). The reader knows that is not what happened. Duras, however, indulges this death in life: "I fall asleep beside him every night, in the black ditch, beside him as he lies dead" (10). In a hysterical inversion, the fear of death turns into necrophilia. "When you think about it later on, you'll be ashamed," says D., her companion (23). Writing can become a transformational object to alleviate shame, but the paradox of writing shame is this: while shame is generated through exposure, the exposure of shame in writing is a form of reparative integration. This is an instance of *Nachträglichkeit*, that is, writing belatedly or in deferred action from within trauma; it is not writing from within the crypt.

Perhaps the most radical writer of the crypt is Samuel Beckett. The scenery of his plays and texts is composed of cryptic architecture: caves, abodes, niches, alcoves, cavities, urns, trashcans, and skulls. His characters are buried in sand, amputated, or otherwise immobilized, representing death in life. His never-ending endgames both anticipate and deny death: still life frozen in images of crypts and vaults, forever immobilized and kept in circulation by proliferating cryptic voices. Beckett writes from a place where it is a pleasure to hide but a disaster not to be found. He breaks language apart into murmurs and stammers, breath and silence, cryptonyms, glossolalia—myriad voices to cover the silence and the void, longing to stop, unable to stop. His writing is about loss, lost ones writing from within the crypt, and a death so slow it becomes invisible: "Here all should die but with so gradual and to put it plainly so fluctuant a death as to escape the notice of even a visitor."[41]

We have seen how intimately the crypt is tied to a psychic void and to gaps in language; it is as if the crypt had voided the world and speech of their vital force. Language becomes haunted by the silence of the tomb, and there is the horror of the void that comes from facing death in life. Toward the end of her life, my mother wrote her war stories. She filled book after book with stories, repeating them over and over with slight variations, just as she had done during the decades of telling them. She had a large, forceful handwriting and left generous spaces between the lines. Increasingly, however, those spaces became intolerable to her. They came to symbolize the void in her life. Finally, she could not bear to look at them and began frantically to fill them with new writing. One day when I took one of her books out of the shelf, I could not believe my eyes: the pages contained layers and layers of stories. It was as if my mother had written on a mystic writing pad. However, rather than erasing the earlier stories, she layered them upon one another. As a result, her manuscript became a completely illegible accumulation of stories. She thus created her own cryptic writing: stories hiding beneath stories under layered traces of grief. She did the same thing with her photo albums, filling every space with new photos from her huge box, arbitrarily almost, until there was a timeless mix of years, layered upon one another, covering one another. The chronology of our lives disappeared beneath a grotesque synchronicity of pictures whose size was out of scale. Looking at this montage of different phases of her and our lives, I felt I was witnessing her involuntary destruction of history—our history. I could not help but think of what I had done as a little child before I could read: my filling in of the spaces of my parents' books with my own stories rendered in illegible squiggly lines. The stories in my first book and my mother's last book were hidden in language. Our stories were reduced to illegible traces.

I see my mother's frantic writing across empty space as an allegory of failed mourning. Empty space, for her, held the threat of abandonment and death. Her layers and layers of stories were a manic defense against the losses of her life and the fear of her own death. They were trying to ward off the pain that came with it. "Pain needs space," Duras writes in *La Douleur*.[42] But sometimes pain cannot tolerate space because space, especially empty space, invites the ghosts of the past and holds the terror of a self that has been evacuated. What if the ghosts of the past bring guilt and shame and pain? Is there a crypt of the perpetrator? Could it be that the perpetrator has encrypted his or her own humanity? If this were true, we would have to ask: How can the perpetrator speak?

> At the very moment where eyes are torn out, where wolves and masks suddenly fly off, the real appears in its extreme concision, more surprising and uncanny than fiction, with its procession of sounds, words and images like closed lips barred by an index finger.[43]

chapterthree

Haunting Legacies
Trauma in Children of Perpetrators

when Iraq is bombed
and I tell her
how enraged I am
at attacks at civilians
no matter what the reasons
because I remember how it feels
to be a child of six
and live in a city
hit by carpet bombing
surrounded by adults
half crazed with terror and hunger
and when I tell her
how it feels
to crawl out from under
after an air raid
to look down the street
and see whose house was hit
and how I cannot forget
adults whispering in horror
that phosphor bombs
missed the railroad station
and hit the slums instead
and people running through the streets
like living torches
screaming until they jumped
into the river

to drown themselves
. . . .
my Greek friend leans back
and I see in her eyes
that I am the child of her enemies
she remembers the atrocities
committed by my people
in her native village
in the mountains of Greece
—Excerpts from Ursula Duba, *Tales From A Child of the Enemy*

The thoughts I am presenting here are a first attempt to formulate my ideas about the traumatic effects of growing up among a generation of children of a perpetrator nation. I was born in Germany after World War II and grew up in a small border town in the south, just across from Switzerland at the outer edges of the Black Forest. I am one of the "children of the enemy," invoked in Ursula Duba's poem. Unlike her, I experienced the carpet bombing only secondhand, through endlessly reiterated war stories. My mother and grandmother's stories about the war have merged with my childhood memories, memory implants that I retain as the first inscriptions of my history. Every evening they would sit in the living room telling the same stories, over and over again. My memories of these stories have an almost eerie quality of lived reality. I remember them differently from the way I remember other stories. Almost as if I had lived through them myself, I remember concrete images, details, fragments of a history I must have hallucinated at the time, thus processing my families' stories as psychic reality: the noise of sirens and approaching bomber planes, people fleeing to the local bunkers or, if it was too late, to their cellars; children sleeping in apple crates through howling sirens and the crashing of bombs; and, above all, the image of masses of people fleeing the burning city through the rubble of smoking houses and the explosions of bombs, people crying and coughing from smoke, screaming, or succumbing to complete disorientation and madness.

I lived the first months of my life with "adults / half crazed with terror and hunger" because fear and starvation persisted through the early postwar years. My parents tell me that as an infant I screamed

68

every night for hours on end from the torments of hunger. They were also still crazed with terror from the war's killing their firstborn, their infant son, and leaving their house in smoldering ruins. Many years later, like Duba, I befriended people—Jewish, French, Greek—upon whom my own people had brought war and genocide. I know the feeling of being the child of the enemy all too intimately. I also know what it feels like to belong to a people whose history has come to stand, in the cultural imaginary of the world at large, for evil incarnate. As I write my thoughts down on growing up in postwar Germany, the United States has invaded Iraq once again and Iraqi people, including children, have been dying. I am a resident alien in the United States now, and as I see the coverage of this new war, memories resurface, the atmosphere of fear and terror, the starvation and despair, the stories that marked my early childhood years. I remember once after a huge peace demonstration in Los Angeles my son, Leon, who was thirteen years old at the time, asked me what I remember from the time after the war. I feel it is time to get my memories and thoughts into a form that I will be able to pass on to him.

When I was born in Germany, Allied signs posted all over the recently defeated country read:

> Here ends the civilized world.
> You are entering Germany.
> Fraternizing prohibited.[1]

Only a few years earlier, an old racist plate, addressed to Jews during the Nazi era, marked the entrance of my hometown:

> Jews are unwelcome in Tiengen.
> Tiengen likes to see foreigners,
> But the Jew better remain far away.
> Because whatever may drive you,
> Remember, Jew,
> Tiengen was, is, and remains German.[2]

I was not born yet when the town addressed its Jewish population in this fashion, and too small to be able to read the Allied sign, but indirectly both signs passed down a legacy through Germany's cultural unconscious. The Allied sign's legacy is complex and difficult to track. Denying Germany the status of the "civilized world," it aligns the German people with a discourse of savagism and barbarism.[3] This discourse continues a familiar legacy of colonialism, casting Germany as the first instance of a "barbarism" that emerges from *within* the civilized world. While the rhetoric of barbarism suggests that Germany broke away from the values and achievements of Western civilization, the Nazis in fact, as Agamben and others have convincingly demonstrated, worked within the logic of modernity and used deeply modern elements to generate the Holocaust.[4] Moreover, it seems important to acknowledge that the German Holocaust, even though unmatched in its cold, mechanistic, and industrialized machinery of death, draws on a relentless drive to subjugate or annihilate other people that reveals many affinities to Western colonialism and imperialism more generally. Ultimately, one would need to ask where the drive to subjugate and annihilate the other comes from, a question that reaches beyond the scope of this chapter.

However one interprets the Nazi assault on the values of Western civilization, the Allied sign challenges the developmental thesis implied in colonial narratives of civilization and progress, raising not only the question of what causes civilization to be undermined from within but also another question regarding the role of the Allied forces in relation to the people under occupation, whom it declares uncivilized. In many ways, the Allied forces' rebuilding of Germany, whose major cities had been destroyed and whose surviving people were starving, can be compared to a colonization, entailing both political subjugation as well as moral and cultural reeducation. We need to be careful, however, in assessing the status of these "transitional interventions" designed to stop a nation's politics of genocide and aggressive invasion of other countries. They depart in particular ways from the utterly unwarranted acts of invasion, aggression, and genocide committed during colonialism against indigenous people. What Germany witnessed after the war was a pervasive cultural reeducation and the imposition of the values of the occupying forces. The United States and the Soviet Union, the two nations that would eventually become the historical protagonists in a relentless cold war, systematically imposed American and Soviet values and propaganda on the German educational and cultural system in the two divided sectors of the country. The division of Germany, eventually enforced by a concrete wall that cut through its former capital, Berlin, into a communist East and a capitalist West, dramatically enacts the conflicts, differences, and divisions internal to what current academic discourses often all too easily homogenize as "the Western tradition."

The denial of Germany's status as a civilized nation rests on a claim that the persecution of Jews and other minorities, the camps, and the Holocaust were aberrations from the values of Western civilization. Recent analyses, particularly Agamben's work, present a systematic attempt to refute this exceptionalist perspective, casting Germany as a significant moment of Western civilization rather than a deviation from it. Exceptionalism rests on the assumption that Germany was either never part of or fell away from mainstream Western civilization because it never took the political turn toward democratization (or French republicanism) or the philosophical turn toward humanist rationalism. We should also not forget that it was the Nazis themselves who first developed an exceptionalist perspective toward German culture, claiming that since antiquity the Germans had developed their own autarky as a civilization. Whether one embraces an exceptionalist or a nonexceptionalist perspective makes a crucial difference in *how* one looks at the historical trauma suffered by Germany's Jewish, gypsy, homosexual, mentally ill, and communist population who became the victims of the Holocaust. It also makes a difference in *how* one assesses the different trauma suffered by the German people during World War II and its aftermath.

Finally, it matters whether German people see themselves as a deviation from Western civilization when they face or refuse to face their own role in a nation of defeated perpetrators. We know that a pervasive silence weighed on Germany after the war, bespeaking a futile attempt to avoid facing the war's atrocities. Yet one cannot escape collective shame and guilt and their transmission across generations. The more the acknowledgment of shame and guilt was silenced in public debates, the more they migrated into the psyche and the cultural unconscious. For the generation of perpetrators, the knowledge of the Holocaust was relegated to a "tacit knowledge" that became taboo in public debates in any but the most superficial ways. For the postwar generation, it became something like a national secret, only to be revealed as brute fact, usually in the early teens, in the cold abstraction of history lessons. There was virtually no public forum for a deeper confrontation and processing of the issues surrounding the Holocaust.

Seeing Germany outside the exceptionalist rubric, as part and parcel of the pervasive history of Western colonial and imperial aspirations, allows one to acknowledge that, among other things, the Nazi atrocities are only the most perniciously inhuman form of the enactment of the myth of Western civilization's superiority. The psychic economy of Germany's isolation from the rest of the West is rather transparent since it allows other countries more easily to avoid confronting their own violent histories and legacies of colonial atrocities and genocide. To take issue with the thesis of German exceptionalism does not mean giving license to turn away from Germany's responsibility for the Holocaust. Rather, it allows one to establish a link between the Holocaust and other histories of violence and genocide. Linking these violent histories is, I think, crucial in order to begin serious thinking about a politics of alliance against oppression, genocide, ethnic cleansing, and imperialist invasions of other countries. Moreover, it may finally prepare some ground for a political dialogue among people and nations that have emerged from or still belong to the victims of such oppression and those who resist the oppression of others from within colonial or imperial nations.

Framing my thoughts in this way will allow me to make a similar argument for a dialogical turn in trauma discourses. These have commonly focused almost exclusively on the victims of trauma. I think we need trauma discourses that look at the dynamic between victims and perpetrators and see that both of them are suffering from the psychic deformations of violent histories, albeit in different ways and with different responsibilities. Pervasive in violent histories is the transgenerational transmission of trauma, or, as Abraham and Torok put it, a history of ghostly hauntings by the phantoms of a silenced past. This haunting transmission of trauma across generations will be the more narrowly defined focus of this chapter.

What are possible concrete manifestations of trauma transmitted across generations? Let me return to the Nazi sign displayed in what later became my hometown: "Remember, Jew, Tiengen was, is, and remains German." This warning prominently exhibits the projective fear of Germans of the war generation of a takeover by another culture. This fear was handed down to postwar children along with the visceral dread of starvation and the horrors of listening to endlessly repeated war stories. The Nazi sign also admonished Germans to distinguish between good and bad foreigners. Living in a border town, the citizens of

Tiengen couldn't really afford to appear xenophobic, but racism was in vogue and one could boast a racist sign without a trace of shame or pang of conscience. After all, racism was, as always, bound up with patriotism and national pride. The fear that German culture and, perhaps more important, German economic monopolies might be taken over by Jews was a familiar excuse to disguise and rationalize Germany's brutal aggression against its German Jewish population as a measure of self-defense. After the war, the fear of a takeover was nearly seamlessly displaced onto the Russians and the communists within Germany. "Wait until the Russians invade us," my grandmother used to threaten me when I didn't follow her rules. She also thought the Russians had changed the weather patterns with nuclear experiments. "They even take over the sky and the clouds," she used to complain. Like so many Germans at the time, she seemed to have succeeded in "forgetting" her memory of Hitler's imperial drive to take over Europe only a few years earlier so that it became easy to project it on the enemy.

It is perhaps telling that I hardly remember any complaints about the takeover of German culture by the United States and France, the occupying forces in southern Germany. Perhaps I should stress that, even though the area where my family lived was under French occupation, we were mainly exposed to the massive infusion into the German cultural and educational sector of North American literature and Hollywood films, as well as a great deal of propaganda. The only open critics of such a refashioning of Germany were the teachers of German literature who shunned the Anglicization of the German language and forbade us to use "foreign" words. They also lamented the fact that postwar children grew up without German literature because it had almost instantly been replaced in school curricula with those allegedly "uncultured" books by such new American authors as Hemingway, Steinbeck, and Pearl S. Buck.

In defiance of our teachers we enthusiastically took to American literature, all the more so because I assume that even before we learned about the Holocaust, we had already internalized that Germany was an inferior nation. At the time I thought I was rebellious and progressive, while in fact I was rather a gullible subject of cultural colonization. This deep ambivalence is symptomatic of the transformation of German culture after the war. Our teachers resisted the colonizing impetus of the American reeducation program, but they did so in terms of an old and problematic nationalism. We students, by contrast, resisted our teachers' nationalism and actively embraced foreign cultures, and we also unwittingly submitted to the propagandistic aspects of the reeducation program. The fact that American literature formed the core of much of this reeducation makes matters even more complicated. The literature we read was itself often ambivalent toward or critical of its own culture. Faulkner, Hemingway, Steinbeck, and Buck, for example, are all authors whose relationship to their own culture is so complex that they can hardly be reduced to a monolithic cultural perspective. Moreover, it was the reception of American literature that reconnected German literature with the modernist and avant-garde movements that were suppressed during the Nazi era. This ambivalence is not unlike the one Fanon describes about the identificatory reception of Shakespeare in colonial education.[5] Literature, we need to remember, is a highly ambivalent and risky tool of colonization or reeducation since it can so easily be appropriated for a much more critical reception than the one intended by the powers that be. Reading American literature, therefore, could hardly be seen as a tool of oppression among postwar German children, and it is symptomatic that when I later studied American literature at the university I actually returned to the books I grew up with. When I eventually emigrated to the United States, I found that I shared a basic canon of literature and other cultural objects, especially Hollywood movies, with my American peers.

The war generation internalized the fear of a takeover as a psychic structure, extending it even to include literature and language more generally. This fear became all-pervasive and came to operate indiscriminately at a more subliminal level. In some of its aspects, the parental generation displaced this fear onto the generation of postwar children. The parents' fear that the children would take over was, in turn, intimately related to the fear that the silenced history might surface and lead to a confrontation with one's own children—a fear that eventually turned real in the 1960s and 1970s and that gave the student movement in Germany its particular transgenerational dynamic. Given that the war generation had retreated into the treacherous refuge of "silence," it is symptomatic that knowledge, education, and particularly language became containers for this fear. The very fact that children could claim a voice of their own became threatening to many parents. The German word "Widerrede" refers to one of the worst transgressions of children against their parents. The word means "talking back" or simply "arguing." "Thou shalt not argue with your parents" as the hallmark of German authoritarian education reaches back, of course, at least to the Bismark era. However, this silencing of children took on a new quality and urgency after the war, when arguing carried the threat of exposing the parents' active or passive complicity as perpetrators. It was not until the 1960s that this pedagogical ethos was connected with the German people's vulnerability to blind obedience under the Nazi regime. With the publication of Adorno's *The Authoritarian Personality* (1950), authoritarianism became finally linked in the German social imaginary with a propensity to fascism. In Germany, the 1960s revolutionary activism was therefore thoroughly overdetermined by the postwar generation's first broad public outcry, which held the parental generation at large accountable for the Holocaust rather than focusing on the few individual perpetrators who were tried at Nuremberg.

This is the psychological climate of a relentless authoritarianism that still reigned during the postwar era. While any sense of true authority was weakened by the loss of the war, the compensatory use of violence toward "inferior" or vulnerable members of a community, including children, often escalated exponentially. Supported by the persistent American ethos of allegedly rebuilding the countries the United States destroys in war, Germans after the war engaged almost instantly in an enormous effort at reconstruction, the *Wiederaufbau*. Psychically, these efforts served a manic defense, mobilized to ward off unbearable feelings of loss and defeat, guilt and shame. This manic defense went hand-in-hand with the ghostly silence about the war atrocities that descended on the defeated nation, a silence that, in turn, generated the crippling "inability to mourn" that Frankfurt School psychoanalysts Alexander and Margarete Mitscherlich analyzed in their book of the same title. The German people after the war had become hardened to a point where they were unable to mourn not only the loss of the six million lives in the camps they had caused. They were equally unable properly to mourn and acknowledge their own losses. How, after all, can one mourn the loss of a few lives in one's own family if your people were guilty of trying to exterminate a whole other people? I am not saying that there was literally no mourning of the dead. But the very process of mourning was thwarted and distorted if not preempted altogether by guilt and shame and an irrevocable sense that as a German you deserved all your losses and more, or indeed were complicit in them. This is a psychic condition that can render one virtually insane with impossible mourning. The conflicted feelings were too intolerable to be processed in the open, let alone publicly. But since one couldn't make them disappear either, they were repressed, split off, and pushed into the cultural unconscious.

The crippling sense of inferiority that smoldered beneath the heat of reconstruction deeply affected the relationship of the war-generation parents to their own children. "The worst thing that can happen to parents is if the children take over," my father used to say. Given the rigidly authoritarian style of my upbringing, I puzzled over his remark and once asked: "What do you even mean by the children taking over?" "Well, that they grow above their parents' heads," he retorted in the familiar colloquial German phrase, "Die Kinder wachsen den Eltern über den Kopf." That fear became a big issue when I wanted to enter Germany's system of higher education, the gymnasium. Unsuccessfully, my parents tried to dissuade me, and, once I was in high school, the battle was often displaced onto language. My father would regularly fly into rages whenever I used a word he did not understand, particularly those new foreign words or terms kids began to use that were blamed for the "Americanization" of the German language. "Don't babble in that learned fashion!" he would shout at me with utter hostility, and I soon learned to watch my words around him just as I watched my steps. Speaking the father's code became my own personal prison house of language, and I rebelled by hardly speaking to him at all. Silencing thus worked at a collective and an individual level.

Written language, too, including poetry and fiction, was considered a dangerous influence. Unable to deter me from reading, my mother tried to screen the books I brought home. I soon learned to give her the books I had already finished, often at night with a flashlight under the blanket. Worst of all were the American comic books. They were treated like poison. To describe them, parents and teachers used the same term they used to describe Nazi propaganda, "*Volksverdummung*," a "stupidification" of the people. I recall a secret reading of a *Mickey Mouse* comic in the forest, after which I tried to determine whether I had really become more stupid and how it could possibly happen. It became nearly a philosophical problem to explore whether language could become a poisonous substance.

Such prohibition placed on language reaches deep, affecting the very core of the self. I grew used to thinking of myself as "the girl without words," and it still haunts me. Now I feel the effects in displaced forms, the most insidious being the guilt and fear associated with claiming a voice as the descendant of a perpetrator nation. The more distant a topic is to my own history and concerns, the easier it becomes to speak. No wonder that I eagerly began to learn foreign languages—starting with French and English, the languages of the occupying forces. No wonder, either, that I ended up as a teacher of foreign literatures and specialized in that most abstract and distancing mode of discourse called critical theory. And if I now for the first time address the legacy of children of perpetrators in a public forum, I do so with some anxiety and unease. While I believe I can and should no longer avoid this confrontation, I still struggle over the issue of claiming a voice. Many years ago, I was invited to lecture at Tel Aviv University. During a lunch with a group of women colleagues, a debate ensued over the recent wave of memoirs of children of Holocaust survivors. One of my friends argued that these writers belittled their parents' unfathomable suffering by exhibiting their own. The descendants of Holocaust survivors should accept an ethical obligation to remain silent, she felt. Others held against her that one cannot silence a whole generation and that no one should be deprived of a voice. I sat there, silently, trying to imagine what they would feel about a German claiming a voice in order to talk about the traumatic legacy of children of perpetrators. After returning to the United States, I put my thoughts on ice for another ten years.

In the meantime, however, psychoanalytic research on the transgenerational transmission of trauma reawakened my concerns. As the only theory able to trace the effects of unconscious experience, psychoanalysis is invaluable in any attempt to face the ghosts of a past one has never lived, or lived only via the detours of its narrative and psychic transmission across generations. Traumatic historical legacies may be transmitted individually via unconscious fantasies of parents and grandparents as well as collectively through the cultural unconscious. Psychoanalysts have theorized such transmission as a form of psychic haunting, arguing that both children of victims and children of perpetrators unwittingly live the ghostly legacies and secrets of their parents and the parental generation. After outlining the basic assumptions of a transgenerational trauma theory, I would therefore like to end with two concrete instances from my personal experience that illustrate such a transmission of trauma across generations.

The debate about whether trauma can be handed down to a next generation that has not experienced the concrete traumatic event dates back to Nicolas Abraham and Maria Torok's theory of transgenerational haunting, published in the 1970s and 1980s. In *The Shell and the Kernel*, Abraham and Torok develop their concept of the crypt, that is, a psychic space fashioned to wall in unbearable experiences, memories, or secrets. Abraham talks about the "phantom effects" that haunt the children of parents who have lived through a traumatic history. Assuming that individuals can inherit the secret psychic substance of their ancestor's lives, Abraham argues that a person can manifest symptoms that do not directly spring from her own life experiences but from a parent's or ancestor's psychic conflicts, traumas, or secrets.[6] Speaking of a *phantom*, a *haunting*, or a *phantasmatic haunting*, Abraham uses a rhetoric of ghosts to suggest a foreign presence in the self. He suggests, in fact, as his editor Rand states, "the existence within an individual of a collective psychology comprised of several generations."[7] As we know from ghost stories and folklore, only the dead who were denied the rite of burial, who died an unnatural death, who committed or were the victim of a crime, or who suffered an unbearable injustice come back to haunt the living. Such haunting is, in other words, the effect of unresolved trauma. A good example to illustrate this dynamic is Toni Morrison's *Beloved*, where the ghost of Sethe's murdered child comes back to haunt her and her family until they work through the trauma of the past. *Beloved* also demonstrates the interweaving of personal and collective trauma. While the story focuses on the familial drama and the personal trauma of those involved in Sethe's killing of her baby, Sethe's act is caused by and cannot be understood without the traumatic history of slavery. In violent histories, the personal is inseparable from the collective and the political.

While Abraham and Torok mainly emphasize a familial framework and the legacies of family histories as they are passed down from generation to generation, their theoretical framework is well suited to include larger communities and peoples with collective traumatic histories. Abraham's concept of the phantom is particularly relevant for an analysis of the transmission of historical trauma though the cultural unconscious. Again, *Beloved* may serve as an example. Toni Morrison uses the figure of a ghost to trace effects of a collective trauma that the protagonists enact unconsciously. It is not only Sethe's personal history as a slave that triggers the killing of her baby daughter; it is also the history of her own mother, who was never allowed to keep any of her own children. Sethe's mother passed down to her the sense that it is better to be dead than to be a slave, and better as a slave not to attach yourself even to your children the way a free mother would. Finally, *Beloved* demonstrates that trauma cannot be healed individually but needs communal support and a joint effort to face the ghosts of the past. In order deal with collective historical trauma, we therefore need a theoretical framework with a transindividual perspective. Abraham and Torok's concept of the phantom and transgenerational haunting not only moves psychoanalysis beyond individual life experiences and their intrapsychic processing but also deals with the cultural legacies or the unfinished business of one or more generations of a people and their transmission to the descendants.

Most cultures share a tendency to silence traumatic histories. Traumatic amnesia seems to become inscribed as cultural practice. Yet trauma can never be completely silenced since its effects continue to operate unconsciously. Suggesting that the silence intended to cover up a traumatic event or history only leads to its unconscious transmission, Abraham speaks of a haunting that spans generations. He calls for a kind of psychoanalytic "cult of ancestors" (as defined by Rand) that allows the dead to rest and the living to gain freedom from their ghostly hauntings.[8] Yet to achieve this freeing from the past requires one first to awaken the dead and to revisit the trauma. This process, in fact, is what we commonly call mourning. To facilitate a collective mourning, communities and nations develop the need to establish a culture of memory. Recognizing the psychic life of our ancestors in our own psychic life means uncovering their unspoken suffering and secret histories, as well as their guilt and shame, their crimes—hence the importance of a family's, a community's, or a nation's "secret" histories. Secrecy in this context does not necessarily mean that there is no conscious knowledge of the past at all. It may also mean that this knowledge is silenced and removed from public life. In this case it becomes tacit knowledge, shared by everyone yet treated like a taboo subject. People who bring it to the surface are often treated with passionate hostility, as if they threatened a fragile sense of balance. The violent and traumatic events have to remain isolated and split off, and in this sense they go unacknowledged even if there are isolated public commemorations or trials of war criminals. Psychoanalysis is, of course, a practice based on an ethics of contained uncovering. It works with the assumption that violent or traumatic events that are repressed or denied will continue to come back in haunting ways until there is a proper working-through. This requires both taking responsibility for one's actions and mourning losses. In uncovering traumatic histories, psychoanalysis at times resembles a paradoxical "unburial," that is, a digging into a community's or a nation's deadly secrets or into the secret life of a dead person who has never been properly buried.

Only a process of breaking traumatic silence and revealing a buried secret can help to exorcise its ghostly alien presence from the inner world. Such a process entails one's taking responsibility for one's actions, working through guilt and shame, and mourning unbearable loss. It also requires that one face the effects of unspeakable violence. This dynamic operates at both a personal and a larger communal or cultural level; it also operates across generations. Of course, the dynamic changes if the acts of perpetration are not your own but belong to the generation of your parents. This makes facing one's historical legacy both easier and more difficult: easier because the guilt is not a personal guilt, and more difficult because you need to face a legacy that has been passed down in complicated, subliminal, and, to a large extent, entirely unconscious ways. Facing historical facts reveals only the tip of an iceberg. Facing the psychic effects of the legacy of violence, guilt, shame, and (impossible) mourning as it has been passed down to the next generation is an excruciatingly complicated process. In the case of Germany, integration of historical trauma means stirring up the past in order to help the postwar generation work through the ghostly legacies of their parents. Such an archeology of the psyche is indispensable for allowing the children of perpetrators to address the unfinished business of their parents. Only then can they gain the agency to deal with the past in their own terms. Without such agency they are bound to remain unconsciously fixated on their parents' traumatic deformation. More often than not this will lead them to try to avoid the issue altogether, thus becoming complicit in the silencing of trauma—even if it is only in feeling guilty about claiming a voice. The exhumation of the buried ghosts of the past is, in other words, also indispensable for trying to avoid the repetition of traumatic history or its displacement onto other people.

Finding a voice—whether it is speaking up or writing a narrative, a poem, or a memoir or simply telling one's story—is crucial in this culture of memory and testimony. Language is the first tool and mode of introjection. Abraham and Torok point out that even the starving infant is less helpless once it finds a way to voice the feeling of hunger, or once "the empty mouth can be filled with words."[9] But how can one find a language for something that is unconscious? How can one tell the story of a history of which one is a protagonist without ever having experienced it directly? Often the story tells itself over and over in fantasies, in the language of the body in pain or distortion, or in the endless compulsive repetition of a particular traumatic rupture. One instance of such an unconscious fantasy has left a deep impression on me.

Margarethe von Trotta, the German filmmaker and director, made a series of films about sisters, among them *Sisters or the Balance of Happiness* (1979) and *Die Bleierne Zeit (Marianne and Juliane)* (1981), a film that was modeled on the life of RAF member Gudrun Enslin and her sister. In a television interview she was asked about her obsession with the topic of sisters, given the fact that she grew up without a sister. In her answer she declared that she never knew why but that ever since she was a small child all her fantasies kept circling around sisters. Some time later an unknown woman contacted her and identified herself as her twin sister. She revealed that their parents had given up one of the twins and kept Margarethe, who was never supposed to know. Unconsciously, however, Margarethe had found a way to enact a family secret that was never revealed to her.

In other instances where a trauma is enacted somatically, the story of the body remains hostage of the buried secret, haunted by an unknown phantom history or presence. A different language is needed to trace the "phantom effect" of a memory without memory, to eliminate the presence of the phantom from the inner world, its encryptment inside the self. In "Notes on the Phantom," Abraham speaks of this language in terms of a "staging of words" that speak traumatic experience.

> Extending the idea of the phantom, it is reasonable to maintain that the 'phantom effect' progressively fades during its transmission from one generation to the next and that, finally, it disappears. Yet, this is not

at all the case when shared or complementary phantoms find a way of being established as social practices along the lines of *staged words*. . . . We must not lose sight of the fact that to stage a word—whether metaphorically, as an alloseme, or as a cryptonym—constitutes an attempt at exorcism, an attempt, that is, to relieve the unconscious by placing the effects of the phantom in the social realm.[10]

This would explain why any ethics that tries to silence personal trauma or traumatic history is doomed to fail. Exploring the possibilities, limitations, and traps of reparation and redress as they are reflected in trauma discourses and, differently, in literature, also entails engaging the silences and phantom effects of traumatic histories. Claiming a voice then becomes part of a larger staging of words to relieve the phantom effects of trauma. Yet it is not as if the act of claiming a voice does not have its own pitfalls and dangers. The "staging of words," while it may contribute to socio-psychic health, is not yet a solution in itself and may, in the worst case, obscure real political processing. Traumatic narratives can become charged melancholic objects that sustain the tie to old traumatic injuries while deflecting from the urgency of addressing new violent histories in the present. This is why it becomes increasingly important to address violent and traumatic histories across national, ethnic, and cultural boundaries and across the divide of victims and perpetrators. Perhaps because I have experienced the guilt of claiming a voice, I have come to believe that both the descendants of victims and the descendants of perpetrators need to break the silence. They also need to escape their mutual isolation and begin talking about their different traumatic histories together, thus creating a dialogue that may help to trace what Abraham calls "shared or complementary phantoms." This dynamic is also related to what Ashis Nandy calls "isomorphic oppression," that is, an oppression that is transferred from one group of victims to another, including the victimization of the oppressors' own kin.

We have arrived at a place in history where we can no longer afford to deal with the histories of victims and perpetrators in isolation. The damages and cultural deformations of these violent histories of colonialism, imperialism, war, genocide, and slavery manifest themselves on both sides of the divide, and only if both sides work through the legacies of these histories can the vicious cycle of repetition be disrupted. Recent postcolonial theories as well as critical race theories have argued in a similar vein.

In his pathbreaking study on the psychology of colonialism, Ashis Nandy points out that while the broad psychological contours of colonialism are now known, the concomitant cultural and psychological pathologies produced by colonization in the colonizing societies are less well known.[11] This is true despite the fact that a theoretical framework to understand this psychosocial dynamic has been available at least since Hegel's analysis of the master-slave dialectic. "Colonialism as a psychological process cannot but endorse the principle of isomorphic oppression,"[12] argues Nandy. This dynamic also underlies, I believe, the psychological deformations of perpetrator cultures more generally. One of the most common deformations is the internalization and hence internal repetition of patterns of violence in the perpetrator culture. Nandy uses Fanon's example of the police officer who tortured the Algerian freedom fighters and then became violent toward his own wife and children to illustrate the dynamic of isomorphic oppression. We have similar evidence of veterans returning from U.S. wars and invasions only to turn violent against their own people and kin. In postwar Germany, there is ample evidence that many German parents transferred the patterns of violence internalized during the Nazi era onto their own children, following a desperate, often unconscious urge to eradicate any trace of "otherness" in them. One of the most invisible and socially unacknowledged effects of war trauma consists precisely in isomorphic oppression. This becomes all the more pervasive if there is a silencing or denial of the history of violence and a concomitant displacement of its effects onto the cultural unconscious. If violent histories are treated like national secrets, they are bound to be reenacted. In her book about the German postwar generation, *What Did You Do in the War, Daddy?*, Sabine Reichel writes:

> The truth is, that Germans have remained tortured too—as they should as oppressors—because what they've committed is an irrevocably guilty act. They haven't survived the cold-blooded annihilation of other people without substantial psychological damage—but they are not aware of it. With every single extinguished life, something in the murderers died with the murdered in the trenches, gas chambers and ovens.[13]

To account for this psychological deformation of perpetrators and their children, it is necessary to expand Abraham and Torok's notion of the "crypt" to include cultural or national crypts. Abraham and Torok define encryptment as a psychic response to trauma in which an intolerable experience becomes walled in, silenced, and removed from consciousness and the public sphere. Such intolerable experiences can occur with victims who cannot face unbearable loss, humiliation, destruction, torture, or genocide. They can also occur with perpetrators who cannot face their own violence, guilt, or shame. Just like intrapsychic crypts, cultural and national crypts harbor the repressed or denied memories of violence. Once they are walled off from a conscious politics of remembrance and public debate, they can no longer be worked through and transformed into a politics of redress. Collectively established crypts become the sources of a cultural and national haunting that cannot be addressed unless the crypt is opened and the silence broken.

Perhaps it is important to stress here that silence need not be complete in order for this dynamic to operate. There may even be—as there was in Germany after the war—an open politics of acknowledgment of war crimes, including the Nuremberg trials and the process of "de-Nazification" as well as the monumentalization of victimage and an official politics of reparation. But unless these acts include a psychosocial politics that addresses the responsibility, complicity, guilt, shame, and psychosocial deformation of the culture at large, it in fact only helps to perpetuate a politics of silencing and denial. In the worst case, historical monumentalization may even aggravate such politics by providing a safely contained outlet to alleviate unconscious feelings of guilt and shame.

I would like to end my thoughts on transgenerational haunting with two concrete examples, one intrapsychic and one cultural, both drawn from my own experience of growing up in postwar Germany. I have thought for a long time about the status of personal experiences and narratives in the attempt to work through the legacies of traumatic histories. Two of my friends to whom I gave this essay cautioned me against including these examples, arguing that they are too personal to be exemplary. I am not sure this is true. I will tell the story of my "phantom brother," that is, the story of my own history as a child who was supposed to replace the brother who had died in the war. While this is a highly personal narrative, we know from the psychoanalytic literature on "replacement children" that the psychic dynamic I am describing is much more widespread that we commonly believe. Parents who lose a child to a violent history are especially vulnerable to turning their next child into a "replacement child." I think that the story is relevant as a concrete example for the transgenerational transmission of a war trauma. In a sense, the stories about my dead brother have become the core of my own visceral experience of what a war means in terms of human loss. I know there are many postwar replacement children with similar stories, and I have met some of them. My second story concerns my hometown and the ghostly erasure, after the war, of the history of its Jewish citizens. This, too, can barely be considered a merely personal experience. I rather think that my discovery of the book about Tiengen's Jews illustrates how pervasive and intricate the silencing of the Holocaust was after the war. Finally, I believe that only by tracing the personal effects of historical violence can we begin to face a responsibility that does not end with the generation of perpetrators.

The Phantom Brother

I was born after the end of the war as the second child of my parents. Their first child, a son named Paul-Jürgen, was born during the war and died when he was only a few months old from the effects of acute smoke poisoning. During an air raid on Freiburg that completely destroyed our family's house, my mother ran with her infant son through the burning city to take refuge in a bomb shelter. The dense smoke poisoned and eventually destroyed his lungs. On their way, they crossed the neighboring playground. A bomb had landed right in the middle, killing the children, tearing their little bodies apart, leaving limbs in the trees and the severed head of a little boy. My mother told the same story over and over since the earliest time I can remember, when I was only three years old. She kept a stern face, reproachful, in fact, and the story, told in a flat, monotone voice, seemed to carry a secret message, a threat of sorts. I always listened mortified, never asking a question. The image of my mother walking with my baby brother through a playground with torn-up children stayed with me through all my life. I carry it inside like a ghostly presence. Sometimes I think that my mother went insane that day. She was never able to cope with the trauma of war, the loss of her first baby, her brother, and her home.

Already my brother's birth, only a few months earlier, had been highly traumatic. My mother went into labor during a previous air raid. The nurses had to rush her into the hospital cellar, and she could hear the bombs hitting right and left while she tried to push her baby out. She nearly died after contracting childbed fever, *Kindbettfieber*. For two months in intensive care, she hallucinated from a fever that would not break. Her doctor saved her with injections of a germ-killing mix of champagne and lemons that my father had to get on the black market. So my mother did survive, only to have her infant son killed a few months later. And even he was already the second casualty in the family after her brother had died on the battlefield during the first days of the war. With their house in ruins, my parents moved with my grandmother to the little border town near Switzerland where I grew up—"to start a new life," as they used to say, already succumbing to the collectively spreading manic defense.

I was already far into my adult life when I figured out that my mother had a form of insanity, a psychotic incapacity to distinguish between reality and fantasy. As a small child, I took her erratic behavior, her unpredictable mood swings, her rages as they came, helpless at first and then defiant. As far back as I can remember, she would call me a changeling, asserting that there was no way I could be her child. "They must have exchanged you in the hospital," she said, "you are the wrong child." Sometimes she tried to convince my father I was possessed by the devil. "I can see the devil in her eyes," she used to scream. To survive psychically, I quite early seemed to have appropriated her narrative of not being her child. My mother read me an entry in her diary from the time I was two years old in which I allegedly told her: "If you are so mean to me, I'm no longer your child, I'll be the child of the man who owns the sun."

It took decades and several years of psychoanalysis to understand finally why I could never be the right child. I was supposed to replace her dead firstborn son, and she kept us both locked in a merciless battle over the impossibility of my ever being able to fulfill this task. I was the wrong child, the wrong gender, the wrong temperament, and, above all else, I didn't bring him back, didn't make those memories go away.

He was still right inside her, encrypted, a living ghost, and, while I was supposed to be him, to replace him, to exorcise him, I always failed. From then on, there was nothing I ever could do right for her. It was not only that I failed to meet her unconscious need; she also displaced her guilt onto me. Ultimately, she took revenge on me for having lost him because I did not bring him back. In this way she enacted an unconscious guilt for being complicit in his death. This sense of mine was supported after my mother's death in a conversation with my younger brother, who told me our mother had relayed to him that she initially didn't want to marry my father because she never wanted to risk having a baby during the war. After their son died she would always harbor a secret blame toward my father and herself for not following through with this precaution.

These processes were, of course, unconscious, a legacy I was born with that even my mother didn't understand. She just acted on it. I was supposed to replace a murdered brother whom my mother could not mourn properly. After all, the war was Germany's fault, and she was weighed down by an unfathomable guilt she could not acknowledge. This sense is encapsulated in a screen memory that belongs to my mother's war stories. When my parents picked up my brother's body in a tiny coffin, my mother broke down in the hospital, only to have the doctor admonish her sharply to pull herself together. "Think of the soldiers who gave their lives to this war," he said, "Your child didn't even have a life yet." Denied the right to mourn her infant son, whose life was too short to count, how could she not have been driven insane by this loss? I recently found a poem of mine in which I wrote "I carried the corpse of my brother in my womb like an identical twin." When I was born, my mother placed her grief into me. I became the crypt, holding my dead brother like a living corpse, taking over my mother's incapacity to mourn him, to let go of him. All my life I sensed, without knowing it, the weight of this legacy. It is a form of survivor's guilt, albeit different from the one experienced by Holocaust survivors. It is the guilt of owing one's life to the death of a sibling. How could I claim a right to live while in my mother's fantasy I was supposed to be my dead brother and in my own fantasy he was dead inside me?

The story of my phantom brother took another turn when I was nine years old. My mother was pregnant with my second brother. A gypsy woman had predicted that she would give birth to a healthy son on a Sunday. "A Sunday child," she called him, a sign of luck. But my mother was taken over by another certitude, namely, that she would die in childbirth. She took me aside one day to talk to me. What she would tell me would have to remain secret forever, she said. Then she revealed to me that she would die giving birth to my new brother and requested that I take her place. "Promise you take care of your sisters and your brother. Make sure your father never marries another woman or sends your grandmother away." Mortified, I could only repeat: "I don't want you to die!" She insisted I needed to take care of the family in her place. Unable to carry the weight of this responsibility, I finally broke down and talked to our local priest during confession. He simply said: "Put your worries to rest, I'll talk to God and tell him to spare your mother."

Again, it took decades to understand what happened at the time. My mother was pregnant with yet another child that was supposed to replace the dead brother. Since the gypsy had revealed to her that it was to be a son, she simply condensed the two children. After all, she nearly died in giving birth to her first son and was never supposed to have survived him. So this time she thought it would happen as it was meant to be: she would be the one who died first, giving birth to him and releasing him to live. One may confidently assume that this fantasy was partly designed to alleviate her survivor's guilt. How then was my mother's trauma transmitted to me? Neither of us knew what was happening, but it seems clear to me that she wanted me to take care of the legacy of a brother who was killed in the war, a son who could not be mourned. First, she wanted me to replace him, and after I failed in doing so, she wanted me to replace her and take care of him. This game of psychic substitution and displacement follows a sacrificial logic of sorts. There was a tacit request from my mother that I sacrifice my own being to become the placeholder of and act as another, first the dead brother and then the soon to be dead mother. How do you love a brother that hovers inside you as a ghost? How do you kill the ghost of a dead brother in order to live, all the while holding on to the love for the baby boy you see on family photos, knowing he had been your brother? How do you live the love for an imaginary older brother who would protect you, having never known him because he had already been killed before you were born? And how do you love a mother who hates you for not being the dead brother and who loves you so much she wants you to take her place?

The Phantom Town

In 1983, I accepted an invitation for a one-year visiting professorship at the University of California–Irvine. I never returned to live in Germany and, in 1986, officially became a "resident alien" in the United States, a designation that fitted like a glove my inner status of feeling alien anywhere in the world, even as a child in my hometown, Tiengen. In 1987, I went back to visit my parents in this town. Browsing in a local bookstore, I came across a book by Dieter Petri entitled *Die Tiengener Juden*. I stared at the book in disbelief. Tiengen's Jews? I hadn't known there had been Jews living in Tiengen; in fact, I had never thought about it. I bought the book and finished it, transfixed, in one reading that night. It felt like unearthing a hidden city under the one I had known as a child. Why had it never occurred to me to ask whether there had been any Jews in Tiengen and what happened to them during the war? Now I recalled that I used to walk through the Judengasse, the Jew's Alley, on my way to church. For me it was just a name, and it never even occurred to me that it was named after the Jews who lived there before the war. So decades after leaving the city I discovered its shameful history in a book written by an author who had, as a child about my age, lived just across the street, above an old restaurant, Blume. In Petri's book, I found out that this very restaurant used to be a Jewish establishment before the war. There was another restaurant, Ochsen, that Petri identifies as the place most frequented by the Jewish citizens. It was right across the street from my parents' first jewelry store, and we used to eat there on Sundays when I was little.

Suddenly, while reading *Die Tiengener Juden*, a fear welled up and took hold of me. The silence had worked after all, had crept into me and blinded me to what I could have seen if I had been more alert. I must have internalized the Germans' denial and silence after the war, despite the fact that, even when I was a child, I had tried to promise to myself that I never wanted to close my eyes before anything, however horrible. My town's erasure of history had caught up with me despite the fact that as soon as I learned about the genocide of Jews and the concentration camps, I was shocked into defiance and suspicion against my country, my parents and teachers, and the people of my childhood town. And yet I had never given a thought about what happened to the Jews, simply assuming the town had always been as it was when I grew up.

The next day I walked through the town, first through the Hauptstrasse and then the familiar old alleys, my favorite solitary places. There was the bakery, Steffen, where I used to buy bread and cake. Now I knew that it once was the house where Berthold Bernheim lived, one of the Jews who owned a dowry business in an old house in the Zubergasse. In the Reichskristallnacht the Nazis got Bernheim at his home, brought him to a district prison, and finally transported him to the concentration camp in Dachau. He survived, returning as a witness of the killing of other Jews from Tiengen, including his brother-in-law. There were many other buildings owned by Jewish businessmen, mainly the Bernheim and Guggenheim families, in the Hauptstrasse. The store where we bought my shoes, for example, used to belong to Julius Guggenheim, who was taken to the concentration camp in Dachau and murdered ten days later. Three years after I was born, his son Ernst was killed as an Israeli soldier.

I then went to the neighborhood next to my elementary school, the old *Volksschule*, where I lived until I was about ten years old. Our backyard had bordered on the Tugoweg, a little alley in which I used to ride my tricycle. Our neighbors across the street were the Albickers. From Petri's book I learned that they had rented out an apartment to Hermann Rabbinowicz before he bought a stately house of his own. He, too, was killed two weeks after being deported to Dachau. I now discovered that it was the Albickers, his former landlords, who took over his house after he was killed and that I used to play in this house with their son Karl. There was an uneasy feeling about being drawn into complicity, without my having a chance to know about it, with a family that actively profited from the murder of their neighbor and former tenant in a concentration camp. It had a haunting quality because it gave me the sense that there was no way to ever escape being tainted by the Nazi violence that occurred before I was even born.

Finally, I went to the Judengasse, but to my amazement the street sign said Turmgasse, Alley of the Tower. After talking to a few people I found out that the alley had been renamed but everybody kept using the name Judengasse. There, I now knew, the Nazis had destroyed the Jewish synagogue and turned it into an apartment house. Around the corner from it, the most beautiful house in Tiengen, a corner house in an old alley with a huge ancient mural depicting a medieval battle between the Germans and the Swiss, had housed the Jewish women's bath. On my way to school, I used to walk by there along a wall made of beautiful stones that Petri identified as the gravestones of the old Jewish cemetery.

I was never able to see Tiengen with the same eyes again and never will. It has become a haunted city, and the erasure of all traces of Jewish life is now but a material manifestation of the German denial of the shoah. There is a material denial of lived experience and affect even where people are willing to acknowledge the historical facts. Moreover, this denial makes it all the more easy to displace certain sentiments formerly harbored against the Jews onto new "others" within. I remember the suspicion, resentment, and rejection while I was growing up of the gypsies who returned to the town every summer, the few communists among Tiengen's inhabitants, but also the German refugees who came to resettle in southern Germany because they had lost their homes. And later, during my teens, the first massive influx of foreign guest workers was met with a new surge of xenophobia and racism. Today some of Tiengen's houses wear commemorative plates that identify their Jewish history. But these speak without speaking, empty signs that point to the denial of history rather than its endurance. "Time does not pass, it accumulates." But here it accumulated a silence that becomes more deadly the longer it lasts. Petri's book was a first step toward breaking this silence, but I met only people of the postwar generation who had read it, while those who were complicit in its history tried to ignore it. It is in this very book where I found the inscription that I quoted at the beginning of this chapter: "Remember, Jew, Tiengen was, is, and remains German." Meanwhile, this invocation has itself become the site of a ghostly haunting. To look at the commemorative plates that encrypt the town's Jewish presence is not to see. Only those who dig deep into the archeology of this town's cultural unconscious can see what the plates tell without telling: the town's hidden history of genocide.

chapterfour

Identity Trouble
Guilt, Shame, and Idealization

There is no help for it: I am a white man. For unconsciously I distrust
what is black in me, that is, the whole of my being.
—Frantz Fanon, *Black Skin, White Masks*

Oh I feel so dumb I can't answer all those questions I don't know
how to be a Kiowa Indian.
—N. Scott Momaday, *The Names*

I . . . hated Germany. I hated being German.
—Sabine Reichel, *What Did You Do in the War, Daddy?*

I was trying to raise myself as a black man in America, and beyond
the given of my appearance, no one around me seemed to know
exactly what that meant.
—Barack Obama, *Dreams of My Father*

We already know that Barack Obama can be many things to many
people, but could anyone have guessed that he would also be a
good German?
—Gregory Rodriguez, "Ich bin ein Obaman"

These five epigraphs can be read as paradigmatic illustrations of particular forms of identity trouble that emerge from emotional conflicts
over ethnic, racial, or national interpellations. Althusser defines interpellation as the hailing of subjects into specific cultural, political, or legal
positions. If we walk down a street, for example, and hear a policeman
shout: "Hey, stop immediately!" we feel interpellated in the same way
as a criminal would even if we have never committed a crime. Rather

than as ontological givens, I argue, race and ethnicity operate on the register of affects and emotions as cultural and political interpellations. These interpellations call on us, demanding that we make them our own, or at the very least requiring that we situate ourselves in relation to them. We become most astutely aware of racial or ethnic attributions when they are imposed on us from outside, either by our own community, by a dominant national or colonial regime, or by members of a foreign culture or religion who stereotype us either by denigration, vilification, or idealization.

In his reflections on the psychic formation of colonized and racialized people in *Black Skin, White Masks*, Fanon makes his famous statement, "I am a white man." With this declaration, he calls our attention to a link between ethnicity and emotion that reaches beneath the surface of overt interpellation. Fanon succinctly points to the vicissitudes of the cultural and racial unconscious. At the level of his reality as a colonial subject, Fanon would simply be interpellated as a black man. He would always be publicly put in his place, so to speak, as a black man by the forces that enact colonial power. However, by tracing the psychic effects of colonization, Fanon reveals that unconscious interpellations are much less straightforward. In a highly conflicted unconscious identification with the aggressor, Fanon detects the traces of a white man's feeling in both his affects and affective dispositions and his self-image. He is forever unable to feel what he could be on his own terms as an uncolonized black man because his ego ideal is that of a white man. An insidious colonization of psychic space hijacks his feelings as a black man. Hence, his affective responses are inextricably bound up with his sense "I am a white man," but they also emulate the white man's rejection of being black. More devastating even than suggested in the title *Black Skin, White Masks*, the racial transference of whiteness is not limited to the surface of a mask. A mask can be taken off. The whiteness Fanon talks about goes to the core of the self. Identity trouble here is based on a tenacious unconscious identification with the white aggressor that persists even within Fanon's conscious struggle for decolonization. "There is no help for it,"[1] he says.

More perniciously even, Fanon's internalization of the colonizer's values inserts a nagging self-denigration into his entire self-relation. "I distrust what is black in me, that is, the whole of my being." Self-esteem, if there is any, must be based for the black man on passing as white, as Other, in the formation of his own self-image. This dynamic operates according to the same logic that Sartre scrutinized in his analysis of the "imaginary child" or the "imaginary personality" of the adult. The mutual influence Sartre and Fanon had on each other is well known. In his psychosocial study of Flaubert, Sartre analyzes cross-gender identifications using the famous phrase that has been attributed to Flaubert: "Madame Bovary, that's me."[2] Imaginary selves routinely cross the boundaries of race, ethnicity, and gender as they are reinvented under the pressures of conflicted interpellations. If it is to be effective, decolonizing the mind will have to reach the bottom of this distrust and self-loathing. It must both integrate conflicting attitudes into the processes of self-fashioning and mourn what has been lost in imaginary reinventions of the self.

Nearly a quarter of a century after Fanon, in another setting of colonial racism, N. Scott Momaday confesses to feeling dumb for not knowing how to be a Kiowa Indian. Undoubtedly, he reacts to an interpellation of a different kind. The Anglo-American culture of a country stolen from his people long ago now expects him to self-identify as a Kiowa. This culture asks him to perform his indigenous identity whenever he enters the public sphere as the writer who is known to have launched the Native American Renaissance in literature. For all practical purposes, however, he was educated within Anglo-American environments and institutions. His ethnic self-consciousness awoke belatedly and had to rely on ethnographic narratives as crutches for what he calls his self-invention as Indian. Many indigenous people have pointed out the bitter irony of having grown up so alienated from their culture of origin that, in order to "reinvent" it, they must turn to their colonizer's narratives. Yet even those who grow up in a more traditional indigenous community experience the identity trouble that inevitably comes with a colonial imposition of values and status.

My third epigraph shifts cultures and sides. "I hated Germany . . . I hated being German." Among other reasons, I also chose this epigraph because it is so unabashedly in your face. Sabine Reichel's almost laconic statement has the quality of a categorical imperative for many who belong to the German postwar generation. "Can anyone understand the experience of growing up among people with such a gruesome past?"[3] she asks as she describes the formation of a negative identity based on guilt and shame. "Guilt can be a feeling, not a fact, and referring to my age never relieved me from the burden of my father's generation."[4] There is, as Reichel asserts, a transgenerational transmission of guilt or, as it is commonly called, collective guilt, *Kollektivschuld*. This is the identity trouble of children of perpetrators, not of victims. Guilt, shame, and self-hatred are major factors in the formation of a negative identity in those who internalize the guilt of perpetration. As a consequence, these children of perpetrators are always on the run, do not want to belong to their own culture, and will never belong to another.

I am, of course, not arguing that all second-generation Germans react in this fashion. There is a wide range of defensive reactions against the knowledge of belonging to a nation of perpetrators. One of them is to remain frozen in guilt and shame; another is to remain lost in denial. But the particular identity trouble I am investigating here—the internalization of guilt and shame and concomitant wholesale affective rejection of one's heritage—is such a common reaction in the generation of German postwar children that it becomes a crucial feature of the national unconscious in postwar Germany. The parental cult of the *Heimat*, the homeland, is superseded by its dark double in the children's desire not to belong.

It was the German war generation that coined the term "inner exile." They used it after the war as an illusory escape from their complicity with, if not excuse for, the Nazi atrocities, whether as active participants or as bystanders. By contrast, their children seem to have inherited "inner exile" as a condition of impossible national belonging. Where Fanon said: "There is no help for it. I am a white man," the German postwar generation would have to say: "There is no help for it. I cannot be German, but I cannot be non-German either." They don't know "how to be" German, but for different reasons than those that inspired Momaday's statement that he doesn't know how to be a Kiowa Indian. To this day, I cringe whenever anybody asks me "Where are you from?" It feels like an interpellation to confess one's legacy of belonging to the most abject people on earth. And even though the dynamic has changed for the third generation, there is no escape from this transgenerational legacy. In *Tales from a Child of the Enemy*, Ursula

Duba concludes her collection of poetry with a poem that exposes the affective dynamic of the third generation's inherited identity trouble in sharp profile:

> what is it you want us to do
> they ask reproachfully
> look at our young people
> weighed down by guilt
> . . . .
> why is everybody still beating that dead horse
> they ask angrily
> *and why do they refuse to forget*
> after all the money we've paid them
>
> they can't understand
> that . . .
> nothing
> absolutely nothing
> will erase the terrible stain
> on their country's history.[5]

National reactions to violent histories are different, often depending on whether the countries have won or lost the war. Some countries may continue to live for centuries in denial of the terrible stain on their history. Such denial, however, does not mean that they can escape the effects of a transgenerational transmission of their violent legacy. The epigraph from Barack Obama takes us into the present of one such transgenerational legacy, namely, racial politics in the United States as this country has nominated and elected a black president for the first time. Obama emphasizes a specific symptom of identity trouble, his goal to raise himself as a black man in America at a time "when no one around . . . seemed to know exactly what that meant." If we compare Obama's statement to Fanon's, we can see how the parameters of interpellation have changed. For Fanon, the ego ideal of a black man was built on the values of a white man. Accordingly, his interpellation as a black man was to suppress those features of identity associated with blackness. By contrast, in Obama's statement, we can detect a wish to raise himself as a man who embraces blackness as a value in a country still profoundly marked by an ongoing, albeit changing history of racism. The fact that no one seemed to know what exactly it meant to be a black man in America reveals not only that racial signifiers have acquired a certain geographical and historical mobility but also that Obama's very desire to raise himself as a black man without quite knowing how to do so is deeply inscribed in America's racial history and bears the traces of transgenerational trauma. We have come a long way since Fanon. Obama may no longer distrust what is black in him, but instead he feels compelled to define himself as black. Yet despite a clearly felt interpellation to define himself in terms of a racially defined identity, he has difficulty doing so.

I could not resist including the final epigraph by Gregory Rodriguez. Playing on John F. Kennedy's imaginary appropriation of German identity in his famous remark "Ich bin ein Berliner," Rodriguez's article "Ich bin ein Obaman" reflects on Obama's speech in Berlin during his election campaign. (Of course, the very term "good German" inevitably conjures connotations of a time when being a "good German"—that is, a German blindly obedient to authority—was actually a bad thing.) More specifically, Rodriguez refers to the revelation in an article titled "The German Obama" in the German newspaper *Die Zeit* that Obama's "great-great-great-great-great-great-grandfather was an upstanding Alsatian farmer named Christian Gutknecht, who shoved off to America on September 13, 1749."[6] From the article's tone, one could almost surmise that it might be easier for Obama to be a "good German" than for a postwar German like Sabine Reichel. Ironically, one might also wonder if it is easier for Obama to be a "good German" while selling his run for the presidency in Germany than it was for him to be a "good American" while growing up.

I also chose to include Rodriguez's statement because it illustrates something fundamental about ethnic identity formation and identity trouble not only in the Americas but also in today's global world. This complication of ethnic identity leads Michael M. J. Fischer to define ethnicity more generally as "a process of inter-reference between two or more cultural traditions":

What emerges as a conclusion is not simply that parallel processes operate across American ethnic identities, but a sense that these ethnicities constitute only a family of resemblances, that ethnicity cannot be reduced to identical sociological functions, that ethnicity is a process of inter-reference between two or more cultural traditions, and that these dynamics of intercultural knowledge provide reservoirs for renewing humane values. Ethnic memory is thus, or ought to be, future, not past, oriented.[7]

How then can we think today about the vicissitudes of racial and ethnic markings? How does one think about cultural belonging from the perspective of the victims of colonization, on the one hand, and of the descendants of perpetrator nations, on the other? How does one think about the political and psychic implications of the negative identity formation that occurs on both sides of the divide? These are the core questions that inform my reflections in this chapter.

Seeing both victims and perpetrators as damaged by historically violent social and economic systems such as colonialism, imperialism, corporate capitalism, or religious fundamentalism by no means implies that the damage done to children of victims can be equated with that of the children of perpetrators. All too often, the children of perpetrators continue to live under privileged economic and social conditions, whereas the children of victims continue to suffer from economic and social discrimination. This is especially true for colonized people. I am focusing here, however, on the psychic damage done both to victims and perpetrators, as well as the mechanisms by which it is passed on to subsequent generations. The stakes in addressing such damage are not merely psychological but also have immense political consequences, especially in cases in which victims and perpetrators are forced to find a mode of conviviality.

In *On the Postcolony*, Achille Mbembe analyzes the effects of oppression on victims and perpetrators who are forced to share a living space in the postcolony. Mbembe detects in both groups a depletion of vitality: "This logic has resulted in the mutual 'zombification' of both the dominant and those apparently dominated. This zombification means that each has robbed the other of vitality and left both impotent."[8] We are reminded once again of how in *The Inability to Mourn*, Alexander and Margarete Mitscherlich see a similar depletion of energy in German culture after World War II. Mbembe's notion of "zombification" also recalls the psychic condition of "death in life" diagnosed in Holocaust victims. In addition to "zombification," "death in life," and psychocultural paralysis more generally, there is also the distortion of history that damages both victims and perpetrators. Fanon alludes to this type of psychohistorical damage when he insists on the need to "show the white man that he is at once the perpetrator and the victim of a delusion"[9] or when he claims that "the white man is the victim of his unconscious."[10]

History bears out what transgenerational studies have shown, namely, that it is the transgenerational transmission of psychic damage that makes future generations vulnerable to repetition and opens history to new cycles of violence. Looking at the psychic damage done to children of perpetrators, however, does not amount to shifting responsibility away from specific individual or collective human agents of history. Rather, this perspective allows one to emphasize why human beings become vulnerable to committing violence against other people if they themselves are victims of systemic violence. This materialist notion of psychology places human violence in the context of the systemic violence we find in certain national, political, economic, or religious formations. We can only understand the psychic aspects of violence if we take into consideration the environment that regulates the material living conditions, the organization of kinship and gender relations and educational systems, and the relationship to other species and the natural environment, as well as the relationship to other people and their histories, including those from different national, racial, ethnic, and religious communities. At the same time, we can only understand the psychic aspects of violence if we look deep into the recesses of the human psyche, including the traces of violence left in the individual and cultural unconscious.

It is perhaps because of my awareness, even as a child, of belonging to a nation of perpetrators that I have developed a lifelong interest in finding out why we feel what we feel and how we become who we are. As a child I wanted to know how I could become less German or, better yet, not German at all. Once I learned about the Holocaust in my early teens, I—like Sabine Reichel—hated being German; I hated my country; I wanted to run away from the crushing feeling of guilt and shame. I also fantasized about and idealized being Other—French, Japanese, Native American, what have you.[11] It was impossible for the German postwar generation to disentangle the highly personal identity struggles of one's teenage years from the problem of national identity.

The infamous German silence about the Holocaust was never successful . . . as the silencing of violence never is. The Holocaust was everywhere and nowhere. We children learned to read between the lines at a
very early age. We found ways to listen to whispers behind closed doors.
We knew there were secrets and horrors that were hushed up before
we knew what they were. We became hypersensitive to the contradictions and hypocrisies in the lives and words of the adults who brought
us up and taught us. Germany in the postwar years became a guilt and
shame culture par excellence. But much of this dynamic was enacted unconsciously. Looking back, I am fairly confident that I felt guilty and
ashamed of being German before I knew the details of Germany's violent
and genocidal history. The feelings were generated by half-understood
stories and allusions, by adults whispering things children were not supposed to hear, by the way Hitler's name was invoked as Germany's own
Satan. German children also absorbed the guilt and shame they could
feel rather than overtly *experience* in their parents. Children have a way
of knowing. Children have a way of listening to the unspoken. Children
also have a way of incorporating their parents' unresolved conflicts,
contradictions, and shameful secrets. This is why children may fall from
the edge of a violent world into a no-man's land of inner uprootedness
that leaves them with a feeling they never belong.

I remember that from my earliest reading of memoirs, fiction, and
poetry written by colonized or persecuted people, I marveled at their
seemingly unquestioned cultural belonging. United in their struggle
against racism and persecution, the Jewish and the indigenous Native
American and African writings I read at the time displayed an unde-
feated cultural pride even as they described the unspeakable humilia-
tions under the Nazi or colonial rule and even as they admitted to the
self-devaluation and identity trouble that comes with the internalization
of colonial contradictions. By contrast, many Germans of my generation
truly abhorred any sense of a national belonging. The national shame
we felt even affected how we received the German heritage of great po-
ets, philosophers, and musicians because by the time we were teenagers
most of us had heard that the Nazis would come home from the gas
chambers and listen to Beethoven.

It took the student revolution finally to provoke a broad public
debate between the generations about Germany's history of genocide

and fascism. In this confrontation, personal conflicts between the generations became inextricably enmeshed with questioning the parental generation's role in the Holocaust. Conflicts over Germany's infamous authoritarian methods of raising children thus became overdetermined by the legacy of fascism. We firmly believed the cruelty of German parents and teachers toward their children could be traced back to the same roots as the Nazi atrocities. During the sixties and seventies, the Frankfurt School—founded by Jewish scholars in exile in California—became a foremost tool of ideological formation in West Germany. Drawing on Marx and Freud, Frankfurt School philosophers theorized the inextricably interwoven relationship between the personal and the political. Adorno's widely discussed work *The Authoritarian Personality* systematically links the repression of emotions and cruelty toward children that comes with German authoritarianism and its excessive emphasis on law and order with a propensity to become complicit in the fascist politics and criminal acts of the Nazi regime.[12] As Sabine Reichel puts it succinctly: "Only people who have personally experienced emotional and physical cruelty and disrespect as children can pass on such contempt for human dignity and can even carry it out with gloating pleasure."[13]

During the student revolution, Germany's postwar generation tried to break the silence and denial about the Holocaust. Dominated by rage, condemnation, bitterness, and accusation, these confrontations ended in deadlock and retaliation. Passed during the backlash years in the seventies, Germany's infamous lustration laws prohibited anyone involved in a leftist organization or in revolutionary activism from working in a public institution. Founded on a politics of revenge, these laws came uncannily close to a new purification of Germany from political dissent. They must be seen as part of the broader dynamic of transgenerational trauma. Silencing or covering up violence, refusal to take responsibility, and failure to acknowledge guilt and shame are major factors in sustaining and passing psychic damage on to subsequent generations. Retaliation against and persecution of internal dissent is only a symptom of a much more toxic overall process that reveals how the contradictions of histories of violence are internalized and reenacted from within.

This persecution of internal dissent not only happened with Germany's war generation but also happened and continues to happen elsewhere, including in the United States. We saw it happen right before our eyes with those who voiced dissent about the war in Iraq. Moreover, a deep rift in the United States today divides those who deny and those who acknowledge that this country was founded on a genocidal history and continues to be immersed in a long history of violence. In the display of official public feelings, however, we also witnessed the manic defenses of a paranoid-schizoid ecology of fear, fueled by a runaway militarism that splits the world along an imagined "axis of evil." Meanwhile, transgenerational haunting in the descendants of the colonizers is largely withheld from public recognition but operates tacitly at the level of the political unconscious. In Germany, by contrast, the effects of transgenerational haunting are much more overt, at least for the postwar generation. The deadlock between generations, however, ties the postwar generation negatively to their parents' war legacy. The sixties rage against the parental generation was an attempt to exorcise forcibly the ghosts of the past and to escape from the guilt and shame that had been passed down. We all too happily bought into a politics of splitting, nourished by the fantasy of good revolutionary German children rebelling against bad fascist parents. It helped us assuage our internalized self-hatred.

Analyzing the psychodynamics of colonial relations, Frantz Fanon coins the term "Manichean delirium" to characterize the agonistic politics resulting from a psychic process of splitting the world into good and evil. The term "delirium" aptly points to a pathological distortion of reality required to split peoples into good and evil or civilized and savage. Melanie Klein characterizes this organization of affects and mode of feeling as a "paranoid-schizoid position." According to Klein, this position marks the organization of an infantile psychic world full of persecutory anxieties, greed and envy, rage and despair.[14] If this paranoid-schizoid position persists into adult life as the exclusive way of modulating and organizing affects, it will feed into offensive politics, chauvinism, militarism, and religious fundamentalisms. Klein admits to the fact that we will always retain residual impulses toward splitting as an affective mode of defense against real or imagined dangers. Sometimes, especially during early childhood or in traumatic circumstances, splitting is necessary for surviving terrifying assaults on our bodies or psyches. However, in order to develop modes of mature coexistence, Klein argues, we need to move toward a "depressive position," characterized by the mourning of losses and injuries. On a collective level, one could equate the depressive position with the mourning and reparation required to take responsibility for one's history of violence.

Alexander and Margarete Mitscherlich argued that the refusal of the German people to take active responsibility for their complicity in Nazi politics pushed their sense of collective guilt into the cultural unconscious. This prevented them from mourning not only those murdered in the camps but also their own losses, including those killed on the battlefield and the bombed cities. Finally, it also prevented them from mourning the loss of their ideals and values. Mourning the losses of victims is, I believe, a necessary precondition for people from perpetrator nations to begin to repair some of the damage to others' as well as to their own psychic health. Twenty years after the appearance of *The Inability to Mourn*, Reichel comes to the devastating conclusion that the German war generation never regained their ability to mourn:

> They are still unable to mourn. I sat in their living rooms, listened to their reflections and ruminations and felt a chill. Their eyes were cold and apathetic; their voices, like my father's, reportorial when they spoke of carnage and calm consciences. They were like impersonators whose performance showed some skill but was essentially hollow, with all feeling cut off. But repressed memories are not forgotten memories—a few scratches are sufficient and all kinds of conflicting emotions erupt. But the memories remain uninvestigated. These people are too old to risk the danger of opening their shrunken hearts, letting that stream of multi-layered, unresolved feelings flow.[15]

I agree with Reichel. The war generation has never mourned in the full sense of mourning. But if there is a transgenerational transmission of guilt and shame, perhaps it is the task of the postwar generation to find ways to take collective responsibility for the guilt of the parental generation and pursue the work of mourning and reparation they aborted—whether because they repressed their guilt or because they were too mortified by their crimes. Perhaps this, too, belongs to the transgenerational legacy.

A similar process seems to be necessary in the United States, where, even centuries after the foundational genocide of indigenous peoples and the atrocities of slavery, the collective work of mourning and reparation has never emerged in a public culture that supports the serious working-through of colonial, racial, and imperial violence. Admissions of broken treaties alone, for example, are not good enough unless they translate into a meaningful politics of reparation. Casino privileges do not belong to such a politics. Mourning, reparation, and the working-through of violent histories require a relational politics, including a politics of emotion that crosses the divide between victims and perpetrators.[16] Such a politics would also need to reflect the interconnectedness of America's foundational violence with more recent wars and violence, including the Vietnam War, the wars in Afghanistan and Iraq, and other forms of neoimperial and neoliberal violence performed to this day.

In *The Colonization of Psychic Space*, Kelly Oliver insists that if we use and further develop psychoanalysis as a social theory, relationality needs to be primary:

> It is relationality that is primary, not one subject or the other, or two self-consciousnesses encountering each other and looking for mutual recognition. . . .
>
> Subjectivity is constituted through response, responsiveness, or response-ability. . . . In addition, I maintain that drives and affects do not originate in one body or one psyche but rather are relational and transitory—they can move from one body to another. Indeed, following Frantz Fanon, I suggest that the negative affects of the oppressors are "deposited into the bones" of the oppressed.[17]

Accounting for this mobility of affect is crucial if we consider the relational working-through of violent histories by both victims and perpetrators, especially in recent attempts to bring victims and perpetrators together for this work of reparation. It is the mobility of affect that enables not only the toxic deposition of negative affects into others but also the sublimation and transformation of negative affects that are constitutive of social bonds and the social more generally. In addition, the deposition of negative affects into others operates not only from the colonizer to the colonized; it also is central to transgenerational transmission because the parental generation tends to disavow negative affects such as guilt and shame, only to deposit them into the unconscious or even conscious processes of subject formation in the next generation.[18] Working through violent histories requires a relational ethics, which, for Oliver, must be grounded in forgiveness and acceptance.[19] It is hard, of course, to imagine reparation and forgiveness for historical violence on the scale of genocide. Certain violent histories, individual or collective, will forever remain beyond reparation and unforgivable.[20]

Ultimately, I think, what we call "reparation" is not a matter of forgiveness. Yet while a destruction on the scale of genocide can never be repaired, what needs reparation is the basis for a less destructive relationality between victims and perpetrators, especially in cases where they are forced by historical circumstances to reside in the same country and to share social and cultural spaces and institutional practices. There is not only transgenerational trauma and haunting but also transgenerational responsibility. In his speech "A More Perfect Union," Barack Obama highlights "that we cannot solve the challenges of our time unless we solve them together."[21] The task he identifies for the current generation of Americans is not only to face the stain left on the nation by "its original sin of slavery" (and we would need to add the genocidal colonization of its indigenous people) but also to overcome the "racial stalemate" and politics of resentment that continue to pervade the American political landscape. The challenge for the descendants of the victims of slavery and colonization, he argues, is to embrace "the burdens of our past without becoming victims of our past." We are reminded, of course, of Fanon's famous statement toward the end of *Black Skin, White Masks*: "I am not a prisoner of history."[22] It is one of the characteristics of trauma that it makes the victim a prisoner of the past. This is why healing trauma also means a release from the past and an opening toward the future. Obama insists on the need to form alliances across racial divides and to move beyond the old racial wounds and the "legacy of defeat" that was passed on to future generations. A politics of redress therefore needs to be future-oriented and grounded in alliances across the historical divides.

A politics of redress, reparation, and reconciliation means, then, acknowledging and integrating the unforgivable in order to repair what is possible at the present time.[23] Moreover, a more comprehensive politics of mourning and reparation that includes the collective work of mourning belongs to a larger politics of what Ngũgĩ wa Thiong'o and others have called "decolonizing the mind." The latter must be shared globally and across the divide between victims and perpetrators because today's world violates and degrades everyone and everything, including other species and the planet at large. For better or worse, in today's brittle ecology of survival, we are in this together.

While these reflections may sound utopian, we should not forget that important work has already been done and continues to be done in this direction. I'm not only thinking about reconciliation movements in South Africa, Australia, and Ireland, for example, that are vitally important despite their shortcomings. I am also thinking about a whole body of scholarly work that explores the conditions and possibilities of living "after evil."[24] In the specific context of transgenerational haunting, Dan Bar-On's groundbreaking work with mixed groups of victims and perpetrators stands out. He was not only the first to interview children of prominent Nazis but also the first to bring Israeli and Palestinian participants together to work in groups on the ongoing violence between their peoples by sharing autobiographical and biographical narratives. Such shared storytelling presupposes working through the asymmetric relationships between victims and perpetrators, even in relationships where the boundaries between the two may be sliding. In the case of Israel and Palestine, for example, Israeli families may have been victims of an attack by Palestinian suicide bombers, while at the same time, because of the brutal occupation of Palestine and oppression of Palestinian citizens, the state of Israel acts as the perpetrator. Dan Bar-On describes the effect of this asymmetric power relation on the dialogue between Holocaust survivors and Israeli Palestinians and Palestinian refugees: "Even before an open dialogue between parties in conflict can take place, when asymmetric power relations persist it is necessary to first empower, recover, and legitimize the stories of the oppressed party."[25]

However, within these asymmetric power relations, Bar-On detects certain related structures of oppression. He develops the concept of a "double wall" in order to describe how both victims and perpetrators tend to erect a wall around the traumatic experiences of the past and then pass this wall on to the next generation.[26]

This "double wall" creates what Bar-On calls a "conspiracy of silence," that is, the silencing or repression of narratives.

> The reasons behind the silence are often different for the survivors than the perpetrators. The former suffer more from existential "survivor guilt" of having lived while many of their family members did not. . . . The perpetrators try to conceal from their offspring and others the atrocities they once committed. . . . The results, however, are similar: The silencing usually transmits the trauma to the following generations. . . . Even if, as some contend, the silencing of these traumatic events was functional during the early years, . . . at later stages the same silencing becomes dysfunctional, especially when it leads to intergenerational transmission of the effects of physical or moral trauma.[27]

The dynamic Bar-On describes in the formation of a "double wall" in victims and perpetrators and their children pertains to a more general phenomenon that Ashis Nandy calls "isomorphic oppression." The notion of "isomorphic oppression" is grounded in the knowledge—available at least since Hegel's work on the dialectic between master and slave—that in relationships of domination both master and slave, colonizer and colonized, or perpetrator and victim are experiencing alienation and psychic damage.

What Nandy calls "isomorphic oppression" still remains largely untheorized. Perhaps this is because the notion of "isomorphism" suggests too much of a parallelism between victims and perpetrators. "Complementary oppression" might be a more accurate description of the necessary decolonization of the mind of perpetrators that Nandy highlights. Looking at the literature about decolonization, there is, as Nandy points out, little about "decolonizing the mind" of colonizers and builders of empire:

> The broad psychological contours of colonialism are now known. Thanks to sensitive writers like Octave Mannoni, Frantz Fanon and Albert Memmi we even know something about the interpersonal patterns which constituted the colonial situation, particularly in Africa. Less well-known are the cultural and psychological pathologies produced by colonization in the colonizing societies.[28]

Nandy argues that the struggle to decolonize the mind needs to work against the denial "that the colonizers are at least as much affected by the ideology of colonialism, that their degradation, too, can sometimes be terrifying."[29] In a similar vein, Reichel asserts that the German people "haven't survived the cold-blooded annihilation of other people without substantial psychological damage—but they are not aware of it. With every single extinguished life, something in the murderers died with the murdered in the trenches, gas chambers, and ovens."[30] Denial of violence and oppression will inevitably come back to haunt the perpetrators. For generations to come, German people will and should be haunted by their past, despite the war generation's denial and, as a transgenerational effect of this denial, an already observable reduced awareness in the generation of grandchildren. This transgenerational haunting is true for other participants in violent histories as well, even in cases where it remains banned from public discourse.

In order to grasp the dynamic of complementary oppression and at the same time remain mindful of the fundamental asymmetry between victims and perpetrators in processes of decolonizing the mind, we need to delineate more specifically the conditions and phases of the struggle for the decolonization of psychic space. Fanon argues, for example, that in their struggle for liberation, colonized people inevitably move through various stages. He characterizes them roughly as:

1. Identification with the aggressor
2. Unilateral rejection of anything identifiable with colonial or racist culture
3. Idealizing fixation on one's own precolonial heritage
4. Integration of one's history as a colonized person and acknowledgment of one's conflicted identity formed in the struggle with a violent history

We see that the phases Fanon identifies are accompanied, if not generated, by different emotional or affective states. Phases 1, 2, and 3 are based on guilt, shame, and idealization, and phase 4 is based on mourning, integration, and reparation. Or, in more Kleinian terms, phases 1, 2, and 3 would belong to a politics of splitting and a paranoid-schizoid position whereas phase 4 would correspond to the depressive

and reparative position. Let us consider for a moment what complementary phases for the "decolonization of the mind" of perpetrators
might look like:

1. Identification with the victim
2. Unilateral rejection of anything identifiable with colonial (or racist) culture
3. Idealizing fixation on the other's precolonial heritage
4. Acknowledgment of one's conflicted identity as participant or
   inheritor of a violent legacy and willingness to assume responsibility and participate in the collective struggle against oppression, violence, and war

Fanon's and Ngũgĩ's works focus on decolonizing the mind from the
perspective of colonized people. With Nandy, I'm interested in exploring equivalent processes for decolonizing the mind of people belonging
to a perpetrator nation. I find the most compelling, if haunting, engagements to be in literature. J. M. Coetzee's *Disgrace*, for example, relentlessly exposes the psychic deformation and transgenerational transmission of trauma in the culture of colonizers in South Africa. While David
Lurie, the central male protagonist, is unable to face his guilt, his daughter, Lucy, internalizes it, taking it on in an act bordering on self-sacrifice.
She acts based on the recognition that there is nowhere to run. The most
devastating aspect of *Disgrace* is perhaps that while there is nowhere
to run, the path toward decolonizing the mind seems foreclosed also.
There is no work of cultural translation and no language that can be
shared by perpetrators and victims. The cycle of violence continues as
both sides live in isolation from each other, even if they share a living
space and kinship arrangement. As power relations turn around, perpetrators become victims, and victims become perpetrators. But it is not
a simple inversion because the former perpetrators enter the new cycle
of violence with guilt and shame, while the former victims enter it with
rage and revenge. Violence is reenacted within a different power grid
rather than worked though collectively. Even minimal hope, however,
seems to hinge on the possibility of such collective work, which cannot
be achieved without acknowledging the psychic damage incurred by
both victims and perpetrators.

Fanon argues that for colonized people, working through identification with the aggressor might prepare the ground for a process of decolonization. He even insisted that the colonized will not be able to reach a phase of integration and self-affirmation without having first gone through a phase of identification with the aggressor. Does a complementary dynamic hold for the colonizer? History makes it hard to conceive of a benign model of cross-cultural identification. We know too well the pitfalls of idealization in the Western imaginary from a long cultural history of Orientalism, philo-Semitism, or images of the noble savage, particularly in the case of the indigenous people in the United States. Historically, the idealization of non-Western cultures emerges from within a racist colonial imaginary, and, inversely, overt racism often carries an unconscious identification in which the Other becomes the container for rejected and split-off parts of the self.

If we take Fanon's scheme of decolonizing the mind seriously, we must explore whether under certain circumstances this idealizing identification with the victim might be mobilized in processes of decolonizing the mind. What if such identification took the form of solidarity with and participation in the victim's struggle against oppression? What if it took the form of an active learning from the cultures and struggles of the oppressed? I am suggesting nothing less than using the cultural imaginary—including the cultural unconscious—to redirect and in a sense invert the psychic energies of colonialism and racism for a decolonization of the mind. This inversion bears certain affinities with a transvaluation of values in the Nietzschean sense, that is, a reprogramming and, in many respects, a turning upside-down of attitudes. It also needs to include what Gayatri Spivak calls a "rearrangement of desire." While remaining part of a colonial legacy, the identification with non-Western cultures can be co-opted, so to speak, for antiracist struggles. Perceiving the identification with oppressed or colonized peoples unilaterally as part of a racist agenda is a theoretical simplification that reduces the psychic ambivalence inherent in idealization. Whenever I think about the complicated status of idealizing the Other, I remember a conversation in which a Chinese American colleague argued that she preferred an honest racist to a philo-Semite. Ruth Kluger, a Holocaust survivor, retorted: "In Auschwitz we would have wished for people idealizing us rather than killing us. I prefer being beaten to being shot or gassed, I prefer being insulted to being beaten, and I prefer being romanticized to being vilified. How could I resent a philo-Semitic friend for creating an idealized image of us after all the negative images the world has created of Jews?"[31]

Politically, the important move is from idealization to historical integration. This corresponds to a move from the first to the fourth phase in Fanon's scheme, or from a politics of splitting to a politics of mourning and reparation. As part of a paranoid-schizoid politics of splitting, idealization remains potentially wedded to its inverse, thus perpetuating negative discrimination in less transparent forms. Fanon's expanded scheme helps to theorize both the conscious and unconscious ambivalence of identification. Even while they belong to a colonial and racist legacy, both the identification with the aggressor and the identification with the victim can be co-opted in the struggle for decolonization.

The psychic dynamic of identification is so complex because it operates on the slippery ground of the cultural unconscious and of imagined communities. Freud argues that in adult life the patterns of identification that are formed within the family of origin are transferred to ties to "artificial institutions," such as, for example, the church and the army. In this process, the patterns of identification may be unconsciously transmitted and remain the same. In a similar vein, in "Filiation, Affiliation," Edward Said reminds us that the deliberate breaking of ties with family, home, class, country, and tradition has reasserted itself throughout the history of modernity as the most pervasive practice of modern self-consciousness.[32] This turn from filiation to affiliation also occurs across the divide between cultures. In "Ethnicity as Text and Model," the anthropologist Michael M. J. Fischer further argues that apart from being socially constructed, ethnicity is "reinvented and reinterpreted in every generation by each individual." He writes:

> Ethnicity is a part of the self that is often quite puzzling to the individual, something over which he or she is not in control. Insofar as it is a deeply rooted emotional component of identity, it is often transmitted less through cognitive language or learning (to which sociology has almost entirely restricted itself) than through processes analogous to the dreaming and transferences of psychoanalytic encounters.[33]

In a world of violent confrontation and oppression, processes of self-fashioning are necessarily wrought with emotional, cultural, and political conflicts and contradictions. More often than we commonly acknowledge, they evolve across cultural, ethnic, and racial divides. Conscious or unconscious identifications with the Other, aggressor or victim, are—for better or worse—integral parts of such processes. In colonialist, racist, or otherwise oppressive cultures, we cannot entirely escape negative psychic deformations that affect our relationships with others, regardless of which side of the divide we are located on. A politics of splitting that leads to vilifications or idealizations of the Other belongs to such deformations. Contradictions will pervade the display of public emotions as well as the affective difference with which we approach and relate to each other.

Moreover, the very display of public emotions must be explored in terms of the vicissitudes of its performativity. In *The Politics of Emotions*, Sara Ahmed draws on Marxism and psychoanalysis to explore the political and psychic work done by publicly displayed emotions. She uses psychoanalytic theory as an economy of emotion to show that affect "does not reside positively in the sign or commodity, but is produced as an effect of its circulation."[34] Performativity enables the circulation and intensification of emotions. As Ahmed emphasizes, "Affective economies are social and material, as well as psychic."[35] However, we also need to acknowledge that in the process of this circulation, certain fixations may occur that project onto others or deposit into others negative or positive affects, thus creating the illusory effect of affects' being "located" there. Ideologically charged projections, I argue, may create a freezing that paralyzes the free circulation of affect. This is a dynamic that Alfred Lorenzer, for example, analyzes in *Sprachzerstörung und Rekonstruktion*, where he describes how certain affective dispositions lead to the rigid formation of psychic clichés that disrupt the dynamic flow of the symbolic order. This is not to contest Ahmed's dynamic theory of affective economies but rather to introduce a specific dynamic in which affective energies may be frozen and produce located emotions. The dynamic identified earlier with Klein as a paranoid-schizoid (dis)position, I would argue, operates with a projective deposition of (unwanted) affect into others. Within an affective economy, the dynamic that Klein identifies as splitting can then also be described in terms of a cutting and freezing of the dynamic flow of affects.

Ahmed, in fact, describes precisely such a dynamic when she analyzes Fanon's description in *Black Skin, White Masks* of how, under
the gaze of the colonizer, the black body is "sealed into that crushing
objecthood."[36] In this context, Ahmed's notion of "sealing" resonates
with my earlier argument that race and ethnicity are an effect of being
"hailed" or interpellated into a subject position. Just as the policeman
freezes the person he hails in his track, so to speak, racial interpellation
freezes the racialized person in his skin:

> A chain of effects (which are at once affects) are in circulation. The
> circulation of objects of hate is not free. In this instance, bodies that
> are attributed as being hateful—as the origin of feelings of hate—are
> (temporarily) sealed in their skins. Such bodies assume the character
> of the negative. That transformation of this body into the body of the
> hated, in other words, leads to the enclosure or sealing of the other's
> body within a figure of hate.[37]

Affects, Ahmed asserts, open up "past histories of association." The
movement between signs and affects "does not have its origin in the
psyche, but is a trace of how such histories remain alive in the present. . . . The production of the black man as an object of fear depends
on past histories of association."[38] This dynamic resembles the transferential relationship between different histories of violence or Rothberg's
theory of multidirectional memory that I outlined in the introduction.
Decolonizing the mind must accordingly be accompanied by a mobilization of multidirectional memory or, as I prefer to call it, a composite and
transferential memory.

What then happens, we need to ask, if past histories of association
are violent and traumatic? Trauma, as we know, generates the most
radical form of the freezing of affect. Individual trauma encapsulates
the unbearable affects generated by a catastrophic event in a space that
will remain sealed off from the everyday and, in most cases, from the
free flow of memory. Splitting is radicalized as complete dissociation.
We may find such forms of encapsulation and dissociation in collective
histories as well, but we may assume that they are more open to het-
erogeneous forms of coping. What at the collective level most resembles
the dynamic of freezing identified above is what Wendy Brown has identified as an involuntary attachment to injury or what Lauren Berlant

calls "wound culture."[39] Ahmed talks about a fetishization of the wound as proof of identity: "Wound culture takes the injury of the individual as the grounds not only for an appeal (for compensation or redress), but as an identity claim, such that 'reaction' against injury forms the very basis of politics."[40] While critics of "wound culture" tend to move away from trauma theory and models of mourning, I suggest we need to look in the opposite direction. It is, I argue, the inability to mourn that generates a fixation on and fetishization of injurious states. It is the encapsulated and fetishized wound that binds affective energies and draws them away from the world. The secondary gain received from claims for redress and compensation does help on a material and economic level, but it does not address or resolve the identity trouble generated by fetishized wounds. Rather, it fixates the very sense of identity on the history of past violence.

Dan Bar-On, in his group work with Jews and Germans, Israelis and Palestinians, addresses both the attachment to injury and the denial of injury as two sides of the same process of psychological defense. He places it in the context of a failure of a dynamic historical memory that both acknowledges and works through violent histories:

> I'm afraid that these breakdowns of memory are still felt today, both in the culture of the victims as well as in the culture of the victimizers and the bystanders. To some extent, many of us are still emotionally incapacitated as a result of the events that happened more than sixty years ago—for some of us, before we were born. It is not clear to what extent we have learned to cry about what was done to our people or about people imposing violence on others in our name. This incapacitation can take different forms. One survivor might become an eternal victim "enjoying" (or more accurately suffering from) the secondary gains of such continuous victimhood. Others might deny the victimization by emotionally distancing themselves from any sign of weakness.[41]

It is important to acknowledge that the denial of injurious states is as pervasive as the fetishistic attachment to them. Both belong to a defensive process that forecloses the mourning of injury. One of the most prominent forms of denial in both victims and perpetrators is the walling-off of the past that Bar-On calls "the double wall phenomenon":

> Another of my concepts, the double wall phenomenon, concerned both the survivors and the perpetrators: they would erect a wall between their past traumatic or atrocious experiences and their present life. Their children who grew up sensing the walls built walls of their own. When, at a later stage, one side wanted to open a window in their own wall, they usually met the wall of the other.[42]

Bar-On's concept of the double wall introduces the crucial notion of the transgenerational transmission of trauma and violence. The feeling and fear that "evil is contagious" is true for trauma as well. This fear of contagion is confirmed by the phenomenon of secondary trauma as families and communities are affected by and indeed traumatized by a victim's primary trauma. It is this affective economy of fear that contributes to generating the erection of walls both between violent histories and present lives and between the generations. Bar-On belongs to those who insist, with psychoanalysis, that only a process that breaks through the barrier of silenced histories and stories can prevent the transgenerational transmission of trauma.

Bar-On's entire life work emphasizes the importance of a collective work of mourning that crosses the boundaries between victims and perpetrators. In his work with groups of Jews and Germans or Palestinians and Israelis, he encounters the crucial role of modulating affect as part of a necessary process of cultural translation. The latter must not only facilitate knowledge between cultures but also address the circulation of affects in the processing of culturally inflected narratives. Storytelling itself requires a form of translation, that is, a psychic processing of cultural narratives and conversion into an individual story. This process becomes more complex if storytelling occurs across the boundaries of different cultures and even more complicated if the cultures in question have been or continue to be involved in violent conflict. One of Bar-On's groups, for example, worked on an experimental school textbook incorporating two distinct and separate narratives, a Jewish Israeli and a Palestinian one, with the goal of leading the group and the potential readers—teachers and schoolchildren—to recognize and legitimize the separateness of the Other's narrative.[43] While this is a way of putting conflicting stories into a mutually interactive public circulation, it is also a way to impact and modulate the circulation of affect across the boundaries of cultures in conflict.

Cultural translation as a process of talking to one another across the abyss between people divided by violent histories thus includes finding conflicted voices to expose guilt, shame, rage, hatred, self-hatred, and injury in all agents of violent histories. As Bar-On's work demonstrates, it also requires finding ways to negotiate affective differences not only between cultures but also between victims and perpetrators. Such learning about and from other cultures, including tolerating and modulating the conflicting affects that arise in the process, is a necessary condition not only for mental decolonization but also for the task of developing a global transcultural literacy. As a basis for global transcultural literacy, cultural translation also fights the danger of monoculturalism and monolingualism. In *Precarious Life: The Powers of Mourning and Violence*, Judith Butler insists on the urgency of cultural translation: "One critical operation of any democratic culture is . . . to take up the challenges of cultural translation, especially those that emerge when we find ourselves living in proximity with those whose beliefs and values challenge our own at very fundamental levels."[44]

Cultural translation addresses the deep chasms opened up by violent histories. But cultural translation is not enough. It does not reach the level of the cultural unconscious or the processes Fischer describes as the transmission of ethnicity through cultural transference. The psychoanalytic concept of "transference" encompasses the processes of projection and stereotyping, of splitting and projective identification that form the cultural unconscious. Working through cultural transference requires doing reparation for the historical damage done by a politics of splitting based on projective identification, stereotyping, and scapegoating. Such work is a form of resistance against the "Manichean delirium" of today's increasingly polarized world. In a model of global cultural literacy, cultural translation therefore needs to be supplemented by the working-through of cultural transference. The latter also needs to include the transference between different violent histories or, as Ahmed calls it, "past histories of association." It is a process that brings the past into the present and is future-oriented. As the work of Dan Bar-On vividly illustrates, telling stories across cultural divides might be a first step toward global transcultural literacy because, in bearing witness to historical violence and damage, storytelling negotiates affective difference and aims toward a rearrangement of affect and desire in the future. The roots of storytelling reach far back into our childhood. Perhaps Fanon is right when he says: "I believe it is necessary to become a child again in order to grasp certain psychic realities."[45]

chapterfive

Replacement Children
The Transgenerational Transmission of Traumatic Loss

BAPTISM OF FIRE

Brother of mine,
you were the war baby
our mother never wanted,
but when you came
she loved you anyway.
Your first scream drowned
in howling sirens,
under bombs exploding
in a baptism of fire,
killing you silently,
black lungs
poisoned by smoke,
body in pain,
your burial, the fallout of war.

BAPTISM OF WATER

A cold shadow death
falls upon the world I enter;
blank fear pushes me out
before a smell of panic
invades my first breath.
My mother who barely survived
her firstborn's birth
in a musty clinic cellar
hallucinates giving birth again
below the eye of an air raid.
When I slip out of her,
smooth like a fish,
I carry my dead brother's soul inside
like the corpse of a Siamese twin
who died in the womb.

Whether we know it or not, writing always carries traces of our lives. Most often these traces remain hidden, or we are satisfied with being only faintly aware of them. Certain experiences, especially traumatic or haunting ones, push for more overt articulation. In order to perceive and integrate their hidden traces, we need transformational objects, that is, objects that evoke a distant, often unconscious memory of the traumatic event or history.[1] Commonly, such memories are not immediately linked to the event as such. Often they are involuntary, like the memories triggered by Proust's famous experience of the *madeleine* that transported him back into his childhood. Memories may also emerge as an evocative mood that touches us as uncannily familiar. We may find a person, a work of literature or art, or a new theory that carries us a step further in our journey to integrate pieces of our lives that orbit outside the core of our selves.

Sometimes a therapeutic encounter facilitates such integration. It was during my psychoanalytic training analysis that I was finally able to confront what I had vaguely known all along: so much of my life was shaped by an older brother who died as an infant during World War II, before I was born. I remember when this recognition first hit me with the clarity of an epiphany. In the summer of 2000, I taught at the International Summer School for Critical Theory in Santiago de Compostela.

Late one night, in a state of reverie, I was suddenly hit by a flash of insight: I always felt guilty for owing my life to the death of my infant brother who was killed during the war. My imagined brother had always played a prominent role in my life. In innumerable fantasies and "family romances" I designed parallel lives for both of us. In some of them, I imagined how the strong and defiant boy I fantasized him to be would have acted in my place. In others, I imagined him as an older brother protecting me. Once I recognized my underlying sense of guilt, writing evolved into a mode of mourning this brother I never knew. I wanted to leave a testimony for him, something that carries his memory for my own sons and perhaps their children. This is when I wrote the sequence of poems from which I selected two as an opening to this chapter to mark the subject position of my reflections. I had not planned to include this personal revelation but realized I would otherwise continue to uphold the silence at the core of his memory in my family of origin. I never talked to my parents or siblings about discovering the psychic legacy left by my brother's death, but I have shared the story with my sons.

In the early stages of putting the story into writing, a colleague pointed me toward a body of psychoanalytic literature on *replacement children*. I had never heard the term or known about this widespread response to the traumatic loss of a child, especially prominent during or after violent histories such as the Holocaust or other genocidal wars. Children born after such wars may feel more than the burden of having to replace the child or children whom their parents lost during the war: they grow up with the sense that their generation must replace the entire generation that was meant to be exterminated. One of the best-known replacement children born after the shoah to Jewish parents is political cartoonist Art Spiegelman who grew up with the sense that he was competing with his "ghost-brother," Richieu. We learn about this ghost brother in *Maus*, an experimental memoir written as a comic book that features the Jewish people as mice and the Nazis as cats (Germans) or pigs (Poles). Spiegelman dedicated *Maus* to Richieu and to his daughter, Nadja, and the work opens with a photograph of Richieu. We learn in the following exchange with Art's wife, Françoise, that this photograph served as the single most tangible object of Art's rivalry with his ghost brother.

"I wonder if Richieu and I would get along if he was still alive."
"Your brother?"

"My Ghost-Brother, since he got killed before I was born. He was only five or six. After the war my parents traced down the vaguest rumors, and went to orphanages all over Europe. They couldn't believe he was dead. I didn't think about him much when I was growing up . . . he was mainly a large blurry photograph hanging in my parents' bedroom."

"Uh-huh. I thought that was a picture of you, though it didn't *look* like you."

"That's the point. They didn't need photos of me in their room. I was *alive!* . . . The photo never threw tantrums or got into any kind of trouble . . . It was an ideal kid, and *I* was a pain in the ass. I couldn't compete. They didn't talk about Richieu, but that photo was a kind of reproach. *He*'d have become a *doctor*, and married a wealthy Jewish girl . . . the creep. But at least we could've made *him* deal with Vladek. It's *spooky*, having sibling rivalry with a snapshot! I never felt guilty about Richieu. But I did have nightmares about S.S. men coming into my class and dragging all us Jewish kids away."[2]

This short dialogue contains the most prominent symptoms of a replacement child. The brother is a ghost brother, killed before the replacement son is born. The parents refuse to accept their firstborn's death and never mourn him properly because "they couldn't believe he was dead." Even though they don't talk much about Richieu, he seems omnipresent. Silence and idealization make him seem larger than life. Prominently displayed as a constant reminder, Richieu's photograph soon begins to function, Art says, as a kind of tacit reproach. The replacement child confronts the bitter irony that the ideal child is a dead child. Richieu becomes the container for his parents' fantasies. Richieu would have fulfilled all their dreams while Art, their living child, fails them. One cannot compete with a dead child, and yet one cannot avoid the ghostly competition handed down with parental fantasies. This tacit competition with a dead sibling is a classical syndrome of replacement children. It is also a prevalent form in which parental trauma is transmitted to the next generation and often to generations to come. Art says he doesn't feel guilty, yet he feels the parents' unspoken reproach via Richieu's photograph and has nightmares that place him in his brother's shoes. In anger at the rival who does everything right, he doesn't hesitate to call Richieu a creep. At the same time, however, he also harbors a tacit fantasy that Richieu could at least have taken over the burden of the survivor trauma of Art's father, Vladek, which continues to affect Art's life in profound ways.

One particular ghostly dimension in Spiegelman's rendition of his life story operates with a curious inversion of history and fantasy. In contrast to Art, who figures as one of the mice in the tale, Richieu figures as a photograph. In Art's life, this photograph made Richieu a ghost brother who, despite his overpowering presence, could never become *real*. By contrast, in Art's comic book, Richieu gains a relatively higher degree of reality than the other characters who, when compared to a real photographic representation, remain, after all, cartoons. Moreover, Françoise's confession that she thought the photograph pictured Art as a child literalizes a confusion that operates throughout Art's life at a psychic level. The confusion of the boundaries between Art and Richieu becomes for the first time explicit in the dying father's last words to Art: "I'm *tired* from talking, Richieu, and it's enough stories for now."[3]

The psychological dynamic of replacement children bears an uncanny resemblance to the logic of supplementarity that Derrida introduces in *Of Grammatology*. Refusing to believe in Richieu's death, Art's parents remain locked up in their inability to mourn the loss of their first son. Instead, they keep Richieu *alive* as a nostalgic, almost hallucinatory presence that denies his actual death. Under these conditions, Art can only move into the position of a supplement to the *real* originary child. He comes to feel like a sign that must replace the absence of the thing itself. Derrida writes:

> But the supplement supplements. It adds only to replace. It intervenes or insinuates itself *in-the-place-of*; if it fills, it is as if one fills a void. If it represents and makes an image, it is by the anterior default of a presence. Compensatory [*suppleant*] and vicarious, the supplement is an adjunct, a subaltern instance which *takes-(the)-place* [*tient lieu*]. As substitute, it is not simply added to the positivity of a presence, it produces no relief, its place is assigned in the structure by the mark of an emptiness.[4]

Occupying this psychological position of supplementarity in parental fantasy, the replacement child will commonly be unable to develop a sense of coming into his or her own place. The confusion of boundaries that sustains this supplementarity is only enhanced by the customary discrepancies between the parents' fantasy and the stories they tell.

Derrida's concept of supplementarity sheds light on a crucial aspect of the psychic and rhetorical function of the replacement child. As the name suggests, the replacement child is a chronotope that operates simultaneously at the level of time and space.[5] At the spatial level, the child "re-places" or, as Derrida says, "it insinuates itself in-the-place-of," "fills a void," or "takes-(the)-place." If the child's place "is assigned by the mark of emptiness," the emptiness is not a mere spatial absence but the absence of time itself, that is, the time of death. The replacement child is supposed to replace what came before its time—to undo time and death.[6]

Theoretically, this emphasis on the replacement child as a chronotope highlights the importance of place in addition to time in the operation of trauma.[7] Replacement children are subjected to the no-place and no-time, "the nothing" of trauma. Replacement children often literally know *nothing* about the child they are supposed to replace. Sometimes, they do not even know of its existence. They are supposed to fill an emptiness, a nothing. This is true even in cases where they are handed down stories (or pictures) of the child who died under tragic circumstances. After all, the dead child remains "nothing" in the sense that it never acquires a real presence. It is a ghost that haunts the living from a no-place.

At the level of discourse, the representation of the dead child often remains a "no-place," too: it inhabits a gap, created either by parental silence or by fragmentary or distorted narratives replete with foreclosure or denial. At the level of fantasy, by contrast, the replacement child is destined to take the place of the dead sibling and thus to undo his or her death. This fantasy operates, of course, unconsciously. It is therefore entirely possible that parents tell the story of their child's tragic death while they at the same time continue to deny it unconsciously. Since the replacement child is the recipient not only of the parents' conscious discourse but also of their unconscious fantasy, he or she inherits the legacy of the sibling's traumatic death and failed mourning. This dynamic is part of the process that hands down the psychic life of trauma across generations.[8]

In recent decades, a rich psychoanalytic literature has emerged that describes the particular identity trouble of so-called replacement children. The role they are assigned in parental fantasies is intimately tied to traumatic loss. But there is more at stake: what comes into play is a culture's changing relationship to loss, death, mortality and mourning. The rational impossibility of replacing a human being has never prevented parents from developing fantasies of a replacement child. Such fantasies follow a psychic, often unconscious economy of seriality and substitution. Since, in the unconscious, the boundaries between discrete entities are permeable and affective energies flow freely between them, people may also become exchangeable. Dreams quite commonly condense different people into one figure. Similarly, our unconscious affective economy can condense different children into one child, regardless of their concrete biological or psychic differences. Psychoanalytic theories of replacement children are based on extensive clinical work with children who experience psychological problems related to the fact that they were meant to replace a child who had died before they were born.

In an essay titled "The Replacement Child," Leon Anisfeld and Arnold Richards provide a provisional definition:

> In the narrowest sense, a replacement child is a child born to parents who have had a child die and then conceive the second child in order to fill the void left by the loss of the first. . . . The psychological dynamics of the parents, who have themselves, survived the trauma of the real or symbolic death of a child, mediate between the sick or deceased child and the sibling who is his or her surrogate.[9]

The death of a child is always a wound and an outrage, an improper death, a death that haunts parents, siblings, or entire communities. Parents are not supposed to survive their children. This is why they are unconsciously compelled to try to undo for themselves and their affective life what should not be. Unconsciously taking in their parents' fantasies, replacement children grow up in confusion about their identity and sometimes about their gender. Supposed to live someone else's life, they never quite come into their own.

The parents' attempt to replace their dead child with another child, even if only in fantasy, entails a refusal properly to mourn and integrate the child's death. Replacement children thus bear the burden of this inability to mourn. In extreme cases they are the products of a manic defense against death. Fantasies of replacement children remain within the regime of violence. Ultimately, they rob the murdered child of a unique death and the replacement child of a unique life. While this theft occurs primarily in fantasy, it has concrete psychic and often somatic effects.

Many children born after war and genocide collectively embody the fate of replacement children: "[A] child born to Holocaust survivors replaces not simply a specific dead child or ancestor, but all those who have perished."[10] Replacement children who are the transgenerational recipients of the trauma of the Holocaust are haunted by a death or even millions of deaths they did not directly experience. The experience of death comes to them secondhand, so to speak, through its effects on the parents. It comes in the form of moods or emotions, taking on many shapes, including grief or anxiety, hypervigilance or numbness, emotional unavailability or uncontrolled rage. Analyzing the fantasies of replacement children, Vamik Volkan speaks of "deposit representations," that is, representations of self or others deposited into the child's developing self-representation by traumatized parents.[11] It is in the form of such representations that replacement children carry the legacy of a parental or generational distortion of mourning after traumatic histories.

Commonly, parents are supposed to function as protective shields against trauma for their children. Traumatized parents instead tend to pass their trauma on to their children. Masud Khan calls the result of this transgenerational transmission "cumulative trauma."[12] A replacement child himself, Anisfeld notes that he was reminded of the children his father had lost in the Holocaust "not because they were ever spoken about but because of his father's periodic 'absences' or dream-like escapes from the present into the past. Thus his father's fugue states became Anisfeld's psychic reality."[13] In "Children of the Holocaust and Their Children's Children," Teréz Virag argues that replacement children grow up in "unconscious identification with the persecuted or exterminated members of the family. . . . The symptoms, the play activity, the dreams, and fantasies of the children made it very clear that they knew about the family 'secrets.'"[14] In the parents' fantasy, the replacement child is supposed to magically restore the lost child to life. As a result of distorted mourning and its pseudo-resolution, the child who has been put in the place of someone else will accordingly be haunted by identity trouble, often in the form of a pseudo-identity.

Anisfeld and Richards point to the high frequency of identity disturbances in Jewish children of the postwar generation. Similar phenomena can be observed in children born in the aftermath of colonialism, slavery, war, or genocide more generally. Andrea Sabbadini argues that a replacement child is "treated more as the embodiment of a memory than as a person in its own right."[15] Survivor guilt is a common response in replacement children. Their life, they feel, is owed to the death of another. James Herzog sees mourning as a precondition for the healing of transgenerational trauma. After the work of mourning is completed, "survivors, children of survivors, and their children can remember, but not relive, and concentrate on the difficult task of being."[16] Silencing traumatic histories constitutes yet another refusal or inability to mourn. Family secrets or taboos placed on shameful histories, Abraham and Torok argue, come back to haunt the children like unknown ghosts of the past and condemn them to become the carriers of another person's or another generation's unconscious. After silenced national or communal trauma, this economy of haunting operates on a collective level as well. After a war, for example, the postwar generation may become the carriers of the war generation's political unconscious.

It is important to acknowledge that this haunting is not restricted to the victims of violence and their children. It also holds for perpetrators and their children, albeit in different ways. Often, the denial, splitting off, and repression of violent histories is even more pronounced in perpetrators than in victims. Postwar Germany provides a vivid illustration of an attempt at silencing that lasted almost half a century, followed by a flood of writings, artworks, and films about the legacy of the past. In Germany, this process is further complicated because the majority of people from the war generation are both perpetrators of the Holocaust and victims of brutal retaliation, air raids, massive civilian casualties, destruction of cities, and years of famine. Since there were innumerable young children among the civilian casualties, postwar Germany has many families with replacement children. Their psychic life is inextricably bound up with the violence of World War II. While the symptoms of replacement children are collectively shared legacies of war, their individual transmissions must be traced in the psychic life of each particular child in order to understand how parental fantasies affect the child's self-representation.

Philippe Grimbert's *Secret*, a recent memoir about replacement children, depicts the transgenerational transmission of the traumatic death of a child to a replacement child in minute psychological ramifications.

This memoir furthered my own thinking about this particular form of transgenerational trauma. Even though Grimbert's story is dramatically different from my own, it functioned as a catalyst, a transformational object that allowed me to view my experience as a replacement child from the distance of another memory. My story as the child of a people of perpetrators was mirrored in the story of the child of a people of victims. But there is more at stake than this uneasy complementary mirroring. In taking over their parents' infamous legacy, the children of perpetrators take on a burden of guilt for the destiny of the victims and *their* children. It is in this sense that I think my generation bears a responsibility for the destiny of Simon, the child in Grimbert's memoir who was killed in Auschwitz.

Born in Paris in 1948, Philippe Grimbert grew up as an only child. Inexplicably to him, throughout his childhood and teen years he succumbed to an unrelenting obsession with an imaginary companion, a brother who in his fantasies had everything he lacked: physical strength, endurance, and the love of his father. During his lonely childhood as an outsider both in his family and at school, Philippe nourished an intense involvement with this imaginary brother, engaging in nightly fantasized fights with him and, at times, involuntary moments of tenderness and attraction. The only person with whom he had an intimate connection during that time was Louise, a close friend who was almost like kin to the family. Philippe spent many hours with her, sharing stories and thoughts, worries and hurts. When he was fifteen years old, Louise revealed to him the family secret that his parents had anxiously guarded: Philippe's family was Jewish, which he never knew or guessed. But the most important revelation was that he had had an older brother who was killed in Auschwitz at age ten, together with his mother, Hannah, who was Philippe's aunt and his father's first wife.

Nearly half a century later, Philippe Grimbert, now an author and psychoanalyst, decided to write down the haunting story of his family, which was formed in all its inner dynamic around this secret. *Secret* appeared in French in 2004 and received the Prix Goncourt des Lycéens in 2004. For many months it stayed on France's best-seller list. The English translation by Polly McLean appeared in 2007. Also in 2007, Claude Miller's movie *A Secret* appeared, based on Grimbert's novel.[17]

Grimbert, the narrator, describes the revelation of the family secret as a transformational experience that would determine the entire trajectory of his life. "Barely had the news fallen from Louise's lips than my new identity started changing me. I was still the same boy but also someone new, someone mysteriously stronger,"[18] he writes. In the weeks following Louise's revelation, Philippe traces the trajectory of his parents' life and experiences "an exodus that took me away from those I loved" (*Secret*, 59). He uses the shards and fragments of Louise's story to spin his own and, after a hiatus of fifty years, he writes his imagined story of his parents' life. "I unwound the tangle of their lives and, much as I had invented myself a brother, created from scratch the meeting of the two bodies from which I was born, as if I were writing a novel" (25). Tropes of haunting guide Philippe's narrative: "The brother I had invented, who had put an end to my solitude, this ghostly big brother had actually existed" (60). "Three dead people loomed out of the shadows. I heard their names for the first time: Robert, Hannah and Simon" (59).

Simon, Philippe's brother, was the child his father, Maxime, had with his first wife, Hannah. Hannah, in turn, had a brother called Robert, who at the time was still married to Tania, who eventually became Maxime's second wife and Philippe's mother. After Hannah and Simon were sent to Auschwitz, Maxime and Tania started a secret relationship. Robert died at the front from an infection and never returned. Maxime and Tania married and eventually had Philippe, the son who, for Maxime, was supposed to replace the first son killed in Auschwitz. Guilt enters the scene in a major way. Families and friends saw the union of Philippe's parents as a betrayal of those who were sent to the camps or the war front. Philippe, the offspring of this union, inherited not only this guilt but also the guilt of feeling he owed his life to the death of another, his brother.

Did Philippe know without knowing? The obsession with his imaginary brother testifies to an unconscious knowledge. Obviously, his parents had passed on their stories and memories to him without ever speaking to him openly about them. Unwittingly, they transmitted the secret through unconscious channels to the next generation. Philippe thus became a vessel for his parents' unconscious, the bearer of their traumatic history.

Uncanny signs of Philippe's unconscious knowledge pervade the story, revealed most viscerally in the anecdote of Philippe's discovery of his brother's stuffed toy dog amid the things buried in the attic. It is this key scene in Grimbert's memoir that testifies to the generative formation of unconscious knowledge. When Philippe's mother opens an old suitcase, he discovers the dusty toy dog on a pile of blankets. Spontaneously, he snatches the dog to cuddle him, but when he notices his mother's sudden shock and discomfort, he puts it back. This incident triggers the invention of his imaginary brother. "That night, for the first time, I rubbed my wet cheek against a brother's chest. He had just come into my life; I would take him with me everywhere" (5). The invention of the imaginary brother is then already a response to the mother's trauma, which Philippe received indirectly when he witnessed her sudden shock. But Philippe cannot share the perception of her response with his mother, and his recognition remains relegated to secrecy. Even though Philippe will not know the family secret for many years, it nonetheless generates distance and loneliness because he apprehends that there is something in his mother's strong reaction that is withheld from him, something unspeakable between them. Family secrets always create distance and loneliness.

During their second visit to the attic, Philippe appropriates the dog and instantly proceeds to call him Sim,[19] a diminutive and indeed a cryptonym of his dead brother's name, which he did not know. This uncanny knowledge could only have been generated unconsciously, perhaps through his unwittingly gleaning a name that had been hushed up. "Where did I get that name? From the dusty smell of his fur? The silences of my mother, my father's sadness? Si, Si! I walked my dog all around the flat, not wanting to notice my parents' distress when they heard me calling his name" (14). The family enters into a pact of silence, all of them knowing more than they are willing to acknowledge. From that moment on, they will relate to one another through the veil of a tacit and uncanny knowledge, covering over the unspeakable death of a child that cannot be properly mourned. The family secret silences the entire violent and traumatic history.

Many years later, after Louise's revelation, Philippe, in turn, opts for silence himself when he decides not to reveal his knowledge to his parents. "The silence was going to continue, and I couldn't imagine what might make me decide to break it. I was trying, in my turn, to protect them" (61). However, the false sense of protection attached to family secrets always backfires, as was the case when Philippe's parents withheld the existence and violent death of his brother from him. In Philippe's case, his relationship to his imaginary brother changes dramatically once he has this knowledge. Unable to feel sorry for his brother, he experiences a silent rage that makes him instantly feel guilty. When Louise confirms the image Philippe had created of a strong and healthy brother unconditionally loved and admired by his father, Philippe must confront the pangs of a cruel jealousy. "Louise had painted a portrait of a seductive child, very sure of his power, identical to the one who crushed me every day. Fully aware of the horror of my desire, I would have loved to feed that image to the flames" (63). Philippe senses that in order to live his life on his own terms, he will have to kill his brother once again, this time symbolically. When Philippe wishes to see the image of the brother go up in flames, knowing he died in the ovens of Auschwitz, he repeats the crime of the perpetrators at a symbolic level—a deed that leaves him crushed under an unfathomable guilt. He becomes engaged in a struggle to the death, a struggle he can never win: "I couldn't have known that one can never beat the dead" (66). Increasingly, Philippe sees his life less as his own than as a repetition of his brother's life:

> Simon also knew the shop in the rue du Bourg-l'Abbé. He too climbed the stairs, ran along the corridors, explored the stockroom. . . . He played at working the till, helped serve the customers . . . I'd been repeating his actions without knowing it. He'd drunk the same hot chocolate in Louise's rooms, sharing his worries and dreams.
> (78)

As if the relationship between the real brother and the imaginary one had been inverted after the revelation, Philippe's life in his own inner perception more and more resembles an imaginary life, a shadow life of Simon's. When he finally discovers an old photo of Simon, he recognizes himself in his brother's image: "At last I had seen Simon: photos of him filled several pages. His face seemed strangely familiar. I could see myself in those features, if not that body" (136).

Out of Philippe's awareness, his guilt also operates as a reenactment of his parents' guilt: in forming their union and conceiving Philippe as their new child, they symbolically replaced his dead brother. In the logic of the unconscious, such a replacement is a paradoxical form of murder: the dead child is killed, yet kept alive in the new child who will have to carry the dead child inside himself like a living ghost.

Permanently damaged by having abandoned him to his fate, and guilty of having built their happiness on his disappearance, my parents had kept him out of sight. I was being squashed by this inherited shame, much as I was beneath the body that ruled over mine each night.

I hadn't realized that it was he who my father saw beyond my narrow chest and spindly legs: that son, his sculptor's model, his interrupted dream. When I was born it was Simon who they'd put once more into his arms, the dream of a child he could mold in his own image. (64–65)

Simon's symbolic murder is not only reenacted in the birth of Philippe but also reenacted once again in the family's silence, that is, in their attempt to erase his history. "Without meaning to, they had wiped him off the list of deaths and also of lives, repeating what his murderers had done but out of love." "Simon and Hannah, obliterated twice over: by the hatred of their persecutors and the love of their family" (65).

Louise, however, carries one more family secret of yet another burden of guilt, even more unspeakable. It is the guilt of Simon's mother, Hannah. Curiously, this guilt is also tied to a fatal silence, a tacit knowledge that Hannah had carried within her but never brought into the open: the attraction between her sister-in-law and her husband. When Hannah learned that Tania had taken refuge with the family in the French village where she herself was to join Maxime soon, she decided, in an impulse of jealousy and despair, to sacrifice herself and take her son with her. During a passport control, Hannah deliberately handed the officer her real passport instead of the fake one she carried. After she identified Simon as her son, the others watched in horror as the two were arrested and transported to Auschwitz, where they were killed the next day. Louise, who witnessed this scene, decided at the time to remain silent and change the story of the willful sacrifice into one of momentary negligence. However, years later she reveals the truth to Philippe, who thus becomes aware of yet another horrifying "murder" of his brother, this time by his own mother. Grimbert comments on this sacrifice: "Timid shy Hannah, the perfect mother, had turned into a tragic heroine; the fragile young woman suddenly became a Medea, sacrificing her child and her own life on the altar of her wounded heart" (107).

Hannah's sacrificial suicide and the sacrifice of her own son may well be the most shocking of a long series of secrets revealed in Grimbert's memoir. By withholding the full emotional impact of this revelation on his own psychic life, Grimbert transfers the haunting quality of this scene to the reader. This textual strategy operates according to a psychological process of delegation; it is almost as if the reader becomes afflicted by what is kept silent in the text and thus subjected to the familial economy of secrecy. Why among all scenes does this particular one make the reader feel the abyss of horrors that haunt this family story? To the extent that the author goes out of his way not to place or misplace blame, he may transfer to the reader a conflicted anger against this mother who sacrificed herself and her son over a broken heart. She had no right to do this, we may feel—how could she selfishly deliver her son to the Nazis over such a trifling matter as her husband's crush on another woman?

The memoir, I think, succeeds in turning readers into recipients of the author's conflicting emotions, which congeal at the nodal point of this scene. One cannot avoid the moral ambiguity, ambivalence, and tragic conflict this scene expresses. In a complex process of transference, displacement, and delegation, we witness this mother's perhaps unwitting yet unbearable complicity with the murderers of her people. Utter despair converges with utter guilt. Isn't it she who assists the perpetrators in completing their task? Rather than a tragic sacrifice, her act may then even appear in this light as a cruel revenge against a husband who, she suspected, had renounced his love for her. She didn't merely take her own and her child's life; she willingly delivered herself and her son to her people's enemies. Sacrifice and revenge merge in an act that seems to proclaim, "Abandoning me, you have become my enemy, and now I complete the murder you have already committed emotionally." This is how readers are made to feel, and perhaps spell out for themselves, the insanity of despair and hopelessness. The raw and brutal fact that a mother's despair becomes the cause for her son's murder in the gas chambers seems impossible to bear, even if one tries to withhold judgment.

But readers may also feel compelled to enter inside this woman, trying in their minds to write her story, much as the author writes his parents stories. How much did she know? Was she aware that they were going to be deported and die in the camps? What if she found this out only after it was too late? What did she feel when her son was ripped from her side? What did she feel in her last minutes, when she knew her son would die the same way that she would? How did she bear her guilt? One may wonder, had she gone insane from this war, perhaps even before she made her fatal decision? These questions illustrate more precisely the process of transference, displacement, and delegation that I referred to earlier. By eclipsing these questions, the narrator delegates the act of asking them to the reader, who, in turn, feels called upon not only to react but also to tolerate the conflicted nature and ambivalence of an array of possible reactions. Moreover, this is also when readers most likely feel sympathy for Hannah and perhaps even want to do what her own family did: cover her story with silence rather than placing blame.

Mourning Hannah and Simon in Grimbert's memoir requires more than integrating the fact that they died senseless deaths without a proper burial: mourning them also requires coming to terms with the familial contradictions surrounding these deaths, including Maxime's and Tania's betrayal of Hannah and Robert and Hannah's unwitting complicity with the murder of her own child. Ultimately, mourning them also includes facing the pain caused by the burial of unfathomable guilt in the tomb of family secrets. In order to mourn properly the death of Hannah and Simon, the family would have had to break their silence. We can see how the trauma of the murder of Hannah and Simon, enhanced by the guilty betrayal of those closest to them, imposed this deadly silence. The family members do what most victims of severe trauma do: they seal off their pain and keep it buried. Philippe, the replacement child, becomes forever entangled in the effects of his parents' failed mourning. He enters a lifelong battle with a phantom brother, a fight he can never win. "Affectionate as they were, my uncles, aunts and grandparents seemed surrounded by an intangible barrier forbidding questions and warding off confidences. A secret club, bound together by an impossible grief" (*Secret*, 47). Yet while it is true that he could never win against a dead brother, we also realize that Louise's revelation at least allows him to abandon the fight and shift his psychic energies toward facing the pain. In this sense, we can say that Louise prepared the ground for healing the trauma he had inherited from his parents and their families. She saved him by restoring him to himself: "I now knew what my father was looking for when he stared into the distance. I understood what silenced my mother. And yet, I was no longer crushed under the weight of that silence, I carried it and it strengthened my shoulders. . . . Since I had been able to name them, the ghosts had loosened their grip" (134).

Transference, delegation, and displacement are crucial in the liberation from a secret that covers up the loss of a child and the guilt associated with it. This process is often facilitated by transformational objects, that is, objects that both evoke and contain, or even bind, the emotions that would otherwise be overwhelming. In Grimbert's narrative, mourning is facilitated by a systematic sequential displacement of emotions attached to the dead child onto a companion animal, first Simon's toy dog, Si; then Philippe's puppy, Echo; and finally the dogs of a perpetrator, buried in a dog cemetery that is reminiscent of a cemetery for children.

In the first instance, Si, the stuffed animal, functions as both a transferential and transformational object. When Philippe's parents see him interact with Simon's toy, they unconsciously transfer the repressed affects that belong to Simon—mourning and guilt—onto Philippe. Later they replace Si with a real dog, Echo, who is killed one day when Maxime fails to prevent him from running in front of a car. Suffering from unrelenting pangs of guilt, Maxime falls into inconsolable grief. Philippe is the one who uncovers the second displacement: when Maxime feels responsible for Echo's death, Philippe allows him to face that he is dealing with a displaced guilt about Simon's death. It took the awareness of this displacement finally to release Philippe's father from his unconscious guilt. And yet the dog's name, Echo, leaves a haunting trace, the imprint of unconscious naming. If this real dog, supposed to replace a ghostly toy, cannot but be the echo of the real Si (Simon), isn't Philippe himself caught in the echo chamber of dead names that have become unspeakable but seem to reemerge from nowhere, as in Philippe's originary naming of the toy dog Si?

Grimbert's narrative is structured like a quest in which names and naming become signposts of an unconscious trajectory. It begins with the unearthing of a ghost brother who was the victim of a violent death, followed by a long period of failed mourning that kills him a second time. It ends with the proper burial of this brother by the one who inherited the impossible task of replacing him. *Secret* is also the story of a belated coming of age, if not indeed the belated psychological birth of Philippe, the replacement child. This birth cannot happen without a proper burial for the original child who was supposed to be replaced. Following the logic of this psychic economy, Grimbert's narrative ends appropriately with a scene at a cemetery that leads to the birth of the memoir. The latter not only inaugurates but also traces the narrator's psychological birth. The narrative unfolds in recursive loops around family secrets, their revelation, and finally their psychic integration. Rather than merely *describing* this psychological birth, Grimbert's narrative *enacts* it.

Even after the secret of his brother's existence and violent death is revealed, Philippe is still haunted by holes in the narrative. "There remained a gap in my story, a chapter whose contents were not known even to my parents" (139). It is as if Philippe needed symbolically to descend into the crypt in which his brother had for too long remained buried alive.[20] He consults the research and documentation center established by Serge and Beate Klarsfeld as part of the Memorial in the Marais in Paris. During his archival work, Philippe unearths bare facts and numbers: the number of the train, the date of Simon's death, and the names of men, women, and children deported to Auschwitz. He comes across the name of Pierre Laval, the minister who had authorized the deportations of children in the name of reuniting families.

In his epilogue, Grimbert reveals that the idea for his memoir was born when he unwittingly came across a small dog cemetery and identified it as the property of Pierre Laval's daughter: "It was in that cemetery, lovingly maintained by the daughter of the man who had given Simon a one-way ticket to the end of the world, that I had the idea for this book. The pain I had never been able to assuage by mourning would be laid to rest in its pages" (150).

The sequence of dogs used as transformational objects comes full circle. These objects allow the emergence of repressed or refused mourning in order to facilitate both its psychic and narrative integration. As a true mourning object, the book enacts a descent into the crypt that coincides with a *rebirthing*, that is, a (re)writing of the story. In giving his dead brother a proper burial, albeit a symbolic one, Philippe Grimbert finds a way to live with the memory of the dead, rather than with their phantom life. After carrying his brother inside like a living corpse, he finds in writing a way of proper mourning, of releasing the ghosts of the past. On his visit to the dog cemetery, his daughter Rose accompanies him. When the idea for his memoir takes hold of him, he sends her away. She leaves and waves to him without looking back. With any luck, writing also becomes a way to halt the transgenerational transmission of trauma.[21]

The memoir Grimbert will write after this visit to the cemetery and that he will call *Secret* persistently demonstrates the inextricable intertwinement of the personal and the political. Even though *Secret* is written as a memoir, it is irreducible to its psychological dimension alone because the political is consistently shown as inherent in the psychological. Family secrets also belong to a larger politics of secrecy and refused mourning. They are part and parcel of a pervasive cultural paralysis resulting from an "inability to mourn."[22]

In response to this public politics of secrecy, Grimbert's narrator becomes involved with the monumental task of unearthing historical knowledge based on the archival work of Serge and Beate Klarsfeld who provided the most extensive documentation of Holocaust victims. Grimbert's archival work performs both the psychic work of integration and the political work of historical testimony. Yet he is also performing this archival work with the knowledge that the archive, as the site where official documents are filed, intervenes only vicariously in a collective politics of secrecy.

In *Archive Fever*, Derrida reminds us that while the archive marks the institutional passage from the private to the public, this does not always coincide with a passage from the secret to the nonsecret.[23] Making official documents about the Holocaust public is political work and may even become part of a process of mourning, but for Grimbert it is not enough. Rather, it serves as a supplement to the more intimate processing of family secrets in the writing of the memoir. In a certain sense, the archive functions psychologically in the opposite way of the crypt in that instead of sealing off the secret, it invites access to it. Both, however, are linked to death and the death drive. The phrase "buried in an archive" describes the polarity of archive and lived memory to each other. The exteriority of the memory aid of the archive is mirrored by the exteriority of what remains outside the archive. Derrida writes: "The archive . . . will never be either memory or anamnesis as spontaneous, alive and internal experience. On the contrary: the archive takes place at the place of originary and structural breakdown of the said memory."[24] Yet this is precisely what is at stake for Grimbert in his archival work:

unearthing an impossible memory, that is, a memory of those who have become victims of genocide.

Like his unconscious personal memories of the murdered brother he never knew, Grimbert's work therefore takes on the tasks and burdens of transgenerational memory, this time in the public sphere of archival conscription. The question is how this archival work not only is related to but also affects the work of mourning that Grimbert performs in his memoir. Derrida asks:

> Is the psychic apparatus *better represented* or is it *affected differently* by all the technical mechanisms for archivization and for reproduction, for prostheses of so-called live memory, for simulacrums of living things which already are, and will increasingly be, more refined, complicated, powerful than the "mystic pad" (microcomputing, electronization, computerization, etc.)?[25]

Perhaps because Grimbert also chose to become a psychoanalyst, another profession involved with memory work, he uses the archive as though it contained the traces of an unconscious knowledge that he follows—one could almost say blindly—until he makes a spontaneous discovery like that of recognizing the name on the cemetery as belonging to the man responsible for the deportation of so many children, including his brother. We may infer that he trusts an unconscious inscription or, as Derrida calls it, a "psychic archive" that cannot be reduced to memory: "Neither to memory as conscious reserve, nor to memory as rememoration, as act of recalling. The psychic archive comes neither under *mneme* nor under *anamnesis.*"[26]

Quite unique in Grimbert's attempt to work through and integrate his transgenerational legacy is that he works in the transitional spaces between three forms of memory work: the archive, writing, and psychoanalysis. For him, these are complementary intersecting spheres rather than separate ones, and he infuses the energies he draws from one into the other. For him all three are simultaneously deeply personal and eminently political.

Similar to this highlighting of the political dimension of his archival work, Grimbert describes his choice to become a psychoanalyst as both a psychological and a political one, relating it to his friendship with Louise, from whom he learned the particular form of listening he uses with his patients. Writing a memoir and doing the psychic labor of a psychoanalyst are, for Grimbert, two complementary forms of working through the personal and political effects of violent histories. Finally, Grimbert's memoir exposes the pain individuals and cultures inflict on others when they relate to human beings according to a conscious or unconscious logic of substitution. Children are not replaceable. Each child is unique and needs to be properly mourned. Grimbert's memoir exhibits an ethics of mourning based on facing and sharing pain rather than on silencing it. It is an ethics that tries to disrupt the vicious cycle of traumatic histories.

Once we become aware of the psychic legacy of replacement children, we realize how widespread and, at the same time, diverse literary renditions of this topic are. One of the most prominent recent examples can be found in the novel *Whale Rider*, by the Maori writer Witi Ithimaera, in which the female protagonist, a girl whose twin brother died at birth, is first rejected and then finally accepted by the grandfather as a replacement child.[27] Like Grimbert, Ithimaera insists that, for children who carry the legacy of replacement children, the psychic and the political are inextricably intertwined. In traditional Maori society, the girl's dead brother would have inherited the role of a leader. A girl cannot take this place. The girl's and her mother's insistence that she is indeed able to fill this place, heralds a profound change in Maori culture regarding traditional gender roles. For the girl, "replacing" her brother on her own terms without submitting to the role of a replacement child is a question of psychic survival. Growing up with the guilt that she has survived as the wrong child with the wrong gender, she fights for the right to fulfill the brother's traditional role. For replacement children, psychological birth is often delayed until they can both face their legacy and gain a role of their own in the family system. In *Whale Rider*, this process unfolds as a process of rewriting the old myth of the male whale rider for a female leader of traditional culture.

Perhaps the most experimental literary figuration of a replacement child can be found in another Maori novel, Patricia Grace's *Baby No-Eyes*. This story is based on actual events that occurred in 1991 in a hospital in New Zealand. After a car accident, a Maori mother was delivered to the hospital with a baby girl who was dead upon arrival. The hospital stole the baby's eyes for purposes of medical research.

Grace's book traces the cultural and political implications of this act of biopiracy, as well as its psychological effects on family members and the community. The two main protagonists are the dead baby—Baby No-Eyes—who has a voice of her own in the novel, and her brother Tawera, born a few years after Baby No-Eyes' death. Tawera grows up as a replacement child, but in ways very different from those described in *Secret* and *Whale Rider*. Tawera's mother does not silence the existence of her dead child, but talks about her as if she were still alive. Immediately after Tawera's birth, his mother tells him:

> "I want you to know you're not an only child."
> "I knew there was someone," I said.
> "You have a sister four years and five days older than you."
> "Now I see her," I said, "Shot. Two holes in her head."
> "You mean she has no eyes," my mother said. "You mean her eyes were stolen."[28]

His "living" dead sister haunts Tawera to the point that he hallucinates her presence. Living a fantasy life with her, he offers himself as her "replacement eyes" in order to describe the world to her. Using the narrative technique of literalizing fantasy, Grace's narrator voices the inner life of characters. We hear the voice of Tawera even when he is still a fetus in the womb, and we hear the voice of his dead sister. As if to counter his sister's blindness, Tawera hallucinates her presence in exceedingly visual terms: "My sister was like this: four years old and dressed in K-Mart Clothes, that is, jade track pants tied at the front with a pink cord, jade T-shirt with a surfer on it riding a great pink wave, colored slippers fastened by velcro straps" (*Baby No-Eyes*, 19). Rather than conveying Tawera's psychic reality as fantasy or imagination, the text literalizes this hallucination, thus endowing the dead sister with a quasi-realistic presence that is also imposed on the reader. Inevitably, this sister, who is invisible to all but Tawera, begins to haunt him. Following him around wherever he goes and sharing his bed at night, she assumes an overbearing presence, always competing with him and occupying the space of his life. "You didn't even have a very good reason for making me," he says to his mother, "It was only so I could babysit my big sister, keep *her* off your back, out of your hair, out of your eyes, your head, your ears" (141). Tawera's reproach targets his mother's delegation of the trauma of her dead child's haunting presence to her son. Consistent with this psychological dynamic, Tawera literally enacts the transgenerational trauma in a performative discourse of externalized psychic life.

In order to highlight the political and cultural dimension of traumatic histories, Patricia Grace's text embeds the story of Tawera and his sister in more encompassing reflections on the collective transmission of traumatic histories. This transmission is facilitated by storytelling, writing, and art. Gran Kura, Tawera's grandmother, speaks of untold stories and family secrets passed on through generations until the silence is broken: "Sometimes there is a story that has no words at all, a story that has been lived by a whole generation but that has never been worded. You see it sitting in the old ones, you see it in how they walk and move and breathe, you see it chiseled into their faces, you see it in their eyes" (28). Despite the fact that Gran Kura insists that every generation has its secrets, she, at a point of high crisis, assumes the role of breaking the silence. She is also the one who, shortly before her death, invites Tawera to exorcise the ghost of his dead sister so that he may live his life on his own terms.

When he becomes an artist Tawera learns to integrate his traumatic history and memory: "I study between the lines of history, seeking out its missing pages, believing this may be one of the journeys that will help me be an artist" (291). After he no longer externalizes the haunting presence of his dead sister, Tawera's psychic space becomes empty: "Inner space. It aches inside me, and in the evenings when I go to my room intending to work, all I can do is stare at absence" (292). This is a figuration of the "no-place, no time" of trauma, a negative chronotope. Only when Tawera is able to transform this space artistically can he begin to heal. Tawera has begun a process of mourning the death of his imaginary sister. Mourning means first facing and then transforming the empty space of absence rather than filling it with phantom life. "But each of these sketches, drawings, paintings, holds a missing piece, a section of paper that is blank. Not one is complete. In each one, space pushes itself outward, and in doing so brings the eye towards it" (292). Mourning pushes space outward and makes the eye face the nothingness at the center. Tawera links this experience with the traditional Maori concept of *Te Kore*, the nothing: "Instead of ending with that little unbreachable gap I begin with it, embrace it, let it be there, make it be there, pushing my drawing further and further to the outskirts. I persist with this, night after night, until one night everything is gone, fallen from the edges of the paper" (293). Tawera thus uses *Te Kore*, a spiritual manifestation of the negative chronotope designating no-place and no-time, as a mourning ritual that facilitates his own psychological birth.

Mourning can only happen when Tawera is able to face the nothingness of death. After having been his sister's eyes for so long, Tawera is for the first time able to see her. His "first incantation of visibility" reveals her to him. This incantation inverts the foreclosure that kept his sister alive as a ghost without eyes. Now Tawera imagines and indeed sees Baby No-Eyes as a dead sister "in a place where she will be my eyes." What Tawera sees with her eyes is a traumatic death, a violation and its impact on the living. "One day I'll bring back the edges of the city," he says (294). This will be the moment when the cycle is broken. Having stared into the heart of his sister's trauma, Tawera will no longer have to pass it on to the next generation. Baby No-Eyes has received a proper burial place; her story has been told.

These texts that depict replacement children vividly illustrate how self-representation is highly fragile and permeable, vulnerable to the fantasies of others and the concomitant anxiety of existential influence. Fantasies may and do affect others, as either enabling visions or as representations of toxic deposits. As Alexandra Piontelli's empirical research with pregnant women and the infants they later raise demonstrates, a mother's fantasies, hopes, and emotions for a fetus in the womb affect the infant's coming into the world and modalities of being.[29] This is what happened to Tawera in *Baby No-Eyes*, and Patricia Grace conveys this unconscious transmission of fantasy by endowing the fetus with a voice of his own. Piontelli also points out that children can grieve the loss of someone they never knew or heard about. A boy who was the only surviving twin, for example, expressed grief about his twin brother who had vanished in the womb.[30] What do these knowledges about the power of cultural and individual fantasies mean not only for the specific destiny of self-formation in replacement children but also for the effect of fantasies on the formation of the self more generally? Ultimately, they pose a fundamental threat to the concept and the reality of a child (or a human being) as a unique and intrinsically valuable entity. The fantasy that children and human beings more generally become replaceable and exchangeable radicalizes the logic of substitution already inherent in industrialization and capitalism. Psychologically, this logic is based on a powerful defense against mortality, if not a phantasm of immortality. The victims of this cultural logic of substitution are the replacement children who become placeholders of a dead child.

I wonder whether we must not also see these fantasies in light of the current wars and mass killings, as well as the relentlessly progressing destruction of the resources of our planet. Are phantasms of immortality a reaction formation against a pervasive anxiety linked to the knowledge that we are threateningly close to destroying our own species? Cultural fantasies of replacement children that emerge after histories of violence, war, and genocide, and the siblings fantasized as replacements for war children who were killed, belong not only to a psychic economy of trauma and refused mourning but also to an economy of denial and defense that enforces the collective work of destruction and death. Psychologically speaking, they belong to a psychic economy of manic defense. They carry the burden of a traumatic legacy and the identity trouble that comes with it. Ultimately, they belong to other related fantasies and phantasms of exchangeability and substitution that are increasingly operative at the level of global capitalism and its mass-media economy. These fantasies operate as a manic defense, allowing us to remain blind to the work of death we perform on a daily basis in the new histories of trauma that we create as we speak.

If substitutions were truly effective in the economy of human relations, we would not be so different from the objects of capitalistic exchange: dispensable and always subjected to an economy of accelerated obsolescence. Children would be haunted by the specter of seriality, replaceable by miniature clones that hover inside the self from birth, like Russian dolls. If love could be shifted that easily, what would be its value except to propel the unending logic of exchange?

In *Mourning and Melancholia*, Freud seems to suggest an alternative to such a logic of substitution. While he casts melancholia as a refusal to bury the dead and let them rest in peace, he declares the process of mourning complete when the mourner is capable of shifting his or her love to a "new object."[31] However, this shift can occur in radically different ways. It is one thing to deny a loss and simply shift one's love to a new object—a replacement child or a replacement lover. But it is quite another to face and mourn that loss and gradually regain the capacity to love again, that is, to live a new and entirely different love. The latter rather resembles what Gayatri Spivak calls the "uncoercive rearrangement of desires."[32] This difference, which Freud's concept of mourning seems to imply but curiously does not explicitly raise, seems to be decisive in understanding the fate of replacement children.

In contrast to Freud, Abraham and Torok distinguish a loss that is denied—in which the lost love object is kept in a crypt inside the self like a living corpse—from a loss that is lived and in which the lost object is granted what they call a "proper burial." The pain of loss can elicit denial; flight from reality; misplaced, repressed, or transformed rage; or manic defense. For Freud, mourning is deemed "proper" only when, after the withdrawal from the world in grief, a space of attachment is gradually reopened to the world and others, including new loved ones. But the fate of replacement children indicates that proper mourning might require something more: it must prepare the path for a new attachment to an *other* that does not unconsciously remain bound to the lost object. This psychoanalytic understanding of mourning operates according to a different psychic economy than the one based on a logic of substitution. Kluger states:

> People aren't reborn. They live or they don't live, their one inalienable life. Schorschi's [her brother] had been taken, and there is no substitute such as 'living on in memory.' We don't want to be pious thoughts in the minds of others; we want the robust substance of our own lives. So throughout the years I felt that I had something which he should have, too, that one of us was the other's shadow, and I was never quite sure which was which.[33]

Substitution inevitably fails to heal the loss it is supposed to erase, or the emptiness it is supposed to fill. Pain, the psychoanalytic concept maintains, cannot be skipped; it can only be repressed and displaced or lived and transformed.

The case of replacement children further shows that pain can be displaced onto the next generation. A new child can be destined to carry the pain for a lost child. Is the only option for replacement children then, in turn, symbolically to kill the original child, the phantom sibling, once again and thereby pass on the pain and guilt?

In *A Child Is Being Killed*, Serge Leclaire tells the story of his analysis of one of his adult patients who had lived his life as the replacement for his older brother Pierre, who had died, not yet a year old, before Pierre-Marie's birth. "Pierre-Marie figures as a replacement child of Pierre, and his problem consists entirely in killing off the representation 'Pierre-Marie' as the living substitute for his dead brother."[34] During his analysis, Pierre-Marie must perform the task of a double symbolic murder: he must kill himself as the replacement child and thereby also kill or exorcise the ghost of the original child:

> What has to be killed so that Pierre-Marie can live is the representation so closely tied to his name and which first appears as that of a consoling child: the dead child's living substitute, destined to be immortal, the unstated figure of his mother's wishes. What is to be killed is a representation presiding, like a star, over the destiny of the child in the flesh.[35]

Haunted by the paralyzing presence of his dead brother, Pierre-Marie thus needs to perform the impossible task of killing him once again:

> What he is looking for in his dreams where he jumps over walls, digs trenches, and discovers tombs in abandoned cemeteries is his brother. He wants to finally get even with the little creep. But how do you kill the dead? As an answer, Pierre-Marie can look at himself, a child vowed immortal by his mother even before he was born, in the place of his dead brother. He burns like a mortuary lamp destined never to go out. And yet, if he wishes to live, he must let that image of light go out and once more kill his brother, thereby wreaking havoc with his mother's dream, doing in the immortal child of her desire: he must kill the very representative he has himself enshrined as the core, however foreign, of his own being.[36]

The literature about replacement children, however, seems to suggest that this symbolic double murder—both of the original child and the self as replacement child—is not enough, and perhaps not even the only option. Just as crucial seems to be what Abraham and Torok call the "proper burial" of the dead child as a precondition for the birth of a child/self allowed to exist on its own terms. Spiegelman's *Maus*, Grimbert's *Secret*, Ithimaera's *Whale Rider*, and Grace's *Baby No-Eyes* present different processes of integrating the fate of a replacement child through a process of symbolic mourning. What emerges in these texts is the function of transformational objects—writing, painting, or ritual—to carry the task of mourning and integration beyond replacement and substitution. In _Memoires for Paul de Man_, Jacques Derrida insists against any logic of substitution on the irreplaceability of loss:

> Is the most distressing, or even the most deadly infidelity that of a _possible mourning_ which would interiorize within us the image, idol, or ideal of the other who is dead and lives only in us? Or is it that of the impossible mourning, which, leaving the other his alterity, respecting thus his infinite remove, either refuses to take or is incapable of taking the other within oneself, as in the tomb or the vault of some narcissism?[37]

Perhaps it takes such a radical ethics of the irreplaceability of a love or a life, a culture or a language, a species or a planet to work against the passing on of violent histories and trauma from generation to generation?

Let me end by giving my reflections a new turn that may serve as a provocation to expand our thinking beyond the present culture of mourning. I opened this essay with a perspective on children who inherit the legacy of replacing a child, if not a generation of children, killed during catastrophic violence, massacres, and genocide. Replacement children are made to act as the involuntary agents in a paradoxical mourning process in which the lost child or children is mourned in a vicarious act that denies their irreplaceable loss. What psychoanalytic theories about replacement children have not asked is whether it is possible to combine proper mourning and the acknowledgment of loss with the desire to have a replacement child. Would that child carry the same legacy of an impossible sense of singularity of self, or would it have a chance, rather, to inherit both a collective memory of a deeply mourned loss and an effort to redress some of the history of violence that caused this loss?

We know about communal and tribal practices of adopting replacement children in indigenous cultures. Some precolonial indigenous cultures in the Americas, for example, practiced the adoption of captive children of the enemy as replacement children for those who had been lost in battle. In "The Politics of Peace (and War) in Preliterate

Societies," Johan M.G. van der Dennen talks about the adoption of children of the enemy as an avenue for preserving peace.[38] He cites as an example an Inca emperor who routinely adopted sons of conquered chiefs. In a different vein, the indigenous anthropologist Ella Cara Deloria, a member of a prominent Yankton Sioux family who studied with Zora Neale Hurston and Ruth Benedict at Columbia University under Franz Boas, refers to the practice of adopting replacement children among native peoples. In her ethnographic novel *Waterlily*, she portrays the retrieval of such a replacement child by the Sioux during intertribal Plains Indian warfare in the nineteenth century:

> The return trip was a complete triumph, for there had been reprisal killings of the enemy in hand-to-hand fights. All the stolen horses were recovered and many of the enemy's finest were taken in addition. Best of all, the young girl was rescued unharmed from the lodge of the chief, where she had been taken in adoption in place of a daughter recently dead.[39]

While in the case described by Deloria the practice of taking replacement children from the enemy did not interrupt intertribal warfare, it nonetheless required seeing the enemy as a human being. In a war culture that dehumanizes the enemy as a people, it would be hard to adopt a child of the enemy as one's own. Dehumanizing the enemy as a people is, in fact, what prepares the ground for turning warfare into genocide. Adoption, by contrast, works with a different logic according to which, as human beings, friend and enemy become interchangeable.

Yet we can imagine a form of adoption that goes even further in an ethics of relating to the enemy. The story with which I want to end my reflections on replacement children is told in Harsh Mander's "Cry, the Beloved Country: Reflections on the Gujarat Massacre" and quoted in Gayatri Spivak's "Terror: A Speech After 9-11":

> I recall a story of the Calcutta riots, when Gandhi was fasting for peace. A Hindu man came to him, to speak of his young boy who had been killed by the Muslim mobs, and of the depth of his anger and longing for revenge. As Gandhi is said to have replied: If you really wish to overcome your pain, find a young [Muslim] boy, just as young as your

son . . . whose parents have been killed by Hindu mobs. Bring up that boy like you would your own son, but bring him up in the Muslim faith to which he was born. Only then will you find that you can heal your pain, your anger, and your longing for retribution.[40]

In this story, Gandhi imagines a replacement child who would inherit the legacy of breaking the cycle of violence, revenge, and retribution. It is the story that invokes the hardest possible task after mourning the loss of a child to an act of violence, namely, imagining oneself as the enemy. Such an act of imagination would transcend a binary structure of thinking and feeling along the divide of victim and perpetrator, or friend and enemy. It would be an imagination that sees histories of violence as systemic and destructive to both sides. Mourning must then be envisioned in conjunction with a redress that encompasses both victim and perpetrator. Any redress aimed at breaking the cycle of violence presupposes imagining the enemy, and indeed the perpetrator, who has violated or killed your own child as a human being.

If this task appears to be larger than human, it is because it requires not only a new ethics but also a profound rearrangement of desires and affect. In today's violent global world, in which wars and genocide belong to the order of the day, we cannot close our eyes to the fact that our affects and structures of feeling are formed under the conditions of a culture of war that divides the world in a paranoid-schizoid way along the lines of enemies and allies. A culture that embraces the dehumanization of enemies is also vulnerable to a politics of revenge and retribution. By contrast, a mourning (and redress) that deserves its name requires an imaginative and affective practice that can only come from within an opposition to such a culture.

The story about Gandhi is not merely a utopian fantasy. It resonates with the actual story of Amy Biehl, the twenty-six-year-old anti-Apartheid activist who was stoned and stabbed to death in a racial hate crime in South Africa in 1993 by four young men who belonged to a crowd shouting antiwhite slogans. The murderers were convicted and sentenced to eighteen years in prison. In 1997, in the context of the Truth and Reconciliation Commission, they petitioned for amnesty. The event was widely broadcast through global media, and the world witnessed the extraordinary public act of Amy Biehl's parents, Peter and

Linda Biehl, an act called "reconciliatory justice" by Angela Davis in her tribute to them. The Biehls publicly supported the amnesty and were crucial in the release of the four men from prison in 1998.

After their release, two of the men, Easy Nofemela and Ntobecko Peni, met with the Biehls to express their sorrow for having killed their daughter. According to Davis, Nofemela uttered the following words: "I know you lost a person you love. I want you to forgive me and take me as your child."[41] In a certain sense, this is exactly what the Biehls did. They involved Nofemala and Peni in the Amy Biehl Foundation, which they had established in order to carry on their daughter's legacy, namely, her work against Apartheid in South Africa. In fact, the Biehls asked Nofema and Peni to work at the Guguletu branch, the town where Amy was murdered. After Peter Biehl died, Linda Biehl bought two plots of land for her daughter's killers so that they could build their own homes.[42] For all practical purposes, then, the Biehls treated the murderers of their daughter as they would have treated their own children, supporting them financially and integrating them into their work against racism and its violent legacies.

Where, then, does this leave us? I began by stating my own investment in scrutinizing this topic as a replacement child. Beyond my scholarly commitment to this exploration, writing this chapter also performs a piece of necessary mourning for the brother I never knew. It is no coincidence, however, that I started the chapter with reflections on mourning and ended with reflections on forgiveness. I had to learn to forgive both my brother and my mother. I had to forgive my brother for occupying the psychic space into which I was born. At the same time, I had to forgive him for never being there in real life, as he was in my fantasies, when I needed him to protect me from my mother's rages. In turn, I had to forgive my mother for never letting me be myself on my own terms. But I also had to begin to learn to understand her. After her many violent outbursts—for which she always blamed me—she would try making up by saying: "Now it is all forgotten!" I could never forget. Yet, decades later, I finally had to learn to forgive and mourn without forgetting. Forgiving meant letting go of my own rage, and mourning meant acknowledging the sadness about an irrevocable disjointing between my mother and me that lasted until the end of her life. It also meant mourning the absence of the mother I perhaps could have had, if she hadn't insisted—as she used to do—that I was a changeling, the wrong child, exchanged at birth in the hospital. What would my mother have been like had she not herself suffered from a lasting war trauma?

More important, what can we learn from the many examples used in these reflections on replacement children that might help us in adjusting our work of mourning loved ones killed in violence to the task of making this a more peaceful world? When is our response to the losses of violence not just mere mourning that tries to replace the loss but a working-through that counters the "work of death" with a "work of life," that is, a work for peace?[43] What, we may ask, is the politics of mourning at work in the stories of Gandhi and Amy Biehl? First, and on the most general level, it is a politics that addresses the ethics of how to learn to live in peace with the other, which also means learning to live with the ghosts of a violent past. In *Specters of Marx*, Jacques Derrida makes a link between such an ethics and the question of justice as distinct from law:

> This being-with specters would also be, not only but also, a *politics* of memory, of inheritance and of generations. . . . No justice—let us not say no law . . . —seems possible or thinkable without the principle of some *responsibility*, beyond all living present, within that which disjoins the living present, before the ghosts of those who are not yet born or who are already dead, be they victims of wars, political or other kinds of violence, nationalist, racist, colonialist, sexist, or other kinds of exterminations, victims of the oppressions of capitalist imperialism or any of the forms of totalitarianism.[44]

A politics of mourning that is mindful of the question of justice and responsibility must be grounded in a politics of memory, of inheritance, and of generations. It must be a politics that orients itself toward a future to come, while taking responsibility for past histories of violence and the ghosts left behind. Such a politics also entails, as Derrida maintains, "some disjointing, disjunction, or disproportion: in the inadequation to self."[45]

The latter, I would add, also bears upon the politics of emotion and affect. Let me therefore end with a few reflections on the issue of public emotions. The Biehls publicly performed mourning as restorative and reconciliatory justice. This is a political statement that sees the violence under Apartheid as a systemic violence that includes victims and perpetrators on both sides of the racial divide. It is important to understand that this form of mourning does not follow—but, on the contrary, counteracts—what we tend to perceive as "natural" emotions. The latter go toward rage, revenge, and retribution. From the hostile reactions that the Biehls received from many corners, we may even infer that it does not come naturally to us to approve of, or even trust, the emotions that sustain this process of mourning and reparation. The fact that this process is performed publicly under global media attention does not help to increase our trust in the emotions displayed.

I vividly recall the sense of shock I first experienced on hearing Amy Biehl's story. I felt right then and there not only that I would never be able to treat the murderer of one of my children as I would treat a child of my own but also that such an act was a betrayal of the murdered child, even though I understood that, in the case of Amy Biehl, the act of forgiveness carried on her own legacy. This form of mourning a murdered child appeared to me almost out of proportion, like a primordial emotional transgression. But this may be precisely the point. Amy Biehl's story made me realize that what we call "humanizing the enemy" does not come naturally. The work of reconciliation, and indeed the work of peace, requires a profound rearrangement of our structures of feeling and desire. And isn't one of the crucial functions of literature and the teaching of literature, as Gayatri Spivak suggests, the "uncoercive rearrangement of desires" and a "training into a preparation for the ethical"?[46]

Perhaps this is what we need to understand and learn when we think about human and civil rights and when we work against racism and war in pursuit of a decolonization of the mind and a different ethics of relating to the Other: we will also have to decolonize our emotions and affects, including our unconscious fears of the Other and perhaps our unconscious desires as well. To invoke Gandhi's words once more: "Only then will you find that you can heal your pain, your anger, and your longing for retribution." And, we may add, only by healing pain and rage and by disrupting the desire that nourishes the vicious cycle of revenge will we be able to reclaim a life in dignity and unabashedly assert the right to live for every human being born on this earth.

chapter six

Deadly Intimacy
The Politics and Psychic Life of Torture

> How can those who tortured and those who were tortured coexist in
> the same land? . . . How do we keep the past alive without becom-
> ing its prisoner? How do we forget it without risking
> its repetition in the future?
> —Ariel Dorfman, *Death and the Maiden*

Torture, Secrecy, Fantasy

"Their secret was death, not sex. That's what the grown-ups were talking about, sitting up late around the table. . . . I wanted to get in on the
forbidden news, the horror stories, fascinating though incomplete as
they always were—or perhaps even more fascinating for their opaque-
ness, that whiff of fantasy they had about them, though one knew they
were true."[1] This is how Ruth Kluger, a child survivor of the Holocaust,
opens her memoir, *Still Alive*. She makes us look at the uncanny proximity of horror and fascination, the lure of secrecy, and our penchant to
invest horror with a "whiff of fantasy." Horror can tap into our most
primordial fantasies to hijack mental and psychic life. My reflections
on the psychic life of torture—presented as a series of hypotheses—will
keep this uncanny proximity in mind. One of the horror stories Kluger
relates concerns her uncle Hans, who as a teenager was tortured in
Buchenwald. She writes: "They had tortured him. What is torture, how
does one stand it, how is it done? But he was alive and back, knock on
wood, let's be thankful."[2] When Kluger meets Hans decades later in
England she asks him about his torture, only to realize she is breaking

a taboo: "The other guests in the stifling space of the tidy English living room want to be left in peace."[3] But Hans tells his story:

> He tells me the minutiae, the contortion of the limbs. He can explain it well. He can even show me; he suffers from back pain dating from that time. And yet these details have a way of leveling the horror, as appeals from Amnesty International never quite get across what they are telling you because the familiar words, black ink on dry white paper, interfere with the mute and essentially wordless suffering—the ooze of pain, if I may so call it—they aim to communicate. Only in Hans's tone of voice is there a hint of the sheer evil, of radical otherness. For the sensation of torture doesn't leave its victim alone—never, not to the end of life. It isn't the pain per se, it's how it was inflicted. . . . What matters is not just what we endure, but also what kind of misery it is, where it comes from. The worst is the kind that's imposed by others with malicious intent. That's the kind from which no one recovers.[4]

This passage raises the question of how we can talk about torture. Even though Hans tells his story with a rhetorical flourish as far as facts and details are concerned, his words "level the horror." "Words," Kluger says, "black ink on white paper, interfere with the mute and essentially wordless suffering." Fixated on facts, Hans's story seems dissociated from the emotional and experiential quality of torture.

Torture attacks language. As Elaine Scarry argues, pain destroys the very ability of language to represent suffering.[5] At its extreme, it leads to the destruction of a meaningful relationship to the world. Trauma theorists call torture's attack against the symbolic order "de-semiosis" or "de-signification." Losing the capacity to symbolize, the victim is reduced to a frightening literality, akin to the processes of de-metaphorization Bateson describes as a characteristic of schizophrenia. At its extreme, torture induces psychotic states, including hallucinations, paranoid delusions, and loss of reality. This de-symbolization includes the body as it is severed from an embodied self. Jean Améry speaks of torture reducing the body to flesh, and Gilles Deleuze, in his interpretation of Bacon, speaks of the body reduced to meat.[6]

Yet for those who witness, hear, or read about torture, the situation is different. As a child, Kluger wanted to "get in on the horror stories," and when, as an adult, she finally dares to ask her questions, her uncle

Hans is a compliant storyteller. He leaves her frustrated, though, because all he can give her is empty words.[7] Dwelling on minutiae and details, his narrative is haunted by the absence of symbolic depth. Hans is unable to deliver precisely what the child Ruth most longed for, namely a narrative that satisfies her fantasy. Only the tone of his voice carries a "hint of the sheer evil." His listener is left with nothing but empty words, unless she fills them with a "whiff of fantasy." Both options seem problematic, one because it colludes with the cold distance of a defensive story, the other because it invests horror with a phantasmatic attachment.

We are reminded of Freud's "A Child Is Being Beaten."[8] The fantasy of the child who is a mute witness to the beating of another child reveals a frightening mobility in subject position: in her imagination, the child can move from being the child who is beaten to the father who is beating the child to the child who watches in horror and fascination. Witnessing the vulnerability of bodies to pain inflicted by an overpowering Other elicits a complex response that includes shifting identifications. Identifying with the aggressor is, of course, a defensive position for the vulnerable witness to a scene of horror, but it is also one that tends to invest the horror with illicit pleasure. In this process, horror and fascination may collapse into each other.

Torture makes the victim regress to a catastrophic helplessness akin to that of an abused child. Reduced to the immediacy, the here and now of physical pain, and an imposed passivity, the torture victim becomes the child being beaten. By contrast, if one witnesses torture or hears stories about it, the power of fantasy allows one not only to identify in empathy with the victim but also to shift position from abused to abusing, from victim to perpetrator. Therein lies our vulnerability to becoming complicit, that is, to sharing the voyeurism or abject pleasure of the child who watches another child being beaten. This can even happen when images of torture are made public and disseminated over the Internet and other media. Perversely enough, this public display of torture can enhance the ecology of fear and fascination that sustains the politics of torture.

Abjection resides in the very fact that human beings can willfully inflict the pain of torture on other human beings. Moreover, if this pain is inflicted "with malicious intent," as Kluger suggests, it is the worst kind of pain, the one "from which no one recovers." Perhaps it is all the harder to recover from this pain because we know that human beings are the only species that torture and that can take pleasure in inflicting pain on another. However, Kluger's notion of a "pain from which no one recovers" needs qualification. What would count as recovery? We know that under favorable conditions, torture victims can reclaim full and creative lives. While mourning and integration may not be able to erase the psychic effects of torture, they may nonetheless support an astonishing recovery that testifies to the power of resilience. Looking at the devastating and annihilating effects of torture, I do not want to lose sight of this capacity for survival.

Minutely describing what is called "initiation torture" at his arrival in Leavenworth, Leonard Peltier grasps both the infliction of pain with malicious intent and the state of catastrophic helplessness it induces in the victim:

> I walked in my shackles and leg-irons up the front steps to the first of a seemingly endless series of steel doors. I thought I could hear distant screams coming from somewhere in the building. Or maybe it was just the wind howling in the razor wire atop the walls. Suddenly your mind begins to play tricks on you . . . you feel as if you're going to wet your pants, you feel like crying, calling out for help . . . when I turned to one of the marshals who was leading me up the stairs, hoping to find some glint of human warmth in his eyes, I saw, instead, not a face at all, but a mask of absolute hatred. . . . He saw my terror and my weakness. . . . He just smiled a devil's smile and said in an almost cheerful voice: "You're dead, you fucking Indian bastard, you'll never get out of this building alive. We'll see to that. We'll get you one way or another."[9]

Under conditions of imprisonment in a hostile environment, the "mind begins to play tricks on you." It turns the victim into a terrified and helpless child and the torturer into a sadistic adult who claims sovereignty over the body and its freedom, over life and death. It is a practice aimed at the destruction of human dignity, that is, a form of dehumanization. At the same time, in calling torture "inhuman," discourses on torture tend to exclude torture from the sense of being human. Torture therefore also emerges as a practice that violates the very boundaries of the human in both victim and torturer.

History, Time, and Duration of Torture

Torture can take many forms. The particular form of assault we call torture presupposes the unity of body, mind, and psyche. We should no longer think of torture as a practice that happens in a torture chamber or dungeon and consists exclusively of the unnecessary and willful infliction of atrocious bodily pain, but as a much more encompassing practice of inflicting unnecessary pain and instrumentalizing pain for punitive and disciplinary measures or for purposes of control. Such an act violates the most basic foundations of human relations, namely, trust and care. Adi Ophir, in fact, takes the infliction of unnecessary pain as the basis of his definition of evil and argues that "unnecessary evils" are those "that could have been prevented or reduced but were not."[10] In a similar vein, Christopher Bollas defines evil as a perversion of trust for the purpose of inflicting grave injury or death.[11]

Historically, it is not so long ago that in official and public discourse and moral law, torture was considered obsolete. It was said to belong to the past, the Middle Ages, the Inquisition. From the end of the eighteenth century to the end of the twentieth century, torture had been delegitimized and considered an unacceptable violation of human rights in most Western countries. While this does not necessarily mean that these countries no longer practiced torture, it means that torture violated moral and practical law.

The Bush administration's recent attempt to relegitimize torture marks a sharp new turn in the legal history of torture by making the boundaries of what officially constitutes torture flexible and subject to negotiation.[12] The attempts in the United States to redefine torture legally proposed to narrow its definition to the infliction of bodily injury that causes complete organ failure or death. This cynical redefinition would, in fact, exclude from definitions of torture all other forms of willful infliction of unnecessary pain, including all forms of long-lasting psychic pain resulting from violations of human dignity. However, in torture the violation of bodily integrity and human dignity have always operated together, and it is the psychic pain of humiliation that often determines the duration of torture long after the healing of physical wounds.

In order to work toward a more humane society, we would therefore by contrast need to widen the definition or torture to include more subliminal and "sustainable" forms of torture that may be inflicted incrementally over time, including their lasting effects. As the African writer, former political prisoner, and torture victim Ngũgĩ wa Thiong'o reminds us in *Detained: A Writer's Prison Diary*, there are insidious forms of detention that practice a more unbounded form of torture, extended over years or even decades. Extended torture has a cumulative effect. It suspends time, causing the victim to feel that his plight is potentially endless. Or it compresses and condenses time, causing the victim to live in a prolonged state of accumulated pain in which experience is so intensified that time feels accelerated. Ngũgĩ writes: "Baudelaire once said of a character: 'He is very old, for he has lived three days in one.' I should say that I have 'aged' considerably for I have lived several years in six months."[13] The time of torture, Ngũgĩ implies, is linked to the integrity of a person. The latter includes being allowed to live one's own time rather than suffering the deprivation of the compressed or expanded time under conditions of imprisonment and the imposition of surplus labor if not slave labor.

In recent decades, the practices of psychological torture have become increasingly refined, often with the help of scientific research. The terrifying images that reach us from Abu Ghraib show that psychological torture and abject humiliation are as indispensable to torture as the infliction of physical pain and injury. At its extreme, torture aims toward the outer limits of pain, operating at the threshold of not only physical but also social and psychic death. To reach this threshold, special secluded and confined spaces for the infliction of pain and terror are designed in which all humane laws of treating others are suspended in a moral vacuum. In recent U.S. history, torture's attacks on selfhood and cultural or religious integrity have been enhanced by two new methods of torture: the violation of cultural and religious sensitivities and the exploitation of individual phobias.[14] While humiliation has always constituted a core element of torture, it has been increasingly refined and moved to center stage. Torturers draw on experts to acquire the cultural literacy necessary to strike at the core of cultural and religious values, including norms of sexual and gender organization.

Deprivation of privacy and elimination of toilets are common devices to induce a primordial humiliation and shame. Sexual humiliation, including rape, is aimed at destroying the most intimate relationality and integrity of the bodies of sexual human beings. The perpetrators at Guantánamo Bay and Abu Ghraib added the violation of cultural and religious sensitivities, such as the desecration of the Koran and the taboo against coming in contact with menstrual blood. In *Frames of War*, Judith Butler points out, however, that the United States relied on a poor anthropological source when it devised its protocols on torture, a work on cultural anthropology from 1970 titled *The Arab Mind*. She argues that the U.S. military used this text to construct "the Arab mind" as an object that it could then manipulate. More importantly, however, Butler insists that torture was used not only to humiliate the prisoners but also, inversely, to produce a certain notion of the Arab subject in military discourse: "The torture was not merely an effort to find ways to shame and humiliate the prisoners of Abu Ghraib and Guantánamo on the basis of their presumptive cultural formation. The torture was also a way to coercively produce the Arab subject and the Arab mind."[15]

Among the increasing refinements of the practices of psychological torture, the "manipulation of time" plays a prominent role. As far back as 1963, we find the following statement in a CIA document on "Techniques of Non-Coercive Interrogation of Resistant Sources":

There are a number of non-coercive techniques for inducing regression. All depend upon the interrogator's control of the environment and, as always, a proper matching of method to source. Some interrogates can be repressed [sic] by persistent manipulation of time, by retarding and advancing clocks and serving meals at odd times—ten minutes or ten hours after the last food was given. Day and night are jumbled. Interrogation sessions are similarly unpatterned [sic] the subject may be brought back for more questioning just a few minutes after being dismissed for the night. . . . A subject who is cut off from the world he knows seeks to recreate it, in some measure, in the new and strange environment. He may try to keep track of time, to live in the familiar past, to cling to old concepts of loyalty, to establish—with one or more interrogators—interpersonal relations resembling those that he had earlier with other people, and to build other bridges back to the known. Thwarting his attempts to do so is likely to drive him deeper and deeper into himself, until he is no longer able to control his responses in adult fashion.[16]

It is worthwhile dwelling for a moment on the rhetorical construction of this torture manual. First of all, the manipulation of time is considered a "non-coercive technique for inducing regression." We may wonder about the notion and use of the term "non-coercive." What can be non-coercive about the forced induction of regression with the malicious intent of driving a person deeper and deeper into himself until he loses the capacity to respond in adult fashion? If one followed the idea behind this rhetoric of non-coercion, the very notion of psychological torture would disappear. However, those who torture during interrogations have long learned from behavioral psychologists and medical researchers that the effects of psychological torture can be even more persistent than those of physical torture. Freud defines psychic trauma as the infliction of invisible wounds. As the suicides and suicidal tendencies among tortured political prisoners may attest, for some of them death seems preferable to living with the invisible wounds of abject humiliation and social death.

Torture thus operates at the most primordial and archaic levels of body, mind, and soul. It uses a violent assault on the senses to break down or kill the self. Torture can operate through sight, sound, smell, and touch. Sensory deprivation and assault—blindfolding, isolation, sleep deprivation, deafening noise, and so on—aim at a fundamental disorientation and disintegration of the self, inducing states akin to psychosis. The CIA, we now know, routinely hires researchers in behavioral science in order to refine the knowledge of how to break a person. A renowned professor of behavioral science conducted experiments to prove that, through mere sensory deprivation such as wearing goggles and earphones in an isolated room, he can induce psychotic states in just forty-eight hours, including hallucinations, severe paranoia, disorientation, and loss of reality.[17]

The psychological equivalent of the threshold of physical death is thus the induction of madness, if not the killing of the self. Psychological torture of this kind pushes the regression to a level of infantile dependency and, at its extreme, to catastrophic helplessness. Psychological torture aims at destroying the conditions of human connectedness and relationality and ultimately the victim's very hold on the world. This induced regression to archaic modes of being and relating is a crucial aspect of torture. Torture manuals emphasize the goal of inducing in the victim a dependency on the torturer that resembles a child's dependency on a parental figure. If we try to imagine a willfully induced state of abject regression in which a victim is reduced to clinging to an interpersonal relationship with his or her torturer, it is hard not to think of the desperate clinging of abused children to the abusive parent. This is not only a "pushing deeper and deeper into the self"; it is a pushing back in time to infantile dependency. The destruction of the victim's relationality to time is then also aimed at the victim's hold on his own lifetime. "Pushing back into himself" also means pushing back in time to the point of shattering the ontological grounding in a spatiotemporal world. The latter becomes the very condition of the torturer's arrogation of sovereign power over body and mind, life and death, sanity and madness.

Scientifically refined, torture increasingly attacks the structures of selfhood. While sensory deprivation is targeted at the victim's relation to the outside world, the systematic deprivation of privacy and dignity violates the bounded inner space of corporeal and psychic integrity. Ngũgĩ describes this assault in vivid terms:

> In prison I see in the clearer light of the 100-watt bulb in my cell that never lets me sleep; I see in the clearer light of the eyes of the key-jangling guards who have completely stripped me of any privacy in eating, washing and shitting; I see it in the clearer light of the sickening nauseating food that I daily have to force down my throat; I see it in the clearer light of the Bleak House, this human zoo where every hour I only look at stone and dust and iron bars, and more stone, dust and iron bars; I see it in the clearer light of the callous police use of disease as a means of torture; I see it in the clearer light of the endless acts of humiliation meant to strip me of the last vestiges of humanness.[18]

Ngũgĩ wa Thiong'o calls torture "the state's psychological terrorism."[19] Extended forms of torture in prisons and detention camps include torture with inedible or rotting food, denial of news and information, forcible breaking up of families by keeping them incommunicado, and systematic neglect of medical care.[20]

Leonard Peltier, a former member of the American Indian Movement, is another case in point. As Peter Mathiessen documents in more than 600 pages in *In the Spirit of Crazy Horse*, Peltier has been unlawfully held in a U.S. prison for almost four decades.[21] Systematically denied adequate medical treatment for his diabetes, Peltier is in danger of going blind. This is the use of illness by the authorities as a form of extended physical and psychic torture. In addition, Peltier suffered both short-term intensive torture and the extended torture of decades of imprisonment under unbearable conditions. In his *Prison Writings: My Life Is My Sundance*, he describes the conditions in the Leavenworth penitentiary:

> Leavenworth was infamous as the Hot House, because there was no air-conditioning here, just big wall-mounted fans that, during the mind-numbing heat of a Kansas hundred-degree summer day, blew the heavy, sluggish, unbreathable air at you like a welding torch. . . . But we still have the noise, always the noise . . . in here every sound is magnified in your mind. The ventilation system roars and rumbles and hisses. Nameless clanks and creakings, flushings and gurglings sound within the walls. Buzzers and bells grate at your nerves. Disembodied, often unintelligible voices drone and squawk on loudspeakers. . . . There is an ever-present background chorus of shouts and yells and calls, demented babblings, crazed screams, ghostlike laughter. Maybe one day you realize one of the voices is your own, and then you really begin to worry.[22]

Exposure to extreme temperatures and assault with unbearable noises or other sensory stimuli are among the most commonly used forms of torture. These extremes serve to destroy the familiar coordinates of orientation in the world, thus inducing a form of madness resembling psychosis.

I have deliberately included examples from the prison diaries of Ngũgĩ wa Thiong'o and Leonard Peltier because they describe forms of torture that are not designed to extract vital and life-saving information, the latter being the most common rationalization of the previous U.S. government to legitimize an inhuman practice. Since it is well known, however, that torture is an unreliable means to extract information that might protect the nation, we may wonder whether it is primarily designed to access information or rather to instill terror and submission on a much larger scale. Reinhold Görling describes this new turn in the politics of torture, arguing that it can be linked to a larger move from a disciplinary society to a society of totalitarian control: "We are specialists of communication and information," he imagines the interrogators saying, "We do not need any information from you. We need you *as* information. We need your bodies as a medium of expression, as a carrier of signs that reveal our control over you."[23] Torture thus becomes part of a pervasive, officially induced and sanctioned ecology of fear, submission, and subjection. Occasional leaks such as the photos from Abu Ghraib ultimately feed back into this logic of torture and the ecology of fear it nourishes. Designed to deter dissent and political action, torture, like the practice of disappearing people, is a form of state terrorism.

Because torture is still widely considered on the international stage to be an illegitimate practice, no state will officially admit to practices of torture and other forms of state terrorism. To maintain torture, legally, morally, and rhetorically, requires extensive operations of defense, splitting torture off from official discourses or, in extreme cases, outsourcing it. We may wonder if splitting has not reemerged as a culturally and politically prominent defense mechanism. Theorizing archaic modes of defense in early infancy, Melanie Klein characterizes splitting as a defensive operation characterized by a paranoid-schizoid hold on the world. Good and evil are neatly separated and whatever emerges as "evil" from within is projected into the outside world and persecuted there. A culture that systematically trains splitting as a defense mechanism is therefore ideally designed to facilitate practices of dehumanization.

Görling argues that we need to write the history of torture in relation to colonialism. Historically, colonialism introduced the mechanism that allowed the colonizer to deny the subjectivity and agency of the colonized. The dehumanization of the colonized makes it possible to refuse empathy and compassion without feeling the guilt such refusal would otherwise cause. Colonialism cannot but operate with massive splitting since the colonizer can no longer afford to perceive the humanity of the colonized. It is this mechanism that can be transferred to other forms of dehumanization. As Aimé Césaire and Hannah Arendt have argued, the Nazis transferred the colonial model of dehumanization onto the Jews, the Gypsies, the mentally ill, and political prisoners. Görling argues that this very model of dehumanization is still available in Guantánamo or Abu Ghraib. He concludes that the defense of subjectivity and psychic space has become a political act of resistance against a culture that is in the process of trying to relegitimize forms of dehumanization such as torture. In order to be effective, the defense of subjectivity and psychic space needs to counter the operations of splitting that allow individuals to split off parts of their selves and project them onto others:

> We need to defend the space of subjectivity, albeit in a new way attuned to the multiplicity of structures that define this space. . . . If we continue to think in terms of a social contract, what the state would have to respect and protect foremost would be the subject's manifold indivisibility and the indivisible multiplicity. Precisely because this indivisibility is a social product, we need to define it politically.[24]

If splitting, projection, and projective identification are the basic psychic and political defense mechanisms that enable both the actual practice of torture and the politics that sanction torture, we need to look more closely at the psychic life of torture from a relational perspective that focuses on the interaction between the torturer and his victim, including the long-term damage torture does to both victim and perpetrator.

Malignant Intimacy, Soul Murder, and Necropolitics

We recall how, listening to her uncle's torture stories, Kluger detects a "hint of the sheer evil" in his voice. Pain willfully inflicted by others with malicious intent lies at the heart of what we call evil. It becomes torture when physical pain is so excruciating or frightening that it reduces the victim to catastrophic helplessness or when psychic pain strips the victim of all foundations of human dignity. Both corporeal and psychic torture, however, attack the self. At its extreme, the pain and suffering will lead to the death of the self. "Enduring massive trauma reacquaints the psyche with the nearness of extinction," writes Sue Grand.[25] Under conditions of torture, the threat of extinction is often directed simultaneously at both corporeal and psychic life. Torture is thus linked to two liminal forms of annihilating human experience: death and evil. While death annihilates the body, evil tends to annihilate the self. Building the threat of death into torture in order systematically to enhance its effects, the torturer—like the despot—usurps the role of absolute sovereign, master over life and death. If the victim survives, she will owe her life to the torturer who could have killed her. The torturer thus establishes a malignant pact against life that guarantees it will not stop with the ending of actual torture but continue to exert its hold on life. A pact, however, requires collusion, and the torturer therefore needs to lure his or her victim into some form of involuntary complicity. Many survivors of torture continue to live within this pact, pursuing the death they should have died in infinite permutations of self-abuse and endangerment. They "want death for having wanted life" under conditions of abject degradation.[26] It is in this respect that they collude with the perpetrator's attack on their life.

Inducing the victim to identify with anti-life or a hatred of life, torture operates according to a logic of the death drive. Psychic numbing and emotional death, sadomasochistic cathexis of anti-life, and vulnerability to compulsive repetition and self-destructive impulses are common symptoms of this malignancy. Torture then does not end with the release of the victim. It continues in the permanent effects on the violated body: the deafness or blindness, the chronic back pain, the missing finger or ear. It also continues in the permanent effects on the psyche: the recurrent nightmares, the flashbacks, the panic attacks, the lifelong depression, the suicidal tendencies, and the compulsion to repeat. A woman subjected to psychological torture and rape by a police officer testified to the fact that four years later she still relives the attack:

> I would fall into depressions. It was such a huge wound, and I felt it was constantly opening and closing. It's a wound without a cure. . . . You live with this 24 hours a day. . . . In the restroom, when you're cooking, when you sleep, you live with this. Sometimes I feel like it's better if they kill you than have to live with such a large wound.[27]

Being condemned to relive the attack—in involuntary memories that clutter the tasks of daily life—is one of the ways in which the wounds of torture reopen again and again.

Proust describes how involuntary memories emerge in response to specific sensory stimuli such as the smell of a pastry one loved as a child, the sound of a familiar tune, a particular inflection of sunlight. Almost like allegorical inscriptions in our body, these sensory memories become placeholders for an entire time or mode of experience. In a similar vein, sensory impressions make a victim of torture vulnerable to involuntary recall. In its extreme manifestation, such recall takes the form of flashbacks that intrude out of the blue and carry the victim back into the time of torture. While victims may be able to control, direct, or even ban the voluntary memories of torture, involuntary memories may assault them at any moment. All they need is the trigger of a sensory stimulus or an internal affect or mood. This is one of the ways in which torture persists beyond the actual event.

Torture's relationship to memory is thus highly ambivalent. Torture attacks memory, one says, but the occurrence of flashbacks shows that it does so only imperfectly. While it is true that human beings can rely on amnesia as a built-in defense mechanism against intolerable memories, sudden involuntary flashbacks break through the protective shield of amnesia and may haunt the victim for years to come. Flashbacks function as split-off memories that intrude on mind or psyche like alien invaders. Jean Améry puts it in the strongest terms: "I dare to assert that torture is the most horrible event a human being can retain within himself."[28] Like rape, torture generates a lasting invisible wound. This is why torture appears to be one of the manifestations of sheer evil.

In talking about torture, Améry also develops a critique of Hannah Arendt's thesis about the "banality of evil." Talking about the ordinary faces of the Gestapo men who tortured him, Améry observes:

> And the enormous perception at a later stage, one that destroys all abstractive imagination, makes clear to us how the plain, ordinary faces finally become Gestapo faces after all, and how evil overlays and exceeds banality. For there is no 'banality of evil,' and Hannah Arendt, who wrote about it in her Eichmann book, knew the enemy of mankind only from hearsay, saw him only through the glass cage. When an event places the most extreme demands on us, one ought not to speak of banality.[29]

Yet Arendt is not simply wrong. While she is trying to understand how human beings who have committed unfathomable atrocities can even go on managing the duties of their daily lives, Améry is looking at a human being in the process of inflicting torture or murder on another. Arendt is right in asserting that, if we look at the entire life of a criminal such as Eichmann, rather than finding a life marked by monstrosity, we will most often find utter banality. In this sense, Eichmann resembles the majority of people we encounter on a daily basis. Améry, however, insists on an important qualification: in the moment in which the torturer, rapist, or murderer acts, he exits the banality of the everyday and enters a space of evil or a state of exception. This is particularly true for the torturer, who, by definition, comes face to face with his victim.

Once again, the psychoanalytic concept of splitting may help one more fully to understand this division of a human being into two separate modes of being. Splitting enables the creation of the moral vacuum within which torture is performed, a vacuum that allows the perpetrators, in Améry's words, to "torture with the good conscience of depravity."[30] In *At the Mind's Limits*, Améry writes: "But with the first blow from a policeman's fist, against which there can be no defense and which no helping hand can ward off, a part of our life ends and it can never again be revived."[31] This is what psychoanalysis calls "soul murder." The violation of humane ethics in torture reaches the very heart of human vulnerability. Torture induces psychic death; the victim experiences the murder of being. The self that operates within the parameters of a basic trust in the world is killed so that the victim experiences not merely a death of the self but an active killing of the self. This killing occurs in a highly performative act that creates a malignant intimacy between the torturer and his victim, who become bound up in a deadly embrace.

Terror, pain-induced regression, and the annihilation of adult personality structures catapult the victim back into an infantile position. Negatively modeled on the early state of an infant's absolute dependency, this intimacy elicits archaic, raw affect states, creating a false "potential space" in which the boundaries between self and other are temporarily obliterated;[32] torturer and victim merge in a deadly symbiosis. The torturer pushes his victim's absolute dependency to the limit of catastrophic helplessness, thus generating a mode of relating akin to malignant symbiosis. "In detention, when one is not reduced to the level of a beast, one is certainly treated like a child,"[33] Ngũgĩ wa Thiong'o says. Within the framework of this malignant symbiosis, the outside world is temporarily eclipsed. While the victim is violently cut off from the outside and reduced to unbearable pain, the torturer operates in a state of dissociation within a moral vacuum. To sustain this vacuum, the torturer needs to split off the parts of the self that harbor humane values such as compassion and the prohibition against willfully inflicting harm. Curiously, however, the torturer must at the same time sustain empathy to access intimate knowledge about the victim's pain. This perversion of empathy, or "empty empathy,"[34] is the single most efficient tool to forge the sadistic bond of a deadly intimacy. "I was being detained on somebody else's assumed knowledge of (my) innermost thoughts and desires," writes Ngũgĩ wa Thiong'o.[35]

Used to describe the dialectics of oppression, Ashis Nandy's metaphor of "intimate enemies" precisely captures the psychic relationship between victim and torturer, whose deadly embrace goes to the heart of evil. Permanently marking both victim and perpetrator, torture causes a form of complementary psychic damage. This damage may include living in a world of permanent psychic splitting or under the thrall of a sadomasochistic pact with death. The death wish can be turned inward against the self or outward against others. Repetition compulsion can go in both directions and manifest as repetition of the victim's victimization and the perpetrator's perpetration. More insidiously, the repetition compulsion may also invert roles and manifest as the victim's perpetration and the perpetrator's victimization of self or extended self. We can see such a compulsion at work, for example, in a torture victim who, in a futile attempt to invert agency and control, returns to torture his own family. Al McCoy describes torture as a "perverse theater that destroys the victims and empowers the perpetrators."[36] I argue that, in the long term, torture destroys not only the victim but also the perpetrator, if only because in order to kill his victim's self, the torturer must also kill his own soul. The latter can occur actively, in the hot-blooded torture that involves the torturer's passion, rage, or enjoyment or in the passive numbing of affect and selfhood. In her essay "On Evil," Hannah Arendt writes: "The greatest evil perpetrated is the evil committed by nobodies, that is, by human beings who refuse to be persons."[37]

After describing torture as a transformation of the tortured person into flesh, Jean Améry adds a crucial thought: "Pain, we said, is the most extreme intensification imaginable of our bodily being. But maybe it is even more, that is: death."[38] The victim of torture experiences a premonition of death mediated through pain. In consequence, Améry argues, torture allows (or imposes upon) a human being a personal experience of death.[39] Drawing on Bataille's existential reading of the death drive, Améry likens the torturer to the sadist who pursues the radical negation of the other and the denial of both the social principle and the reality principle. The torturer "wants to nullify this world, and by negating his fellow man, who also in an entirely specific sense is 'hell' for him, he wants to realize his own total sovereignty."[40] As a consequence, it is as if the victim of torture becomes forever a stranger in a world that is based on basic trust in a social contract:

> If from the experience of torture any knowledge at all remains . . . it is that of . . . a foreignness in the world that cannot be compensated by any sort of subsequent human communication. Amazed, the tortured person experienced that in this world there can be the other as absolute sovereign, and sovereignty revealed itself as the power to inflict suffering and to destroy.[41]

In "Necropolitics," Achille Mbembe writes: "The ultimate expression of sovereignty resides . . . in the power and the capacity to decide who may live and who must die."[42] I submit that the practice of torture extends this sovereignty to the life and death of the soul. To understand this violent arrogation of sovereignty over self, we must think beyond biopower and the infliction of physical pain and move humiliation to the core of thinking about torture. Torture, as I argued earlier, works under conditions that proclaim a state of exception that moves the practice above and beyond the law.

Torture is, as Elaine Scarry further argues, an attempt to destroy language, meaning, and agency and reduce the victim to bare life. Yet it is more than that: it is a soul murder that attempts to reduce the victim to a being less than human. Torture is designed to induce a state of depravation that attacks more than self-understanding, self-consciousness, and self-representation. It is aimed at destroying the human being's core of dignity. If, as Mbembe claims with Hegel, the human being truly becomes a subject in the struggle and the work though which he or she confronts death,[43] then torture forces upon the victim a confrontation with death that obliterates the agency and thus the "work" of such confrontation.

Moreover, soul murder creates a form of "living death" in which the victim becomes the phantom that haunts his or her own life before the actual death of the body. The victim, in other words, becomes his or her own ghost. This, too, is a form of social death. Mbembe reminds us of the fact that this death-in-life has its roots in slavery and the plantation system. "The slave is . . . kept alive but in a *state of injury*, in a phantom-like world of horrors and intense cruelty and profanity. . . . Slave life, in many ways, is a form of death-in-life."[44] We can see such an exercise in state sovereignty that radicalizes the subjugation of life to the power of death, for example, in the revival and sanction of torture by the U.S. government after September 11. This is what Mbembe calls "necropolitics," which, he claims, "profoundly reconfigure[s] the relations among resistance, sacrifice, and terror."[45] It is part of a larger construction of "*death-worlds*, new and unique forms of social existence in which vast populations are subjected to conditions of life conferring upon them the status of *living dead*."[46]

The Eroticization of Torture's Malignant Intimacy

Under specific conditions, the intimate enmity between the torturer and his victim may assume a malignant, sadomasochistic intimacy. Torturers have always known how to sexualize torture; rape, after all, is the most common and widespread form of torture and soul murder, practiced both within and outside of torture chambers. If the victim internalizes the torturer's sadism, she becomes an unwitting accomplice in the act. Sometimes this violence is eroticized. In eroticized submission, the victim not only enacts a compulsive repetition but also regains an imaginary agency. This dynamic is exposed in Liliana Cavani's 1974 film *The Night Porter*, in which Lucia, a child survivor of the Holocaust, meets Max, her sadistic torturer, years after the liberation. When she solicits him for a voluntary reenactment of their sadomasochistic pact, they fall into the thralls of a deadly repetition compulsion.

The film is set in Vienna in 1957 after the departure of the Soviet occupation troops. The Viennese people are engaged in a collective attempt to repress their memory of the war, fascism, and genocide in a willful return to pseudo-normality. Cavani confesses in the preface to the film that she was impressed by a woman survivor who always spent her summer vacations in Dachau. "It was the victim returning to the scene of the crime," Cavani writes, "Why? One must seek an answer in the unconscious."[47] *The Night Porter* tries to give such an answer. The two main protagonists, Lucia and Max, replay the past in a regressive madness that precipitates their murder, which is, at the same time, a joint suicide. They become embodiments of the complementary damage and oppression resulting from the concentration-camp experience. Both victim and perpetrator have acquired a deadly knowledge of human depravity and evil in the camp. Neither of them can forget and neither of them can live again in the outside world. Unable to return to a basic trust in the social contract, they are nothing but simulacra of normal or real selves. While in their social lives they successfully play their respective roles as night porter and wife of a musician, their psychic life and reality is still that of the camp. This is what drives them back to each other. Teresa de Lauretis writes about Cavani's vision in *The Night Porter*: "It is a harsh, unadorned, cruel view of the depth of one's self."[48] We may add that it is also a view into the abyss of traumatic abjection.

One may describe the psychodrama in *The Night Porter* as a folie à deux that emerges from a repetition compulsion. Yet repetitions are never the same. The crucial difference here lies in the agency of voluntary reenactment. We encounter a paradox at the core of this reenactment: since we know that a repetition compulsion overrides a subject's will, what seems voluntary is so only at the surface. At a deeper level, the deadly pact follows the logic of deferred traumatic action. The belated enactment of the couple's sadomasochistic passion is obscene. The film challenges, even violates the boundaries of figurations of the Holocaust. By actively exposing the psychodynamic of what Kluger calls "Holocaust kitsch,"[49] it confronts us with our morbid fascination with evil, our thrill with violence, or, to use Kluger's term, that "whiff of fantasy" that aggregates around horror stories. Thus exposing our potential complicity, *The Night Porter* violates our sense of a safe boundary between perpetrator and victim or good and evil.

Ariel Dorfman's *Death and the Maiden*, by contrast, exhibits the malignant intimacy between the torturer and his victim in the latter's dynamic exploration of justice and revenge. Dorfman, in exile from Pinochet's dictatorship in Chile, began writing *Death and the Maiden* when Pinochet was still in power, but he was unable to complete the play until Chile once again became a democracy and he was able to return after seventeen years of exile. While Dorfman's play dramatizes the lingering psychic life of torture after the fall of Pinochet's dictatorship, it addresses, as Dorfman states in his afterword, "problems that could be found all over the world, all over the twentieth century, all over the face of humanity through the ages."[50] In *Death and the Maiden*, Paulina, a former political prisoner, by chance meets one of her torturers after the country's return to democracy. Holding him captive in her house, she coerces her husband to perform a privately staged trial in which the torturer is supposed to give a confession. In the process, Paulina tells him that, after her captors let her go, she was unable to return to her pro-military parents.

> Isn't it bizarre, that I should be telling you all this as if you were my confessor, when there are things I've never told Gerardo, or my sister, certainly not my mother. She'd die if she knew what I've really got in my head. Whereas I can tell you exactly what I feel, what I felt when they let me go. That night . . . well, you don't need me to describe what state I was in, you gave me a quite thorough inspection before I was released, didn't you? We're rather cozy here, aren't we, like this? Like two old pensioners sitting on a bench in the sun.[51]

Paulina's story of torture has become largely unspeakable. Like Kluger's uncle, Hans, she can give information and tell facts, but her words remain empty and disconnected. No one will understand unless they have the intimate knowledge of a witness to her abjection. Paradoxically, it is therefore the former perpetrator who knows her better than anyone in her family. Paulina sarcastically invokes and draws on this malignant intimacy as she prepares the stage for her belated enactment of a healing drama of revenge.

Trauma attacks language and memory, but at the same time it retains, as I argued earlier, an entire arsenal of deadly intimate sensorial memories. Seventeen years after her release, Paulina recognizes her torturer in the tone of his voice, his smell, and the texture of his skin. "It's not only the voice I recognize, Gerardo. I also recognize the skin. And the smell. Gerardo. I recognize his skin."[52] Paulina's corporeal memory is entirely consistent with the logic of her regression to catastrophic helplessness during her prolonged torture. Dr. Miranda, in fact, reminds her of his role as sovereign who decides about life and death of his victims by asserting that he took great care of her and made sure she survived. As Miranda's language and her hold on the world was destroyed, she was forcibly returned to mere sensory perception, to a life without agency, rights, or sovereignty. She experienced the world like an infant under attack, struggling for bare survival. And like an infant, she recorded traces of her sensory environment. Her memory would forever be marked by the traces of her torturer's voice and touch and smell. Over a decade later, Paulina now stages an inverse reenactment of the torture scene. This enactment functions as a transformational practice, an exorcism of sorts, designed to expel the mnemonic traces of her malignant intimacy with her torturer. As Gerardo remarks, the encounter with the torturer *is* her therapy.

Dissociation, Psychic Splitting, and Isomorphic Deformation

In *La Douleur*, translated as *The War*, Marguerite Duras vividly describes a torture scene that figures as an instance of a performative externalization of the internal aggressor. *The War* contains a section titled "Albert of the Capitals" that deals with the torture of a former informant to the Gestapo by members of the French Resistance. In a short preface, Duras identifies the story as autobiographical: "Therèse is me. The person who tortures the informer is me. . . . I give you the torturer along with the rest of the texts. Learn to read them properly: they are sacred."[53] How do we read a text about torture as a sacred text? What is this notion of the sacred? Is it because the text takes us to the emotional core of the torturer and her intimate relationship to the victim? Is it because it takes us beyond suffering to the heart of terror?

After the liberation, members of the former Resistance capture an informer. The men ask the informer to undress and decide to let "Therèse," alias Duras, interrogate the captive. "Therèse wonders if it's really necessary to make him undress. Now that he's there, it's no longer urgent. She feels nothing any more, nothing, neither hatred nor impatience. Nothing. The only thing is, it's slow. Time is dead as he undresses. . . . D. has given him to her. She has taken him. She's got him. She wants to sleep. She says to herself, 'I'm asleep.'" And later: "I'm at the cinema" (*The War*, 124–25). What Duras describes here are classic symptoms of dissociation and derealization. The perpetrator splits a part of herself off and leaves the other part exterior to this self in the moral vacuum of the torture chamber. Her "torturer self" faces the victim: "Now he's naked. It's the first time in her life that she's been with a naked man for any other purpose than making love. He's standing, leaning on the chair, his eyes lowered. Waiting" (128). The victim's state of vulnerable nakedness creates a sense of abject intimacy as he occupies, in Thérèse's fantasy, a position that oscillates between that of a helpless child and that of a despondent lover.

Then the men begin to beat the victim. As Thérèse questions him, she experiences a moment of recognition: "True, it's a serious matter: they're torturing someone" (130). Bloods flows; an eye is damaged; the victim is crying, reduced to catastrophic helplessness. "What color was the identity card that got you into the Gestapo?" Thérèse asks. Torture needs a script. Thérèse's script identifies the victim as perpetrator. Again and again the question about the color of the identity card. But as it turns out, the interrogation is not about the extraction of information. The color of the identity card is utterly irrelevant and useless as a piece of information for the torturers. Rather, it is the ritual of asking questions to extract information that is part of an unofficial torture script. Thérèse's question performs the arbitrariness of the signifier—in this case the color of the card—in the script of interrogation. Meanwhile the torture script has taken its own course:

> Whether he dies or survives no longer depends on Thérèse. . . . They hit better and better, more coolly. The more they hit and the more he bleeds, the more it's clear that hitting is necessary, right, just. Images arise out of the blows. Thèrese is invaded, spellbound by images. A man standing against a wall falls. Another. Another. Unendingly.
> (132–133)

This is dissociation, disrupted by the recognition that she is truly part of a torture scene and simultaneously an observation that almost conjures a justification for torture as "necessary, right, just." Thérèse then adds a distancing reflection: "It's like an efficient machine. But where does it come from, man's ability to strike, to get used to it, to do it as if it were a job, a duty?" (134). The recognition is chilling. Duras must remember this is the excuse of prison guards in the concentration camps: It was my job. I just fulfilled my duty. She continues: "He's afraid of dying. But not enough. He still goes on lying. He wants to live. Even lice cling to life" (134). Another chilling recognition: "lice" is what the Nazis called the Jews, using an old colonial technique of dehumanizing labeling.[54]

This is how Duras reflects upon and makes her readers face her own dehumanization during her participation in the informant's torture. Unsettling the boundary between victim and perpetrator sits uncomfortably within our desire to divide the world into good and evil. Duras also makes us face her internalization of the aggressor's dehumanizing sadism: "Now you can't compare him to anything that's alive," she writes. "There's no point in killing him. And there's no longer any point in letting him live" (*The War*, 136): death-in-life, emblem of the tortured victim. Thèrèse insists it's not enough yet continues the interrogation, asks for the color of the identity card, speaks "as if to a child" (139). Duras makes us witness the deadly intimacy of the torturer and her victim. We are made to recognize the process of Duras/Thèrèse becoming perpetrator. This entire dynamic of a slippage between victim and perpetrator is a symptom of complementary oppression and psychic deformation. "He's not even suffering. It's just terror," she realizes (139). Finally the informer breaks and shouts out that the color was green. "'Yes,' says Thèrèse. 'It was green.' As if stating something known for centuries. It's over" (140). It never was about the information. It's over. Thèrèse starts to cry. How long does it take a one-time torturer to do it as a job, a duty? And what has this act done to Thèrèse/Duras? Already this first time, she experienced how easy it is to dissociate from the act of cruelty one is committing and how easy it is to numb oneself to the pain of others. But she also experienced how easy it is to dehumanize the enemy and become caught in the rush toward escalating violence.

Torture induces psychic splitting in both the victim and the torturer. According to the British psychoanalyst Christopher Bollas, the "annihilation of the other occasions a sense of dissociation."[55] Both victim and torturer succumb to dissociation as an extreme form of splitting. The torturer splits off a part self that, identified with anti-life, acts as an entire self. The victim, in turn, dissociates under the impact of intolerable pain and becomes the container for the torturer's identification with anti-life. The splitting off of a hateful or dead core self and its projection into the victim is matched by the victim's internalization of the aggressor. It is the victim who subsequently experiences and lives what should be the aggressor's shame, including the need to split it off and persecute it in her own self. Torture creates its ghostly shadow double after the fact when the victim has internalized the violence, almost like an ego ideal, and sets out to finish the task of the torturer.

This largely unconscious identification with the aggressor explains some of the suicidal tendencies in victims of torture. This dynamic creates a complementary psychic deformation in both torturer and victim. The torturer's mental forces are dominated by a totalitarian belief or ideology that requires the obsessive elimination of doubt, ambiguity, ambivalence, or the polysemy of the symbolic order. It is this freezing of the symbolic order and its polysemy or the foreclosure of doubt that creates a moral vacuum. When, decades after the war, decades of silence, Duras gives us her story of torture, she admonishes us to read her words properly. Does she call them "sacred" because they work against torture's destruction of memory and language and thus open a pathway to the unspeakable? Maybe she hesitates about releasing her story because she has become attached to it like to a traumatic wound and doesn't want to let it go. And this is perhaps why she offers the story to her readers like a sacred gift because externalizing her internal aggressor is a way of letting go.

Destruction of Memory and Language

The defense of subjectivity and psychic space includes a defense of memory and language as the most basic tools in the formation of psychic life. The regression to catastrophic helplessness that torture induces in the victim reactivates modes of experience from before the formation of language, thought, and the symbolic order. Ultimately, it is this radical regression that results in the particular destruction of language that theorists have called traumatic de-semiosis or de-signification. Elaine Scarry writes: "Intense pain is also language-destroying: as the content of one's world disintegrates, so the content of one's language disintegrates."[56] Meaning, thoughts, and words are eliminated. The destruction of language is meant to last beyond the confines of actual torture, rendering torture unspeakable, if not unmemorable. The destruction of language is a second crime. Even though the practice of torture is performed according to an elaborate script, the effects of torture push the limits of representation. The attack on language entails an attack on memory; the victim's catastrophic regression and helplessness prevent her memory of torture from being integrated into the story of the self. If it does not succumb to amnesia, memory remains experiential and corporeal rather than verbal. While torture memories leave a hole in mind and self, the unconscious inscription of torture in the body may, as recent research in the neurosciences shows, permanently alter the processing of danger and pain signals in the brain as well as the hormonal responses to threatening stimuli.[57] This is why traumatic body memory and its effects on neurological and hormonal functioning belong to the lasting effects of torture.

If torture attacks memory and language, it would seem that telling torture helps the process of healing. Telling is an act of reclaiming life and self. Yet there are complicated issues of confession and spectatorship that may create resistance to telling one's story and enforce complicity in secrecy. Moreover, telling torture, as Kluger says, often levels the horror of the victim's mute and wordless suffering. Erasing language, torture is said to hold the victim captive in a space beyond words. Kluger tells of a scene in which she witnesses her mother's torture. Forced to kneel for hours on a sharp wooden log, her mother falls apart, screaming wildly. Kluger writes:

> I stood next to her, helpless, witnessing something indecent: my mother being punished. This scene is perhaps my most vivid and lurid memory of Birkenau. And yet I have never talked about it. I thought, I can't write this down, and planned instead to mention that there are events that are indescribable. Now that I have written it, I see that the words are as common as other words and were no harder to come by.

Yet even this reflection entails a leveling of the horror of both the mother's torture and the daughter's helpless witnessing: "The memory is connected with an overwhelming sense of shame, as if a superego had been dragged into the ditch water of the id," Kluger adds.[58] The only way to write about torture is from within the distance of memory. The pain of torture—physical, psychic, and mental—hides in language. Failing to convey a thick description, the narrative leaves us outside the quality of felt experience even when pain is described. Dwelling on mere facts absorbs torture into the banality of everyday life, which might be even more terrifying.

This is the epistemological challenge a victim faces in writing about torture. Writing torture needs a paradoxical writing about something that defies language but needs acknowledgment, which is needed precisely because torture induces a de-signification or de-semiosis. To put it differently, writing about torture needs to find a way to access the unconscious and thereby touch, in Abraham's words, "the founding silence of any act of signification."[59] To designate such discourse beyond rhetoric, Abraham coins the neologism "anasemia." Despite being, as Abraham says, "antisemantic," anasemia may occur subliminally even in a discourse that operates at the semantic level. What is needed is a discourse that is marked by the imprints of "the structures and psychic movements,"[60] as well as the somatic imprints of trauma.

Abraham asserts that poetry can function in this way as anasemic discourse: "From a purely semantic point of view, psychic representatives, like the symbols of poetry, are mysterious messages from one knows not what to one knows not whom; they reveal their allusiveness only in context, although the 'to what' of the allusion must necessarily stop short of articulation."[61] Duras's text seems to draw some of its effects from an anasemic dimension that alludes to an unspeakable core of trauma. Words and other forms of witnessing, trauma theorists argue, help the victim survive and live with a pain that can never be healed because they "re-signify" and reintegrate an unspeakable experience into the symbolic order. But to do so, Abraham suggests, they need to be words capable of reaching beyond their semantic dimension. Duras's telling of her own act of torture takes on a related challenge: finding words to help the perpetrator face and take responsibility for guilt and shame that may be explained but can never be voiced fully and perhaps never be completely healed. At the same time, Duras's text is perhaps also an appeal to her readers to take the evidence of human proclivity to violence and thus help her restore the humane compassion she had lost in the story she tells.

Poetry as evidence and appeal is also what Judith Butler emphasizes in her reading of the Guantánamo poems written by the prisoners under harshest conditions:

> So what do these poems tell us about vulnerability and survivability? They interrogate the kind of utterance at the limits of grief, humiliation, longing, and rage. The words are carved in cups, written on paper, recorded onto a surface, in an effort to leave a mark, a trace, of a living being—a sign formed by a body, a sign that carries the life of the body. And even when what happens to a body is not survivable, the words survive to say as much. This is also poetry as evidence and as appeal, in which each word is finally meant for another.[62]

Writing thus works in the service of survival, if only as a trace. It counters the "work of death" in a necropolitical environment designed to dehumanize others to the point that they become reduced to an existence of "death-in-life." Yet the living dead will always return.

Torture's Psychic Blowback: Transgenerational Transmission of Trauma

If we think about the history of torture in the context of other histories of dehumanization, such as, for example, slavery and colonialism, torture can also be seen as a way of bringing terror and dehumanization home. I argue that this is even the case when countries "outsource" torture in order to remove it from the reach of the law. A country that sanctions torture—in whichever twisted way—will not be able or willing to confine it to its illegitimate institutions in other countries, if only because torture itself already constitutes an attack on its own constitution.

Ngũgĩ wa Thiong'o called torture a form of state terrorism. In the United States, the recent attempt to relegitimize torture was rationalized as a response to terrorism. However, as many have argued, terrorism itself constituted a form of terror moving "home," albeit in a different sense. In *Blowback*, Chalmers Johnson argues that the emergence of terrorism on a global scale is linked to the "unintended consequences of American empire."[63] The terror inflicted on other countries and peoples in the assertion and expansion of empire "blows back," so to speak, including terrorist attacks at the heart of empire. The so-called war on terror is no longer a war in which the enemy is located elsewhere. In fact, it is almost impossible to "locate" the enemy until after the fact. Yet even though the terrorist must be imagined as a moving target, the figure of the terrorist has become a fixed icon in the cultural imaginary. One could even argue that the torture of prisoners suspected of connections with Al Qaeda is partly designed to constitute the figure of the terrorist. It is the figure that America abjects as radical otherness and sheer evil. As such, the terrorist becomes an almost ideal object of projection, including the projection of internal aggression, both national and personal. This is why the figure of the terrorist can also be used in attempts to rationalize and legitimize increasing infringements on civil and human rights, including the use of torture. Hard to confine to an abjected elsewhere, violence and terror always seem to find ways of blowing back home.

Seen from a different angle, we could also say that a people that allows the torture of enemies will eventually internalize the practice of soul murder and find enemies within its own ranks. On February 9, 2006, the German newspaper *Die Zeit* published an article about the torture of hundreds of thousands of German postwar children in youth homes of the newly founded republic, mostly under the guidance of the Catholic Church. Children were institutionalized in these homes simply because they had difficulties at school or at home, their single mothers were suspected of improper care, or minors were found kissing. In postwar Germany, only 10 percent of families were considered healthy. Holding children from infancy to age twenty-one (the legal age of adulthood at the time), these homes used children primarily as a cheap labor force, imposing long hours of forced labor, including weekends. Extreme forms of punishment amounting to torture included prolonged incarceration in dark isolated cells with bread and water, frequent severe beatings, shaving of the head for girls, systematic humiliation and psychological torture, as well as refusal of both privacy and contact with family and the outside world. From 1949 until 1967, the conservative religious right dominated the political and cultural climate in Germany. Peter Wensierski writes: "Many directors of these homes as well as their educators executed after 1945 a punitive and redemptive pedagogy that was invented at the turn of the century and further developed by the NS-regime."[64]

What we find here could be seen as a form of blowback from fascism in which the terror returns home. This is not to say there was no cruel treatment of children in Germany before. On the contrary, Germany has a strong tradition of harshly authoritarian and cruel childrearing. As Adorno and Horkheimer have convincingly argued, the formation of an authoritarian character helped to forge the culture of obedient German citizens unwilling or unable to question the Nazi regime. The perspective of a "blowback," rather, emphasizes the connections and feedback loops between practices of dehumanization in different societal spheres. Once dehumanization is established as a viable practice, it cannot be contained. Accordingly, torture's malignant attack on life and dignity will create enemies without and within a people that embraces this practice. Once torture is sanctioned it cannot be confined. It will, as I argued earlier, always return home.

Let me end with a few reflections on a new type of torture increasingly prominent in today's global war zones. It occurs during the training of child soldiers, some no more than eight years old. Estimates are that currently there are at least 300,000 children serving as soldiers around the world, possibly many more.[65] Children have always been central figures in contested cultural definitions of the boundaries of the human. Analyzing the increasing recruitment and exploitation of children in war, we cannot ignore how violent political conflicts that rely on children as principal actors historically change the very notion of childhood. Upon their recruitment, many child soldiers—for whom joining the military or a rebel group is often the only mode of survival—undergo the most cruel initiation torture imaginable. They are forced to kill a member or members of their family as proof of both their solidarity with the leader and their callousness and suitability as soldiers. This "initiation torture" is designed not only as a form of soul murder that turns the child into a killing machine but also as a way to sever permanently all ties to the child's family and community. Many of the child soldiers are no longer welcomed back because the community fears that the violence they were forced to commit has permanently marked them.

Currently, the recruitment and torture of child soldiers receives a lot of media attention. Among the growing wave of memoirs of child soldiers and their commodification in a global media culture, the marketing of Ishmael Beah's *A Long Way Gone: Memoirs of a Boy Soldier* at Starbucks and the career of the author, who received an M.F.A. at New York University and is now working for the U.N., is perhaps the most striking example. Within the overarching topic of transgenerational trauma, child soldiers play a crucial role because they are forced to carry not only the psychic legacy of violent histories but also the concrete material and political legacy as well. Child soldiers are coerced to put their bodies and lives on the line for wars handed down to them by the parental generation. Perhaps the most abject torture imaginable, the torture of child soldiers is not confined to their initiation. Perhaps the most insidious aspect of this torture is that the child is forcibly turned into a perpetrator and thereby initiated into the brutalization required to become a vagrant soldier who is forced, again and again, to kill other children. From then on, the entire life of a child soldier becomes a form of extended and cumulative torture. In *A Long Way Gone*, Ishmael Beah describes this type of brutalization:

> We opened fire until the last living being in the other group fell to the ground. We walked toward the dead bodies, giving each other high fives. The group had also consisted of young boys like us, but we didn't care about them. We took their ammunition, sat on their bodies, and started eating the cooked food they had been carrying. All around us, fresh blood leaked from the bullet holes in their bodies.[66]

This description conveys several aspects relevant to understanding what cumulative torture means for the child soldiers. Part of their brutalization consists in the fact that they don't feel tortured in the moment in which they kill the other children. In fact, they rejoice and congratulate one another, just as if they were children playing war. Trauma registers belatedly and after the fact.[67] It will consist, as it did for Beah, in torturing images and flashbacks of a violence not even recognized any longer. The brutalization of these children lies in the fact that they are turned into merciless killers while their psychic life still bears the marks of childhood. Yet they no longer own their lives or, for that matter, their bodies. Upon their recruitment, their military owners brand them like slaves:

> Young boys were immediately recruited, and the initials RUF [Revolutionary United Front] were carved wherever it pleased the rebels, with a hot bayonet. This not only meant that you were scarred for life but that you could never escape from them, because escaping with the carving of the rebels' initials was asking for death, as soldiers would kill you without any questions and militant civilians would do the same.[68]

Branded like slaves and confined in a prison without walls among the rebels, the children live a psychic life of prolonged torture, marked by excruciating headaches, nightmares and flashbacks, and above all the feeling of a slowly progressing psychic death:

> I didn't want to show my friends the pain I felt from my headache. In my mind's eye I would see sparks of flame, flashes of scenes I had wit-

nessed, and the agonizing voices of children and women would come alive in my head. I cried quietly as my head beat like the clapper of a bell.[69]

"How many more times do we have to come to terms with death before we find safety?" he [the author's friend Saidu] asked.

He waited a few minutes, but the three of us didn't say anything. He continued: "Every time people come at us with the intention of killing us, I close my eyes and wait for death. Even though I'm still alive, I feel like each time I accept death, part of me dies. Very soon I will completely die and all that will be left is my empty body walking with you. It will be quieter than I am."[70]

Perhaps the torture inflicted upon child soldiers exceeds the horror of other forms of torture precisely because it erases the boundaries between victim and perpetrator. One could argue that being forced to become a perpetrator does not constitute perpetration in the proper sense of the term. However, this is and is not true. For the child soldier, part of the torture consists in being turned into a perpetrator: "Our innocence had been replaced by fear and we had become monsters. There was nothing we could do about it."[71]

Most of the child soldiers will never be able to return home, even after being rescued from their military or rebel unit. Many families will not take their children back because they have committed war crimes and the families fear their brutalization. Hardly any of them will find a way to use writing to work through the war trauma and find a career like Ishmael Beah, who is, after all, being commodified like a poster-child soldier. Most will live with wounds that will never heal completely. Even though groups have been founded that work toward healing the social wounds between child soldiers and the villages they attacked, this is only a first step and not enough to heal the psychic wounds.[72] But it is a step nonetheless, and many child soldiers, like other torture victims, can reclaim a life for themselves. Unless they find a way to work through the trauma, however, their past will remain a haunting legacy passed on to the next generation.

As Ngũgĩ wa Thiong'o reminds us, torture does not end with the victim's release. After his release as a political prisoner, Ngũgĩ himself was forced into twenty-two years of exile. Only in 2004, after the election of a new Kenyan government, was he able to return to his home country. Accompanied by his family, he received an overwhelming welcome. One day, however, four armed men attacked him in his hotel, held him at gunpoint, burned his face with cigarettes, and raped and stabbed his wife, Njeeri, in front of him. The person who orchestrated the crime, according to Ngũgĩ, was a distant relative. It is well known in Kenya that the previous regime routinely hires and pays high prizes to family members for carrying out assaults against political dissidents. The psychic pain of betrayal by family becomes part of the torture. If the worst misery is the one imposed by others with malicious intent, the pain is even worse when these others are your kin. Once torture is sanctioned, it cannot be confined. It kills the self, the family, the community, the country. In essence, it attacks not only the victim's but also the perpetrator's hold on life. Fighting against torture and defying the attacks on language and memory with words is a way to reclaim one's life, even if it means having to live with an open wound. Every instance of fighting for peace, justice, and dignity is a victory over the perpetrator. Every creative act, every moment of joy, is a victory even as we learn to live again with our open or hidden wounds.

> I will know the ecstasy
> and the pain
> of freedom.
> I will be ordinary again.
> Yes, ordinary,
> that terrifying condition,
> where all is possibility,
> where the present exists and must be faced.[73]

Notes

1. Introduction

1. See Diana Fuss, *Identification Papers* (New York: Routledge Press, 1995), 1–19.

2. Ruth Kluger, *Still Alive: A Holocaust Girlhood Remembered* (New York: The Feminist Press, 2001), 80.

3. Ishmael Beah, *A Long Way Gone: Memoirs of a Boy Soldier* (New York: Farrar, Straus and Giroux, 2008), 52.

4. See W. R. Bion, "Attacks on Linking," in *Second Thoughts: Selected Papers on Psychoanalysis* (1967; London: Karnac, 2005), 93–109. See also Mary Jacobus, "The Pain in the Patient's Knee," *Diacritics* 28, no. 4 (1998): 99–110.

5. Beah, *A Long Way Gone*, 103.

6. I need to emphasize that my specific reflections on postwar Germany draw exclusively on my own experiences of growing up in West Germany under French occupation. The difference between dealing with the legacies of the Holocaust in West and East Germany, then under Russian occupation, are enormous and cannot be treated here. They would have to be the object of a different comparative study. I am grateful for many discussions with Claudia Sadowski-Smith and hope for a future collaboration on this topic.

7. Jacques Derrida, "Fors," trans. Barbara Johnson, *Georgia Review* 31 (1977): 75.

8. Ibid., 78.

9. Ibid., 99.

10. Sabine Reichel, *What Did You Do in the War, Daddy?* (New York: Hill and Wang, 1989), 9.

11. See Wendy Brown, *States of Injury: Power and Freedom in Late Modernity* (Princeton, N.J.: Princeton University Press, 1995); Lauren Berlant, "The Face of America and the State of Emergency," in *Popular Culture: A Reader*, ed. Raiford Guins and Omayra Zaragoza Cruz (London: Sage Press, 2005), 309–23; and Mark Seltzer, "Wound Culture: Trauma in the Pathological Public Sphere," *October* 80 (Spring 1997): 3–26.

12. Shoshana Felman and Dori Laub, *Testimony: Crises of Witnessing in Literature, Psychoanalysis, and History* (New York: Routledge Press, 1992), xx.

13. I use the concept of "unthought knowledge" as developed by Christopher Bollas in *The Shadow of the Object: Psychoanalysis of the Unthought Known* (New York: Columbia University Press, 1988). The term is further elaborated for literary and art objects in my essays, "Words and Moods: The Transference of Literary Knowledge," *SubStance* 26, no. 3 (1997): 107–27, and "Cultural Texts and Endopsychic Scripts," *SubStance* 30, nos. 1 and 2 (2001): 160–76.

14. For further elaboration of the concept of transformational literary and artistic objects see Schwab, "Words and Moods" and "Endopsychic Scripts."

15. See Renate Lachmann, *Memory and Literature: Intertextuality in Russian Modernism*, trans. Anthony Wall (Minneapolis: University of Minnesota Press, 1997), and Jan Assmann, "Kollektives Gedächtnis und kulturelle Identität," in *Kultur und Gedächtnis*, ed. Jan Assmann and Tonio Hoelscher (Frankfurt: Suhrkamp, 1988), 9–19.

16. See Aleida Assmann, *Erinnerungsräume: Formen und Wandlungen des kulturellen Gedächtnisses* (Munich: Beck, 1999); Aleida Assmann and Ute Frevert, *Geschichtsvergessenheit — Geschichtsversessenheit: Vom Umgang mit der Deutschen Vergangenheit Nach 1945* (Stuttgart: Deutsche Verlags-Anstalt 1999); Aleida Assmann, *Der Lange Schatten der Vergangenheit: Erinnerungskultur und Geschichtspolitik* (Munich: Beck, 2006).

17. Dominick LaCapra, "Representing the Holocaust," in *Probing the Limits of Representation: Nazism and the "Final Solution,"* ed. Saul Friedlander (Cambridge, Mass.: Harvard University Press, 1992), 110.

18. Ibid., 110.

19. Ibid., 125.

20. Recent debates on the inclusion of the personal in writings about violent histories have largely focused on the "authority of experience." The perspective of transference shifts the debate in a different and, I think, more pertinent direction. See Gayatri Chakravorty Spivak, "Terror: A Speech After 9-11," *boundary* 2 31, no. 2 (2004): 81–111.

21. LaCapra, "Representing the Holocaust," 125.

22. Ibid., 122.

23. Eric L. Santner, "History Beyond the Pleasure Principle," in *Probing the Limits of Representation: Nazism and the "Final Solution,"* ed. Saul Friedlander (Cambridge: Harvard University Press, 1992), 144.

24. Ibid., 145.

25. Ibid., 150.

26. Ibid., 153.

27. Ibid., 151.

28. Alexander Mitscherlich and Margarete Mitscherlich, *The Inability to Mourn: Principles of Collective Behavior*, trans. Beverley R. Placzek (New York: Grove Press, 1975).

29. Karl Jaspers, *The Question of German Guilt*, trans. E. B. Ashton (New York: Dial Press, 1947).

30. Jürgen Habermas, "Concerning the Public Use of History," trans. Jeremy Leaman, *New German Critique*, no. 44 (1988): 44.

31. Mitscherlich and Mitscherlich, *The Inability to Mourn*, xviii.

32. Marianne Hirsch, *Family Frames: Photography, Narrative, and Postmemory* (Cambridge, Mass.: Harvard University Press, 1997).

33. Ibid., 12.

34. Ibid., 13.

35. Ibid., 22.

36. Ibid., 34.

37. Naomi Mandel, *Against the Unspeakable: Complicity, the Holocaust, and Slavery in America* (Charlottesville: University of Virginia Press, 2006), 116.

38. Michael G. Levine, "Necessary Stains: Spiegelman's *Maus* and the Bleeding of History," *American Imago* 59, no. 3 (2002): 338.

39. Geoffrey Hartman, "The Longest Shadow," in *Testimony: Contemporary Writers Make the Holocaust Personal*, ed. David Rosenberg (New York: Times Books, 1989), 437.

40. Shoshana Felman, *The Juridical Unconscious: Trials and Traumas in the Twentieth Century* (Cambridge, Mass.: Harvard University Press, 2002), 153.

41. Amy Hungerford, *The Holocaust of Texts: Genocide, Literature, and Personification* (Chicago: University of Chicago Press, 2003), 73–74.

42. Ibid., 157.

43. This introduction is not the place to go into a more detailed discussion of the rhetorical functions of prosopopoeia and the debates that have linked this figure to a politics and poetics of mourning, except to mention the extensive work of Hillis Miller (from *The Ethics of Reading: Kant, De Man, Eliot, Trollope, James, Benjamin* [New York: Columbia University Press, 1989] to *Versions of Pygmalion* [Cambridge, Mass.: Harvard University Press, 1990]) on the topic, who has discussed prosopopoeia as the figure of reading itself.

44. Hungerford, *The Holocaust of Texts*, 155.

45. Ibid., 156.

46. Ibid., 156.

47. Ibid., 73.

48. Ibid., 153.

49. Ruth Leys, *Trauma: A Genealogy* (Chicago: University of Chicago Press, 2000), 285. For Leys, the notion that one can inherit a trauma that one experiences only secondhand implies a conflation of boundaries between history and memory as well as the individual victim and the group to which he or she belongs. "The group is thus imagined as having the same psychology as the individual, so that history itself can be conceptualized in traumatic terms." Leys traces the idea of transgenerational trauma to Freud's interest in Lamarck's theory of inheritance of acquired characteristics. This move, however, all but ignores the fact that none of the theories of transgenerational trauma argues that children born in the wake of a major traumatic history literally (and mysteriously) inherit some kind of substance. Rather, the claim is that they inherit the trauma through the effects it has on their parents' behavior or even body language. They become witnesses not of the original trauma but of the concrete traces it has left on the victims, such as, for example, expressions of unremitting grief, depression, uncontrollable rages, silences, and fugue states. They may also inherit trauma secondhand via an acquired knowledge of atrocities of such proportions that it shakes the foundations of their belief and trust in humanity and a humane world.

50. Gary Weissman, *Fantasies of Witnessing: Postwar Efforts to Experience the Holocaust* (Ithaca, N.Y.: Cornell University Press, 2004), 22.

51. Ibid., 9.

52. Elie Wiesel, quoted in ibid., 16.

53. Weissman, *Fantasies of Witnessing*, 7.

54. See Veena Das, *Life and Words: Violence and the Descent Into the Ordinary* (Berkeley: University of California Press, 2007).

55. For an extended discussion of the transitional space of literature and narrative as a transformational object see my earlier work: *Subjects Without Selves: Transitional Texts in Modern Fiction* (Cambridge, Mass.: Harvard University Press, 1994); *The Mirror and the Killer-Queen: Otherness in Literary Language* (Bloomington: Indiana University Press, 1996); "Words and Moods"; and "Cultural Texts and Endopsychic Scripts."

56. Charlotte Delbo, quoted in Weissman, *Fantasies of Witnessing*, 113.

57. In a similar vein, the genocide of the indigenous peoples of the United States has been worked through in new ways in recent decades, which has led to a vibrant revival of indigenous cultures and languages. This is not to deny that there are indigenous peoples that live their lives in "disassociation" from their genocidal legacy. Rather, I argue that the disassociation may operate at a level of daily lives and practices, while the working-through and integration may hap-

pen in communal spaces of commemoration, storytelling, and the continuance of traditional cultural practices.

58. Peter Novick, *The Holocaust in American Life* (Boston: Houghton Mifflin, 1999), 7. In this context, Novick asserts that he is not concerned with the centrality of the Holocaust in Germany, Israel, and other European countries where the preoccupation with its legacy seems necessary.

59. One could argue that, merged with the memory of the Holocaust, Israel becomes another common denominator.

60. Novick, *The Holocaust in American Life*, 9.

61. Ibid., 15.

62. While Novick's argument against Jewish exceptionalism is well taken, it should not lead to the silencing of the Holocaust in American life. Rather, it may productively further the debates in two directions: first, toward linking the Holocaust with other histories of violence and, second, toward increasing awareness about the inevitably transferential relationship to histories of violence and their immense vulnerability to commodification. What Adorno said about the "freezing of memory in the commodity form" also affects the narrative fetishization and institutionalization of painful memories of the Holocaust and other historical violence. In *Twilight Memories: Marking Time in a Culture of Amnesia* (New York: Routledge, 1995), Andreas Huyssen makes an intriguing link between this freezing of memory in the commodity form and a postmodern culture of amnesia, arguing that a boom of memory and trauma culture can nonetheless buy into and help to sustain a culture of amnesia.

63. Andreas Huyssen, "Transnationale Verwertungen von Holocaust und Kolonialismus," unpublished manuscript, 11.

64. Michael Rothberg, *Multidirectional Memory: Remembering the Holocaust in the Age of Decolonization* (Stanford, Calif.: Stanford University Press, 2009), 13.

65. Nicolas Abraham and Maria Torok, *The Shell and the Kernel: Renewals of Psychoanalysis*, vol. 1, trans. Nicholas T. Rand (Chicago: University of Chicago Press, 1994), 172.

66. Angelika Bammer, *Displacements: Cultural Identities in Question*. Bloomington: Indiana University Press, 1994.

67. Erin McGlothlin, *Second Generation Holocaust Literature: Legacies of Survival and Perpetration* (Rochester, N.Y.: Camden House, 2006), 16.

68. Ibid., 9.

69. Eric L. Santner, *Stranded Objects: Mourning, Memory, and Film in Postwar Germany* (Ithaca, N.Y.: Cornell University Press, 1990), p. 35.

70. Dan Diner, "Negative Symbiosis: Germans and Jews After Auschwitz," in *Reworking the Past: Hitler, the Holocaust, and the Historian's Debate*, ed. Peter Baldwin (Boston: Beacon Press, 1990), 185.

71. Eva Hoffman quoted in McGlothin, *Second Generation Holocaust Literature*, 32.

72. Ibid., 230.

73. Sigrid Weigel, "Generation as a Symbolic Form: On the Genealogical Discourse of Memory Since 1945," *The Germanic Review* 77, no. 4 (2002): 269.

74. McGlothlin, *Second Generation Holocaust Literature*, 229.

75. Ibid., 24.

76. Marianne Hirsch, "Surviving Images: Holocaust Photographs and the Work of Postmemory," *The Yale Journal of Criticism* 14, no. 1 (2001): 12.

77. Vamik Volkan, "Traumatized Societies and Psychological Care: Expanding the Concept of Preventative Medicine," *Mind and Human Interaction* 11, no. 3 (2000): 186.

78. Even the growing body of work on reconciliation movements, transitional justice, redress, and reparation rarely asks how transgenerational legacies and the transferential dynamic they impose inevitably limit and shape these movements. For me, the most important exception has been the pathbreaking work of Dan Bar-On. He worked as an Israeli psychiatrist with groups of victims and perpetrators, including Israelis and Germans, as well as Israelis and Palestinians. I will repeatedly return to Bar-On's work in *Haunting Legacies*. His books *Legacy of Silence: Encounters with Children of the Third Reich* (Cambridge, Mass.: Harvard University, 1989), and *Tell Your Life-Story: Creating Dialogue Among Jews and Germans, Israelis and Palestinians* (Budapest: Central European University Press, 2006), leave their traces on my writing, even beyond the instances where I directly discuss them.

79. See Kelly Oliver, *The Colonization of Psychic Space: A Psychoanalytic Social Theory of Oppression* (Minneapolis: University of Minnesota Press, 2004). I use Kelly Oliver's term in order to link trauma theory with Oliver's psychoanalytic social theory of oppression.

80. See Ngũgĩ wa Thiong'o, *Decolonizing the Mind: The Politics of Language in African Literature* (London: James Currey Press, 1986). This book has shaped my thinking throughout. In addition to Ngũgĩ's focus on mind and language, I want to highlight the decolonization of psychic space and, in a sense, the decolonization of the unconscious.

81. Rothberg, *Multidirectional Memory*, 11.

82. Ibid., 22.

83. Ibid., 25.

84. Ibid., 11.

85. Arjun Appadurai, *Modernity at Large: Cultural Dimensions of Globalization* (Minneapolis: University of Minnesota Press, 1996).

86. Huyssen, "Transnationale Verwertungen von Holocaust und Kolonialismus," 5.

87. Rothberg, *Multidirectional Memory*, 18.

88. Judith Butler, *Frames of War: When Is Life Grievable?* (London: Verso Press, 2009), 31.

89. Ibid., 52.

90. Ibid., 32, 52.

91. Ibid., 63.

92. Ibid., 75.

93. See Hannah Arendt, *The Origins of Totalitarianism* (New York: Harcourt, 1968), 186–97.

94. I use the term "transitional object" as it has been developed by Christopher Bollas and elaborated in my own theory of literature as a transformational object. See Schwab, "Cultural Texts and Endopsychic Scripts."

95. Even though Karl Jaspers introduced the notion of "collective responsibility" in Germany, the debates in Germany have to this day largely focused on "collective guilt" (*Kollektivschuld*).

96. Barack Obama, *Dreams of My Father: A Story of Race and Inheritance* (New York: Random House, 2004), 76.

97. In my chapter I will exclusively focus on Grimbert's book rather than including a reading of Claude Miller's film, *A Secret*, which is based on Grimbert's novel and was released in 2007. The film does not add anything specific to the topic of replacement children, and Grimbert's text allows for a more detailed reading than the film of the use of cryptography as well as the role of the archive in reconstructing silenced histories.

98. Michael Wessells, *Child Soldiers: From Violence to Protection* (Cambridge, Mass.: Harvard University Press, 2009), cover copy.

99. Nancy Scheper-Hughes and Carolyn Sargent, eds., *Small Wars: The Cultural Politics of Childhood* (Berkeley: University of California Press, 1999), 3.

2. Writing Against Memory and Forgetting

1. Samuel Beckett, "The End," in *Samuel Beckett: The Complete Short Prose*, ed. S. E. Gontarski (New York: Grove Press, 1995), 99.

2. Serge Leclaire, *A Child Is Being Killed: On Primary Narcissism and the Death Drive*, trans. Marie-Claude Hays (Stanford, Calif.: Stanford University Press, 1998), 53.

3. While Freud uses the term "*Schicksalsneurose*" primarily to describe the effects of an individual's "repetition compulsion," Nicholas Abraham and Maria Torok's work suggests that repetition compulsions may also be unconsciously transferred across generations. See Abraham and Torok, *The Shell and the Kernel: Renewals of Psychoanalysis*, vol. 1, trans. Nicholas T. Rand (Chicago: University of Chicago Press, 1994).

4. See Alexander Mitscherlich and Margarete Mitscherlich, *The Inability to Mourn: Principles of Collective Behavior*, trans. Beverley R. Placzek (New York: Grove Press, 1975).

5. Hannah Arendt, *The Origins of Totalitarianism* (New York: Harcourt Press, 1968), 186. Subsequent references are cited parenthetically in the text.

6. Aimé Césaire, *Discourse on Colonialism*, trans. Joan Pinkham (New York: Monthly Review Press, 2000), 36. Subsequent references are cited parenthetically in the text.

7. Ashis Nandy, *The Intimate Enemy: Loss and Recovery of Self Under Colonialism* (Oxford: Oxford University Press, 1983), 31.

8. There is not the time here to comment on the particular anthropomorphism and speciesism that Césaire takes over from the colonizer in the very rhetoric of "treating . . . like an animal" and "transform[ing] into an animal." Animals do not treat one another with this "superfluous cruelty," which Adi Ophir defines as the signature of evil. See Adi Ophir, *The Order of Evils: Toward an Ontology of Morals*, trans. Rela Mazali and Havi Carel (New York: Zone Books, 2005), 14. Animals are not known to have committed genocide, mass murder, or willful torture. This lapse is all the more astonishing as shortly after this passage we find another one in which Césaire describes colonization as the disruption of the natural and viable indigenous economies adapted to the indigenous population; economies, in other words, in which the relationship to animals forms an integral part.

9. W. G. Sebald, *Austerlitz*, trans. Anthea Bell (New York: Modern Library, 2001), 139–40.

10. For a discussion of internal focalization, see Shlomith Rimmon-Kenan, *Narrative Fiction: Contemporary Poetics* (London: Routledge, 2002), 72–86.

11. Sebald, *Austerlitz*, 179.

12. For a more detailed discussion of this subliminal somatic and existential memory, see Gabriele Schwab, "Words and Moods: The Transference of Literary Knowledge," *SubStance* 26, no. 3 (1997): 107–27, and "Cultural Texts and Endopsychic Scripts," *SubStance* 30, nos. 1 and 2 (2001): 160–76.

13. Simon J. Ortiz, *from Sand Creek* (Tucson: University of Arizona Press, 1981), 47.

14. Abraham and Torok, *The Shell and the Kernel*, 165.

15. Toni Morrison, *Beloved* (New York: Alfred A. Knopf, 1987), 274–75.

16. William Heyen, *Crazy Horse in Stillness: Poems* (New York: BOA Editions, 1996), 254–55.

17. Quoted in Dee Brown, *Bury My Heart at Wounded Knee: An Indian History of the American West* (New York: Holt, Rinehart and Winston, 1970), 442.

18. Ortiz, *from Sand Creek*, 43.

19. See Abraham and Torok, *The Shell and the Kernel*, 152–53. The story of the Wolf Man is one of Freud's famous case studies in which he further develops his concepts of anal eroticism and the castration complex. The name refers to the patient's dream with wolves in a tree, resulting in a wolf phobia. The case is particularly relevant for cryptic writing or cryptonymy because the associations of the Wolf Man often draw on his different languages—German,

English, Russian, Latin—to create condensed new words or cryptonyms. See Freud, "From the History of an Infantile Neurosis" in *The Standard Edition of the Complete Psychological Works of Sigmund Freud*, ed. James Strachey, 17:7–12 (London: Hogarth, 1953–1974).

20. Abraham and Torok, *The Shell and the Kernel*, 7.

21. Ibid.

22. In this respect there are certain affinities to the project developed by Alfred Lorenzer in *Sprachzerstörung und Rekonstruktion* (Frankfurt: Suhrkamp, 1973). Lorenzer defines the psychoanalytic cure as a resymbolization of language after the destruction of its symbolic function and the reduction of meaning to what he calls a "cliché."

23. Abraham and Torok, *The Shell and the Kernel*, 8.

24. Ibid., 135. See also Rand's editor's notes on pages 18 and 100.

25. Ibid., 168.

26. Ibid., 174.

27. Ibid., 174–75.

28. Ibid., 176.

29. Ibid., 105.

30. Ashraf H. Rushdy, *Remembering Generations: Race and Family in Contemporary African American Fiction* (Chapel Hill: University of North Carolina Press, 2001), 2.

31. Dominick LaCapra, *Writing History, Writing Trauma* (Baltimore, Md.: Johns Hopkins University Press, 2001), 215.

32. Warren Motte, "Reading Georges Perec," *Context: A Forum for Literary Arts and Culture*, online edition no. 11 (2002): http://www.centerforbookculture .org/context/no11/Motte.html.

33. Ibid.

34. Georges Perec, *W, or the Memory of Childhood*, trans. David Bellos (Boston: David R. Godine, 1988), 1. Subsequent references are cited parenthetically in the text.

35. Significantly, Perec published his childhood memoirs the year after finishing his psychoanalysis.

36. Derrida, "Fors," trans. Barbara Johnson, *Georgia Review* 31 (1977): 116.

37. Sigmund Freud, "Screen Memories," in *The Standard Edition of the Complete Psychological Works of Sigmund Freud*, ed. James Strachey (London: Hogarth Press, 1957), 3:299–322.

38. Christopher Bollas, *The Shadow of the Object: Psychoanalysis of the Unthought Known* (New York: Columbia University Press, 1987), 4.

39. Derrida, "Fors," 111.

40. Marguerite Duras, *The War: A Memoir*, trans. Barbara Bray (New York: Pantheon, 1986), 4.

41. Samuel Beckett, *The Lost Ones* (New York: Grove Press, 1972), 18.

42. Duras, *The War*, 7, my translation of the French original: "La douleur a besoin de place" in Marguerite Duras, *La Douleur* (Paris: P.O.L., 1985), 14. While the English translation uses the term "room," I prefer to translate it as "space."

43. Leclaire, *A Child is Being Killed*, 83.

3. Haunting Legacies: Trauma in Children of Perpetrators

1. Sabine Reichel, *What Did You Do In the War, Daddy?* (New York: Hill and Wang, 1989), 4.

2. "*Juden* sind in Tiengen nicht erwünscht. In Tiengen sieht man Fremde gern, / Doch der Jude bleibe fern. / Denn merk Dir Jude, was dich auch treibt, / Daß Tiengen Deutsch war, ist und bleibt."

3. Roy Harvey Pearce, *Savagism and Civilization* (Berkely: University of California Press, 1953).

4. Giorgio Agamben, *Homo Sacer: Sovereign Power and Bare Life*, trans. Daniel Heller-Roazen (Stanford, Calif.: Stanford University Press, 1998), 166 80.

5. See Frantz Fanon, *The Wretched of the Earth* (New York: Grove Press, 2004), 156. In some colonial contexts, the introduction of Western literature is even more complicated. For Native Americans forced to attend boarding schools, for example, Western literature was not used as a reformatory device as it was in other contexts. As Leslie Silko notes, the U.S. government was "not interested in teaching us the canon of Western classics . . . [like] Shakespeare," which had the interesting effect of "encouraging [Native people] to maintain [their] own narratives" (Leslie Marmon Silko, *Yellow Woman and a Beauty of the Spirit: Essays on Native American Life Today* [New York: Simon & Schuster, 1996], 57). This is one of the many contradictions of colonialism.

6. Nicolas Abraham and Maria Torok, *The Shell and the Kernel: The Renewals of Psychoanalysis*, vol. 1, trans. Nicholas T. Rand (Chicago: University of Chicago Press, 1994), "Introduction" and 166.

7. Ibid., part 5, "Secrets and Posterity: The Theory of the Transgenerational Phantom," editor's note, 166.

8. Ibid., 167.

9. Ibid., 114.

10. Ibid., 176.

11. Ashis Nandy, *The Intimate Enemy: Loss and Recovery of Self Under Colonialism* (Oxford: Oxford University Press, 1983), 30.

12. Nandy, *The Intimate Enemy*, 31.

13. Reichel, *What Did You Do in the War, Daddy?*, 190–91.

4. Identity Trouble: Guilt, Shame, and Idealization

1. Frantz Fanon, *Black Skin, White Masks*, trans. Charles Lam Markmann (New York: Grove Press, 1967), 191.

2. Jean-Paul Sartre, "Flaubert," in *Flaubert: A Collection of Critical Essays*, ed. Raymond Giraud (Englewood Cliffs, N.J.: Prentice Hall Press, 1964), 13–20.

3. Sabine Reichel, *What Did You Do in the War, Daddy?* (New York: Hill and Wang, 1989), 7.

4. Ibid., 4.

5. Ursula Duba, *Tales from a Child of the Enemy* (New York: Penguin Books, 1995), 151–53.

6. Gregory Rodriguez, "Ich bin ein Obaman," *LA Times*, July 28, 2008.

7. Michael M. J. Fischer, "Ethnicity and the Arts of Memory," in *Writing Culture: The Poetics and Politics of Ethnography*, ed. James Clifford and George E. Marcus (Berkeley: University of California Press, 1986), 201.

8. Achille Mbembe, *On the Postcolony*, trans. A. M. Berrett, Janet Roitman, Murray Last, and Steven Rendall (Berkeley: University of California Press, 2001), 104.

9. Fanon, *Black Skin, White Masks*, 225.

10. Ibid., 175.

11. Finally, I wanted to know how to direct and avoid feelings we were not supposed to have. The latter was mainly an outgrowth of the fateful combination of Christian—in my case Catholic—and Prussian authoritarianism that determined so much of my generation's upbringing. Preachers, teachers, and parents neatly divided appropriate emotion from inappropriate emotion. Feelings and their public display were subject to rigid censorship, with inappropriate feelings, especially anger, becoming a source of secretly felt shame. Worse than being ashamed of an act of transgression, the shame about inappropriate feelings addressed the core of one's self and generated, along with a lingering hidden shame, the concomitant lack of self-esteem.

12. See Theodor Adorno, Else Frenkel-Brunswik, Daniel Levinson, and Nevitt Sanford, *The Authoritarian Personality* (New York: Harper and Row, 1950).

13. Reichel, *What Did You Do in the War, Daddy?*, 184.

14. Klein essentializes such infantile emotions as innate and ubiquitous whereas a perspective anchored in social constructivism would allow one to see persecutory fantasies as an effect of the frustrations and damages stemming from the child's material and social environment. See Melanie Klein, "A Contribution to the Psychogenesis of Manic-Depressive States" (1935), in *Love, Guilt, and Reparation and Other Works, 1921–1945* (New York: Delacorte Press, 1975), 262–89.

15. Reichel, *What Did You Do in the War, Daddy?*, 188.

16. What if we read public policies and the display of public feelings about histories of violence in different nations as symptoms of different cultural attitudes, and therefore as differences in the formation of national identities? Think, for example, of the different ways in which Germany, South Africa, Australia, and the United States deal with their histories of colonialism, racism, and the violence associated with them. Germany places the emphasis on the judicial system and public expression of guilt and material reparations to victims, with only a superficial effort to integrate German-Jewish relationships, as well as relationships to other victims such as political refugees and certain immigrant populations. South Africa places the emphasis on relations between perpetrators and victims through confession and an often all too fast and superficial reconciliation. Australia goes out of its way to take public responsibility for its violence against the aboriginal people, and it cultivates and even legislates the display of public feelings of remorse. Today no public event can take place in Australia without acknowledging the violence against aboriginal people and extending an expression of sorrow and the hope for a more peaceful coexistence with the original owners of the stolen land in the future. Superficial as these rhetorically coded gestures may seem, they at least are gestures of acknowledgment. The United States is the only country that displays a stunning lack of public guilt, shame, and acknowledgment of its multiple histories of perpetration. Rather, a triumphalist tone continues to pervade narratives about America's early colonial invasion of the continent and genocide of indigenous people, as well as the more recent invasions and wars with other countries from South Korea to Vietnam, Afghanistan, and Iraq. Vietnam is so far the only war that has generated a broad national debate, mainly because of the civil rights movement and the student revolution that generated nationwide massive protests.

17. Kelly Oliver, *The Colonization of Psychic Space: A Psychoanalytic Social Theory of Oppression* (Minneapolis: University of Minnesota Press, 2004), xviii–xix.

18. For Volkan's concept of "deposit representations," see Vamik D. Volkan, "Traumatized Societies and Psychological Care: Expanding the Concept of Preventative Medicine," *Mind and Human Interaction* 11, no. 3 (2000): 177–94.

19. Oliver, *The Colonization of Psychic Space*, 195–200.

20. We would have to consider here that Derrida calls for the "forgiving of the unforgivable." For lack of space this discussion will have to remain unaddressed here.

21. Barack Obama, "A More Perfect Union," available online at: http://my .barackobama.com/page/content/hisownwords.

22. Fanon, *Black Skin, White Masks*, 229.

23. Politics that focus on mourning and reparation as part of a national staging of public feelings—such as the Truth and Reconciliation Commis-

sion in South Africa or the Politics of Public Acknowledgement and Apology for Past Violence in Australia—will remain shallow unless they become embedded in new modes of communication and engagement across cultural, ethnic, national, and religious divides. None of them suffices unless it addresses the continued economic, environmental, and psychological racism in today's global world.

24. Robert Meister, "After Evil," unpublished manuscript.

25. Dan Bar-On, *Tell Your Life-Story: Creating Dialogue Among Jews and Germans, Israelis and Palestinians* (Budapest: Central European University Press, 2006), 26.

26. Ibid., 51.

27. Ibid., 37.

28. Ashis Nandy, *The Intimate Enemy: Loss and Recovery of Self Under Colonialism* (Oxford: Oxford University Press, 1983), 30.

29. Ibid., 30.

30. Reichel, *What Did You Do in the War, Daddy?*, 191.

31. Quoted from memory of a personal conversation in the early nineties.

32. Edward Said, "Secular Criticism," in *The World, the Text, and the Critic* (Cambridge, Mass.: Harvard University Press, 1983), 18.

33. Michael M. J. Fischer, "Ethnicity as Text and Model," in *Anthropology as Cultural Critique: An Experimental Moment in the Human Sciences*, by George E. Marcus and Michael M. J. Fischer (Chicago: University of Chicago Press, 1986), 173.

34. Sara Ahmed, *The Cultural Politics of Emotion* (New York: Routledge, 2004), 45.

35. Ibid., 46.

36. Quoted in ibid., 57. The original quotation from Fanon can be found in *Black Skin, White Masks*, 109.

37. Ahmed, *The Cultural Politics of Emotion*, 57.

38. Ibid., 63, 66.

39. Lauren Berlant, "The Face of America and the State of Emergency," in *Popular Culture: A Reader*, ed. Raiford Guins and Omayra Zaragoza Cruz (London: Sage Press, 2005), 309–10. See also Mark Seltzer, "Wound Culture: Trauma in the Pathological Public Sphere," *October* 80 (Spring 1997): 3–26.

40. Ahmed, *The Cultural Politics of Emotion*, 58.

41. Bar-On, *Tell Your Life-Story*, 46.

42. Ibid., 51.

43. See a detailed discussion in ibid., 26.

44. See also Judith Butler's recent insistence on the urgency of cultural translation in Judith Butler, *Precarious Life: The Powers of Mourning and Violence* (London: Verso Press, 2004), 90.

45. Fanon, *Black Skin, White Masks*, 190.

5. Replacement Children: The Transgenerational Transmission of Traumatic Loss

1. For a more detailed analysis of transformational objects, see Christopher Bollas, *The Shadow of the Object: Psychoanalysis of the Unthought Known* (New York: Columbia University Press, 1987), 13–29. See also Gabriele Schwab, "Words and Moods: The Transference of Literary Knowledge," *SubStance* 26, no. 3 (1997): 107–27, and "Cultural Texts and Endopsychic Scripts," *SubStance* 30, nos. 1 and 2 (2001): 160–76.

2. Art Spiegelman, *Maus II: A Survivor's Tale: And Here My Troubles Began* (New York: Pantheon, 1991), 15–16.

3. Spiegelman, *Mauss II*, 136.

4. Jacques Derrida, *Of Grammatology*, trans. Gayatri Chakravorty Spivak (Baltimore, Md.: Johns Hopkins University Press, 1974), 145.

5. I owe these reflections to Ruth Ginsburg, who pointed out to me that the replacement child as a chronotope should be part of my theoretical reflections on trauma, especially since trauma studies has historically tended to undervalue the importance of space in the experience of trauma. See also Ruth Ginsberg, "Ida Fink's Scraps and Traces: Forms of Space and the Chronotrope of Trauma Narratives," *Partial Answers: Journal of Literature and the History of Ideas* 4, no. 2 (June 2006): 205–18.

6. At the same time, this replacement child is also an instance of psychic displacement in the psychoanalytic sense. The German term *"Verschiebung"* illustrates more clearly than its English equivalent—"displacement"—that psychic displacement is itself a chronotope since *Verschiebung* means both to dis-place and to defer in time. Both play a crucial role in the space and time of mourning.

7. Historically, trauma studies has tended to overvalue time at the expense of space. Abraham and Torok's concept of the crypt, which is itself a chronotope, introduces the first influential shift in this tendency. See *The Shell and the Kernel: Renewals of Psychoanalysis*, vol. 1, trans. Nicholas T. Rand (Chicago: University of Chicago Press, 1994).

8. Of course, the wish to replace a lost child is as old as history and may even be psychologically and culturally ubiquitous. Diverse cultures have developed manifold practices designed to fulfill this wish. At the same time, the forms this wish takes are highly culture-specific, emerging in the cultural imaginary predominately among peoples who have lost children during colonization, war, genocide, periods of starvation, or epidemics. It also is a common wish in environments with high infant mortality.

9. Leon Anisfeld and Arnold D. Richards, "The Replacement Child: Variations on a Theme in Individual and Collective History and Psychoanalysis," *Psychoanalytic Study of the Child* 55 (2000): 303.

10. Anisfeld and Richards, "The Replacement Child," 304–5.

11. Vamik Volkan and Gabriele Ast, *Siblings in the Unconscious and Psychopathology: Womb Fantasies, Claustrophobias, Fear of Pregnancy, Murderous Rage, Animal Symbolism* (Madison, Wis.: International Universities Press, 1997), 7.

12. Masud Khan, "The Concept of Cumulative Trauma," *Psychoanalytic Study of the Child* 18 (1963): 286–306.

13. Anisfeld and Richards, "The Replacement Child," 55: 305.

14. Teréz Virag, "Children of the Holocaust and Their Children's Children: Working Through Current Trauma in the Psychotherapeutic Process," *Dynamic Psychotherapy* 2 (1984): 47–60.

15. Andrea Sabbadini, "The Replacement Child," *Contemporary Psychoanalysis* 24 (1988): 528–47.

16. James Herzog, "World Beyond Metaphor: Thoughts on the Transmission of Trauma," in *Generations of the Holocaust*, ed. Martin S. Bergmann and Milton E. Jucovy (New York: Basic Books, 1982), 103–19.

17. I will not discuss Miller's film in this chapter since it does not add anything more specific beyond the book version to the topic of replacement children.

18. Philippe Grimbert, *Secret*, trans. Polly McLean (London: Portobello Books, 2008), 57; subsequent references appear in the text.

19. The authorized English translation of the memoir has changed the French name Sim into Si.

20. I use the term the "crypt" in the psychological sense developed in Abraham and Torok, *The Kernel and the Shell*.

21. The framework of this chapter doesn't allow me to explore the psychic density of Grimbert's novel in full detail. I want to mention, however, that there is a rich arsenal of cryptonyms in the text that support my reading of cryptic mourning. Naming and renaming, as well as the tracking of names to find information about the destiny of Hannah and Simon, become crucial moments of displaced mourning. Shortly after Philippe's birth, for example, Maxime causes tension because he changes the family name from Grinberg to Grimbert. "Grinberg will be washed clean of its 'n' and 'g', those two letters that had become harbingers of death" (Grimbert, *Secret*, 130). Or: "An 'm' for an 'n', a 't' for a 'g'; two tiny changes. But of course M for mute hid the N of Nazism, while G for ghosts vanished under taciturn T" (9). Grimbert, if fact, links these cryptonymic renamings to the transgenerational transmission of trauma: "The destructive mission undertaken by killers a few years before my birth thus continued underground, spreading secrets and silences, cultivating shame, mutilating names and engendering lies. In defeat, the persecutor continued to triumph" (8). Another example is the name of Laval, who had sent Simon to his death and whom Philippe tracks through his daughter's dog cemetery. When, in his baccalaureate oral exam, he draws a card stating his topic, it is the name Laval. He freezes and can only stammer a sentence on collaboration. He fails the exam and needs to

repeat the class. This is yet another instance in which "the persecutor continued to triumph" (139,150). There is also a dense play of repetitions, substitutions, and "echoes" at work over and above the dynamic of the replacement child. In the chapter, I analyze the role of the dog Echo who, in many ways, becomes the replacement dog for Si and, as such, a substitute for Simon in Maxime's unconscious. This becomes evident in his displaced guilt when he takes responsibility for Echo's death. Finally, the father repeats the psychological dynamic of the sacrifice of Hannah and Simon as he takes Tania with him when he commits suicide by throwing himself from the balcony (152).

22. See Alexander Mitscherlich and Margarete Mitscherlich, *The Inability to Mourn: Principles of Collective Behavior*, trans. Beverley R. Placzek (New York: Grove Press, 1975).

23. Jacques Derrida, *Archive Fever: A Freudian Impression*, trans. Eric Prenowitz (Chicago: University of Chicago Press, 1998), 2–3.

24. Ibid., 11.

25. Ibid., 15.

26. Ibid., 92.

27. See Witi Ihimaera, *Whale Rider* (New York: Harcourt, 1987).

28. Patricia Grace, *Baby No-Eyes* (Honolulu: University of Hawaii Press, 1998), 19; subsequent references appear in the text.

29. Interestingly, this work empirically confirms ideas Paracelsus propagated as early as the sixteenth century. See Alessandra Piontelli, *From Fetus to Child: An Observational and Psychoanalytic Study* (London: Routledge, 1992), 1–25.

30. Piontelli, *From Fetus to Child*, 108–80.

31. Sigmund Freud, *Mourning and Melancholia*, in *The Standard Edition of the Complete Psychological Works of Sigmund Freud*, ed. James Strachey, 24 vols. (London: Hogarth Press, 1957), 14:249.

32. Gayatri Chakravorty Spivak, "Terror: A Speech After 9-11," *boundary 2* 31, no. 2 (2004): 93. I owe this insight and particular reading of *Mourning and Melancholia* to Travis Tanner.

33. Ruth Kluger, *Still Alive: A Holocaust Girlhood Remembered* (New York: The Feminist Press, 2001), 83.

34. Serge Leclaire, *A Child Is Being Killed: On Primary Narcissism and the Death Drive*, trans. Marie-Claude Hays (Stanford, Calif.: Stanford University Press, 1998), 8.

35. Ibid., 9–10.

36. Ibid., 11.

37. Jacques Derrida, *Memoires for Paul de Man*, trans. Cecile Lindsay, Jonathan Culler, and Eduardo Cadava (New York: Columbia University Press, 1986), 6.

38. Johan M. G. Van der Dennen, "The Politics of Peace (and War) in Preliterate Societies," http://rechten.eldoc.ub.rug.nl/FILES/root/Algemeen/overigepublicaties/2005enouder/PEACE3/PEACE3.pdf, 17.

39. Cara Ella Deloria, *Waterlily* (Lincoln: University of Nebraska Press, 1988), 89.

40. Mander, "Cry, the Beloved Country: Reflections on the Gujarat Massacre," quoted in Spivak, "Terror," 97.

41. Angela Davis, "Are Prisons Obsolete?" speech at the First Congregational Church of Oakland on July 26, 2003, transcribed by Paul Goettlich from a recording by KPFK, 15.

42. In my retelling of Amy Biehl's story, I follow the information provided by Angela Davis in the speech cited above.

43. I use the term "work of death" in the sense defined by Achille Mbembe, "Necropolitics," trans. Libby Meintjes, *Public Culture* 15 (2004): 11–40.

44. Jacques Derrida, *Specters of Marx: The State of the Debt the Work of Mourning, and the New International,* trans. Peggy Kamuf (New York: Routledge, 1994), xix.

45. Derrida, *Specters of Marx,* xix.

46. Spivak, "Terror," 93, 83.

6. Deadly Intimacy: The Politics and Psychic Life of Torture

1. Ruth Kluger, *Still Alive: A Holocaust Girlhood Remembered* (New York: The Feminist Press, 2001), 15.

2. Ibid.

3. Ibid., 17.

4. Ibid., 18.

5. Elaine Scarry, *The Body in Pain: The Making and Unmaking of the World* (Oxford: Oxford University Press, 1985), 27–59.

6. See Gilles Deleuze, *Francis Bacon: The Logic of Sensation,* trans. Daniel W. Smith (Minneapolis: University of Minnesota Press, 2003).

7. Nicolas Abraham and Maria Torok write: "Failing to feed itself on words to be exchanged with others, the mouth absorbs in fantasy all or part of a person—the genuine depository of what is now nameless" (*The Shell and the Kernel: The Renewals of Psychoanalysis,* vol. 1, trans. Nicholas T. Rand [Chicago: University of Chicago Press, 1994], 128). It is as if we choke on the object because we cannot represent it in language.

8. Sigmund Freud, "A Child Is Being Beaten," in *The Standard Edition of the Complete Psychological Works of Sigmund Freud,* ed. James Strachey, 24 vols. (London: Hogarth, 1957), 17:175–204.

9. Leonard Peltier, *Prison Writings: My Life Is My Sundance,* ed. Harvey Arden (New York: Crazy Horse Spirit and Arden Editorial Services, 1999), 155–56.

10. Adi Ophir, *The Order of Evils: Toward an Ontology of Morals,* trans. Rela Mazali and Havi Carel (New York: Zone Books, 2005), 14.

11. See Christopher Bollas, *Cracking Up: The Work of Unconscious Experience* (New York: Hill and Wang, 1995), 180–220, esp. 182.

12. However, the outsourcing of torture is an attempt to remove the contested and unacknowledged practice not only from the U.S. legal system but also from the eyes of the public, a goal that is increasingly difficult to achieve in an age of cell phone cameras and global access to the Internet. In cases where offensive torture practices become public through pictures that circulate widely around the globe, the defense usually uses a "bad-apple theory," flatly disavowing that in most cases torture is calculated, if not encouraged by those from the very top. Rhetorically and legally denied, torture thus works on the basis of a tacit awareness that, contrary to official declarations, torture is unofficially sanctioned, desired, and rewarded. This tacit sanctioning of torture includes the calculated risk that in cases of public outcry—such as after the discoveries of torture chambers in Guantánamo Bay and Abu Ghraib—some of the actual torturers will receive a sacrificial punishment. More symbolic than actual, this punishment serves to maintain the public illusion of moral law.

13. Ngũgĩ wa Thiong'o, *Detained: A Writer's Prison Diary* (Nairobi: East African Educational Publishers, 1981), 187–88.

14. See Amy Goodman, "A Question of Torture," interview by KPFK, Studio City, Calif., February 17, 2006.

15. Judith Butler, *Frames of War: When Is Life Grievable?* (London: Verso, 2009), 126.

16. CIA, *KUBARK Counterintelligence Interrogations*, "C. Techniques of Non-Coercive Interrogation of Resistant Sources, Regression," July 1963; quoted in Tom Burghardt, "Torture and Madness at Guantanamo Bay," Global Research.ca, http://www.globalresearch.ca/index.php?context=va&aid=8857.

17. Al McCoy, *A Question of Torture: CIA Interrogation from the Cold War to the War on Terror* (New York: Metropolitan Press, 2006); quoted in Goodman, "A Question of Torture."

18. Thiong'o, *Detained*, 187.

19. Ibid., 147.

20. See ibid., 183. As a form of humiliation, Ngũgĩ wa Thiong'o was—after many months of refused treatment—finally sent to a gynecologist for the treatment of his backache. Even medical care is perverted into a tool of sexually inflected humiliation.

21. Peter Matthiessen, *In the Spirit of Crazy Horse* (New York: Viking Press, 1983).

22. Peltier, *Prison Writings*, 5–6.

23. Reinhold Görling, "Folter und Wissenschaft. Was heißt kulturwissenschaftliche Forschung über Folter?" unpublished manuscript, 2007, 7; my translation.

24. Ibid., 9.

25. Sue Grand, *The Reproduction of Evil: A Clinical and Cultural Perspective* (Hillsdale, N.J.: The Analytic Press, 2000), 13.

26. Ibid., 88, 112.

27. Hector Becerra, "Deputy's Rape Victim Recalls Ordeal," *LA Times*, March 2, 2006.

28. Jean Améry, *At the Mind's Limits: Contemplations by a Survivor on Auschwitz and Its Reality*, trans. Sidney Rosenfeld and Stella P. Rosenfeld (Bloomington: Indiana University Press, 1980), 22.

29. Ibid., 25.

30. Ibid., 31.

31. Ibid., 29.

32. I use Winnicott's term "potential space" because the regression in the victim of torture induces a confusion of boundaries between self and other or what comes from inside and what comes from outside. A torturer may take advantage of this confusion and pervert this space for malignant purposes. See D. W. Winnicott, *Playing and Reality*, New York: Routledge, 2005.

33. Thiong'o, *Detained*, 140.

34. The concept is developed in E. Ann Kaplan, *Trauma Culture: The Politics of Terror and Loss in Media and Literature* (New Brunswick, N.J.: Rutgers University Press, 2005).

35. Thiong'o, *Detained*, 186.

36. McCoy, *A Question of Torture*; quoted in Goodman, "A Question of Torture."

37. See Hannah Arendt, "On Evil," in *Responsibility and Judgments* (New York: Schocken, 2003), 110.

38. Améry, *At the Mind's Limits*, 33.

39. Ibid., 34.

40. Ibid., 35.

41. Ibid., 39.

42. Achille Mbembe, "Necropolitics," trans. Libby Meintjes, *Public Culture* 15, no. 1 (2003): 11.

43. Ibid., 14.

44. Ibid., 21.

45. Ibid., 39.

46. Ibid., 40.

47. Teresa De Lauretis, "Cavani's *Night Porter*: A Woman's Film?" *Film Quarterly* 30, no. 2 (1976/1977): 35–38.

48. De Lauretis, "Cavani's *Night Porter*," 38.

49. Ruth Kluger, "Missbrauch der Erinnerung: KZ-Kitsch," in *Von hoher und niedriger Literatur* (Gottingen: Wallstein Verlag, 1996), 29–44.

50. Ariel Dorfman, *Death and the Maiden* (New York: Penguin, 1991), 74.

51. Ibid., 29.

52. Ibid., 38.

53. Marguerite Duras, *The War: A Memoir*, trans. Barbara Bray (New York: Pantheon Books, 1986), 115; subsequent references appear in the text.

54. Chivington said before the Sand Creek massacre of indigenous American children, "Nits make lice." See Ward Churchill, *A Little Matter of Genocide: Holocaust and Denial in the Americas, 1492 to the Present* (San Francisco: City Lights Books, 1997), 129–288.

55. Christopher Bollas, *The Shadow of the Object: The Psychoanalysis of the Unthought Known* (New York: Columbia University Press, 1987), 3.

56. Scarry, *The Body in Pain*, 35.

57. Among the many recent studies in this field, I want to direct the reader particularly to Yoram Yovell, "From Hysteria to Posttraumatic Stress Disorder: Psychoanalysis and the Neurobiology of Traumatic Memories," *Neuro-Psychoanalysis: An Interdisciplinary Journal for Psychoanalysis and the Neurosciences* 2, no. 2 (2000):171–81.

58. Kluger, *Still Alive*, 111.

59. Abraham and Torok, *The Shell and the Kernel*, 84.

60. Ibid., 85.

61. Ibid., 86.

62. Butler, *Frames of War*, 59.

63. See Chalmers Johnson, *Blowback: The Costs and Consequences of American Empire* (New York: Henry Holt, 2000).

64. Peter Wensierski, "Das Leid der frühen Jahre," in *Die Zeit*, February 9, 2006, http://www.zeit.de/2006/07/Heimkinder?page=all, page 6 of 13. Translation mine.

65. See Michael Wessells, *Child Soldiers: From Violence to Protection* (Cambridge, Mass.: Harvard University Press, 2007), cover copy.

66. Ishmael Beah, *A Long Way Gone: Memoirs of a Child Soldier* (New York: Farrar, Straus and Giroux, 2007), 19.

67. Freud's concept of *Nachträglichkeit*, translated commonly as "belatedness," refers to this deferred action or traumatic response.

68. Beah, *A Long Way Gone*, 24.

69. Ibid., 103.

70. Ibid., 70.

71. Ibid., 55.

72. See Wessels, *Child Soldiers*.

73. Peltier, *Prison Writings*, 33.

Bibliography

Abraham, Nicolas, and Maria Torok. *The Shell and the Kernel: Renewals of Psychoanalysis.* Vol. 1. Trans. Nicholas T. Rand. Chicago: University of Chicago Press, 1994.

Adorno, Theodor, Else Frenkel-Brunswik, Daniel Levinson, and Nevitt Sanford. *The Authoritarian Personality.* New York: Harper and Row, 1950.

Agamben, Giorgio. *Homo Sacer: Sovereign Power and Bare Life.* Trans. Daniel Heller-Roazen. Stanford: Stanford University Press, 1998.

Ahmed, Sara. *The Cultural Politics of Emotion.* New York: Routledge, 2004.

Améry, Jean. *At the Mind's Limits: Contemplations by a Survivor on Auschwitz and Its Reality.* Trans. Sidney Rosenfeld and Stella P. Rosenfeld. Bloomington: Indiana University Press, 1980.

Anisfeld, Leon, and Arnold D. Richards. "The Replacement Child: Variations on a Theme in History and Psychoanalysis." *Psychoanalytic Study of the Child* 55 (2000): 301–18.

Appadurai, Arjun. *Modernity at Large: Cultural Dimensions of Globalization.* Minneapolis: University of Minnesota Press, 1996.

Arendt, Hannah. *Responsibility and Judgment.* New York: Schocken, 2003.

——. *The Origins of Totalitarianism.* New York: Harcourt, 1968.

Assmann, Aleida. *Erinnerungsräume: Formen und Wandlungen des kulturellen Gedächtnisses,* Munich: Beck, 1999.

Assmann, Aleida. *Der Lange Schatten der Vergangenheit: Erinnerungskultur und Geschichtspolitik.* Munich: Beck 2006.

Assmann, Aleida, and Ute Frevert. *Geschichtsvergessenheit — Geschichtsversessenheit: Vom Umgang mit der Deutschen Vergangenheit Nach 1945.* Stuttgart: Deutsche Verlags-Anstalt 1999.

Assmann, Jan. "Kollektives Gedächtnis und kulturelle Identität." In *Kultur und Gedächtnis,* ed. Jan Assmann and Tonio Hoelscher, 9–19. Frankfurt: Suhrkamp, 1988.

Bammer, Angelika. *Displacements: Cultural Identities in Question.* Bloomington: Indiana University Press, 1994.

Bar-On, Dan. *Legacy of Silence: Encounters with Children of the Third Reich.* Cambridge, Mass.: Harvard University, 1989.

——. *Tell Your Life-Story: Creating Dialogue Among Jews and Germans, Israelis and Palestinians.* Budapest: Central European University Press, 2006.

Beah, Ishmael. *A Long Way Gone: Memoirs of a Child Soldier.* New York: Farrar, Straus and Giroux, 2007.

Beckett, Samuel. "The End." In *Samuel Beckett: The Complete Short Prose,* ed. S. E. Gontarski, 78–99. New York: Grove Press, 1995.

——. *For to End Yet Again and Other Fizzles.* London: John Calder, 1976.

——. *The Lost Ones.* New York: Grove Press, 1972.

Berlant, Lauren. "The Face of America and the State of Emergency." In *Popular Culture: A Reader,* ed. Raiford Guins and Omayra Zaragoza Cruz, 309–23. London: Sage Press, 2005.

Bion, Wilfred. "Attacks on Linking." 1967. In *Second Thoughts: Selected Papers on Psychoanalysis,* 93–109. London: Karnac, 2005.

Bollas, Christopher. *Cracking Up: The Work of Unconscious Experience.* New York: Hill and Wang, 1995.

——. *The Shadow of the Object: Psychoanalysis of the Unthought Known.* New York: Columbia University Press, 1987.

Brown, Dee. *Bury My Heart at Wounded Knee: An Indian History of the American West.* New York: Holt, Rinehart and Winston, 1970.

Brown, Wendy. *States of Injury: Power and Freedom in Late Modernity.* Princeton, N.J.: Princeton University Press, 1995.

Burghardt, Tom. "Torture and Madness at Guantanamo Bay." GlobalResearch. ca. http://www.globalresearch.ca/index.php?context=va&aid=8857.

Butler, Judith. *Frames of War: When Is Life Grievable?* London: Verso Press, 2009.

——. *Precarious Life: The Powers of Mourning and Violence.* London: Verso, 2004.

Caruth, Cathy. *Unclaimed Experience: Trauma, Narrative, and History.* Baltimore, Md.: Johns Hopkins University Press, 1996.

Césaire, Aimé. *Discourse on Colonialism.* Trans. Joan Pinkham. New York: Monthly Review Press, 2000.

Churchill, Ward. *A Little Matter of Genocide: Holocaust and Denial in the Americas, 1492 to the Present*. San Francisco: City Lights Books, 1997.

Das, Veena. *Life and Words: Violence and the Descent Into the Ordinary*. Berkeley: University of California Press, 2007.

Davis, Angela. "Are Prisons Obsolete?" Speech at the First Congregational Church of Oakland on July 26, 2003. Transcribed by Paul Goettlich from a recording by KPFK, Studio City, Calif.

De Lauretis, Teresa. "Cavani's *Night Porter*: A Woman's Film?" *Film Quarterly* 30, no. 2 (1976–1977): 35–38.

Deleuze, Gilles. *Francis Bacon: The Logic of Sensation*. Trans. Daniel W. Smith. Minneapolis: University of Minnesota Press, 2003.

Deloria, Ella Cara. *Waterlily*. Lincoln: University of Nebraska Press, 1988.

Dennen, Johan M. G. van der. "The Politics of Peace (and War) in Preliterate Societies." http://rechten.eldoc.ub.rug.nl/FILES/departments/Algemeen/overigepublicaties/2005enouder/PEACE3/PEACE3.pdf.

Derrida, Jacques. *Archive Fever: A Freudian Impression*. Trans. Eric Prenowitz. Chicago: The University of Chicago Press, 1996.

——. "Fors." Trans. Barbara Johnson. *Georgia Review* 31 (1977): 64–116.

——. *Memoires for Paul de Man*. Trans. Cecile Lindsay, Jonathan Culler, and Eduardo Cadava. New York: Columbia University Press, 1986.

——. *Of Grammatology*. Trans. Gayatri Chakravorty Spivak. Baltimore, Md.: Johns Hopkins University Press, 1976.

——. *Specters of Marx: The State of the Debt, the Work of Mourning, and the New International*. Trans. Peggy Kamuf. New York: Routledge, 1994.

Diner, Dan. "Negative Symbiosis: Germans and Jews After Auschwitz." In *Reworking the Past: Hitler, the Holocaust and the Historian's Debate*, ed. Peter Baldwin, 423–30. Boston: Beacon Press, 1990.

Dorfman, Ariel. *Death and the Maiden*. New York: Penguin, 1991.

Duba, Ursula. *Tales from the Child of the Enemy*. New York: Penguin, 1995.

Duras, Marguerite. *La Douleur*. Paris: P.O.L., 1985.

——. *The War: A Memoir*. Trans. Barbara Bray. New York: Pantheon Books, 1986.

Fanon, Frantz. *Black Skin, White Masks*. Trans. Charles Lam Markmann. New York: Grove Press, 1967.

——. *The Wretched of the Earth*. New York: Grove Press, 2004.

Felman, Shoshana, *The Juridical Unconscious: Trials and Traumas in the Twentieth Century*. Cambridge, Mass.: Harvard University Press, 2002.

Felman, Shoshana, and Dori Laub. *Testimony: Crises of Witnessing in Literature, Psychoanalysis, and History*. New York: Routledge Press, 1992.

Fischer, Michael M. J. "Ethnicity and the Arts of Memory." In *Writing Culture: The Poetics and Politics of Ethnography*, ed. James Clifford and George E. Marcus, 194–223. Berkeley: University of California Press, 1986.

Fischer, Michael M. J. "Ethnicity as Text and Model," In *Anthropology as Cutural Critique: An Experimental Moment in the Human Sciences*, ed. George E. Marcus and Michael M. J. Fischer, 173–77. Chicago: University of Chicago Press, 1986.

Freud, Sigmund. "A Child Is Being Beaten." In *The Standard Edition of the Complete Psychological Works of Sigmund Freud*, ed. James Strachey, 17:175–204. London: Hogarth, 1953–1974.

——. "From the History of an Infantile Neurosis." In *The Standard Edition of the Complete Psychological Works of Sigmund Freud*, ed. James Strachey, 17:7–12. London: Hogarth, 1953–1974.

——. "Mourning and Melancholia." In *The Standard Edition of the Complete Psychological Works of Sigmund Freud*, ed. James Strachey, 14:237–60. London: Hogarth, 1953–1974.

——. "Screen Memories." In *The Standard Edition of the Complete Psychological Works of Sigmund Freud*, ed. James Strachey, 3:301–20. London: Hogarth, 1953–1974.

Fuss, Diana. *Identification Papers*. New York: Routledge, 1995.

Ginsburg, Ruth. "Ida Fink's Scraps and Traces: Forms of Space and the Chronotrope of Trauma Narratives." *Partial Answers: Journal of Literature and the History of Ideas* 4, no. 2 (June 2006): 205–18.

Görling, Reinhold. "Folter und Wissenschaft. Was heißt kulturwissenschaftliche Forschung über Folter?" Unpublished manuscript. 12 pages. 2007.

Goodman, Amy. "A Question of Torture." Interview by KPFK, Studio City, Calif. February 17, 2006.

Grace, Patricia. *Baby No-Eyes*. Honolulu: University of Hawaii Press, 1998.

Grand, Sue. *The Reproduction of Evil*. Hillsdale, N.J.: The Analytic Press, 2000.

Grimbert, Philippe. *Secret*. Trans. Polly McLean. London: Portobello Books, 2007.

Habermas, Jürgen. "Concerning the Public Use of History." Trans. Jeremy Leaman. *New German Critique*, no. 44 (1988): 40–50.

Hartman, Geoffrey. "The Longest Shadow." In *Testimony: Contemporary Writers Make the Holocaust Personal*, ed. David Rosenberg, 425–39. New York: Times Books, 1989.

Herzog, James. "World Beyond Metaphor: Thoughts on the Transmission of Trauma." In *Generations of the Holocaust*, ed. M. S. Bergmann and M. E. Jucovy, 103–19. New York: Basic Books, 1982.

Heyen, William. *Crazy Horse in Stillness: Poems*. New York: BOA Editions, 1996.

Hirsch, Marianne. *Family Frames: Photography, Narrative, and Postmemory*. Cambridge, Mass.: Harvard University Press, 1997.

——. "Surviving Images: Holocaust Photographs and the Work of Postmemory." *The Yale Journal of Criticism* 14, no. 1 (2001): 5–37.

Hungerford, Amy. *The Holocaust of Texts: Genocide, Literature, and Personi-fication.* Chicago: University of Chicago Press, 2003.

Huyssen, Andreas. "Transnationale Verwertungen von Holocaust und Kolo-nialismus." Unpublished manuscript.

——. *Twilight Memories: Marking Time in a Culture of Amnesia.* New York: Routledge, 1995.

Jacobus, Mary. "Pain in the Patient's Knee." *Diacritics* 28, no. 4 (1998): 99–110.

Jaspers, Karl. *The Question of German Guilt.* Trans. E. B. Ashton. New York: Dial Press, 1947.

Johnson, Chalmers. *Blowback: The Costs and Consequences of American Em-pire.* New York: Henry Holt, 2000.

Kaplan, E. Ann. *Trauma Culture: The Politics of Terror and Loss in Media and Literature.* New Brunswick, N.J.: Rutgers University Press, 2005.

Khan, Masud. "The Concept of Cumulative Trauma," *Psychoanalytic Study of the Child* 18 (1963): 286–306.

Klein, Melanie. "A Contribution to the Psychogenesis of Manic-Depressive States." 1935. In *Love, Guilt, and Reparation and Other Works, 1921–1945,* 262–89. New York: Delacorte Press, 1975.

Kluger, Ruth. "Mißbrauch der Erinnerung: KZ-Kitsch." In *Von hoher und niedriger Literatur,* 29–44. Gottingen: Wallstein Verlag, 1996.

——. *Still Alive: A Holocaust Girlhood Remembered.* New York: The Feminist Press, 2001.

LaCapra, Dominick. "Representing the Holocaust: Reflections on the Histori-ans' Debate." In *Probing the Limits of Representation: Nazism and the "Fi-nal Solution,"* ed. Saul Friedlander, 108–27. Cambridge, Mass.: Harvard University Press, 1992.

——. *Writing History, Writing Trauma.* Baltimore, Md.: Johns Hopkins Uni-versity Press, 2001.

Lachmann, Renate. *Memory and Literature: Intertextuality in Russian Modern-ism.* Trans. Anthony Wall. Minneapolis: University of Minnesota Press, 1997.

Leclaire, Serge. *A Child Is Being Killed: On Primary Narcissism and the Death Drive.* Trans. Marie-Claude Hays. Stanford, Calif.: Stanford University Press, 1998.

Levine, Michael G. "Necessary Stains: Spiegelman's *Maus* and the Bleeding of History." *American Imago* 59, no. 3 (2002): 317–41.

Leys, Ruth. *Trauma: A Genealogy.* Chicago: University of Chicago Press, 2000.

Lorenzer, Alfred. *Sprachzerstörung und Rekonstruktion.* Frankfurt: Suhrkamp, 1973.

Mandel, Naomi. *Against the Unspeakable: Complicity, the Holocaust, and Slav-ery in America.* Charlottesville: University of Virginia Press, 2006.

Matthiessen, Peter. *In the Spirit of Crazy Horse.* New York: Viking Press, 1983.

Mbembe, Achille. "Necropolitics." Trans. Libby Meintjes. *Public Culture* 15, no. 1 (2003): 11–40.

——. *On the Postcolony.* Trans. A. M. Berrett, Janet Roitman, Murray Last, and Steven Rendall. Berkeley: University of California Press, 2001.

McCoy, Al. *A Question of Torture: CIA Interrogation from the Cold War to the War on Terror.* New York: Metropolitan Press, 2006.

McGlothlin, Erin. *Second Generation Holocaust Literature: Legacies of Survival and Perpetration.* Rochester, N.Y.: Camden House, 2006.

Meister, Robert. "After Evil." Unpublished manuscript.

Miller, J. Hillis. *The Ethics of Reading: Kant, De Man, Eliot, Trollope, James, Benjamin.* New York: Columbia University Press, 1989.

——. *Versions of Pygmalion.* Cambridge, Mass.: Harvard University Press, 1990.

Mitscherlisch, Alexander, and Margarete Mitscherlich. *The Inability to Mourn: Principles of Collective Behavior.* Trans. Beverley R. Placzek. New York: Grove Press, 1975.

Momaday, N. Scott. *The Names: A Memoir.* Tucson: University of Arizona Press, 1976.

Morrison, Toni. *Beloved.* New York: Knopf, 1987.

Motte, Warren. "Reading Georges Perec." *Context: A Forum for Literary Arts and Culture,* online edition no. 11 (2002): http://www.centerforbookculture .org/context/no11/Motte.html.

Nandy, Ashis. *The Intimate Enemy: Loss and Recovery of Self Under Colonialism.* Oxford: Oxford University Press, 1983.

Novick, Peter. *The Holocaust in American Life.* Boston: Houghton Mifflin, 1999.

Obama, Barack. *Dreams of My Father: A Story of Race and Inheritance.* New York: Random House, 2004.

——. "A More Perfect Union." http://my.barackobama.com/page/content/ hisownwords.

Oliver, Kelly. *The Colonization of Psychic Space: A Psychoanalytic Social Theory of Oppression.* Minneapolis: University of Minnesota Press, 2004.

Ophir, Adi. *The Order of Evils: Toward an Ontology of Morals.* Trans. Rela Mazali and Havi Carel. New York: Zone Books, 2005.

Ortiz, Simon J. *from Sand Creek.* Tucson: University of Arizona Press, 1981.

Pearce, Roy Harvey. *Savagism and Civilization.* Berkeley: University of California Press, 1953.

Peltier, Leonard. *Prison Writings: My Life Is My Sundance.* Ed. Harvey Arden. New York: Crazy Horse Spirit and Arden Editorial Services, 1999.

Perec, Georges. *La Disparation.* Paris: Gallimard, 1989.

——. *Les Revenentes.* Paris: Julliard, 1997.

——. *W, or The Memory of Childhood.* Trans. David Bellos. Boston: David R. Godine, 1988.

Piontelli, Alessandra. *From Fetus to Child: An Observational and Psychoanalytic Study*. London: Routledge, 1992.

Rand, Nicholas T. "Introduction." In Abraham and Torok, *The Shell and the Kernel: Renewals of Psychoanalysis, Vol. 1*. Chicago: University of Chicago Press, 1994.

Randall, Kate. "US Doctors Tied to Torture at Guantanamo, Abu Ghraib." World Socialist Web Site, January 13, 2005, http://www.wsws.org/articles/2005/jan2005/tort-j13.shtml.

Reichel, Sabine. *What Did You Do in the War, Daddy?* New York: Hill and Wang, 1989.

Rimmon-Kenan, Shlomith. *Narrative Fiction: Contemporary Poetics*. London: Routledge, 2002.

Rodriguez, Gregory. "Ich bin ein Obaman." *LA Times*, July 28, 2008.

Rothberg, Michael. *Multidirectional Memory: Remembering the Holocaust in the Age of Decolonization*. Stanford, Calif.: Stanford University Press, 2009.

Rushdy, Ashraf H. *Remembering Generations: Race and Family in Contemporary African American Fiction*. Chapel Hill: University of North Carolina Press, 2001.

Said, Edward. "Secular Criticism." In *The World, the Text, and the Critic*, 1–30. Cambridge, Mass.: Harvard University Press, 1983.

Sabbadini, Andrea. "The Replacement Child." *Contemporary Psychoanalysis* 24 (1998): 528–47.

Santner, Eric L. "History Beyond the Pleasure Principle." In *Probing the Limits of Representation: Nazism and the "Final Solution,"* ed. Saul Friedlander. Cambridge: Harvard University Press, 1992.

——. *Stranded Objects: Mourning, Memory, and Film in Postwar Germany*. Ithaca, N.Y.: Cornell University Press, 1990.

Sartre, Jean-Paul. "Flaubert." In *Flaubert: A Collection of Critical Essays*, ed. Raymond Giraud, 13–20. Englewood Cliffs, N.J.: Prentice Hall Press, 1964.

Scarry, Elaine. *The Body in Pain: The Making and Unmaking of the World*. Oxford: Oxford University Press, 1985.

Scheper-Hughes, Nancy, and Carolyn Sargent, eds. *Small Wars: The Cultural Politics of Childhood*. Berkeley: University of California Press, 1998.

Schwab, Gabriele. "Cultural Texts and Endopsychic Scripts." *SubStance* 30, nos. 1 and 2 (2001): 160–76.

——. *The Mirror and the Killer-Queen: Otherness in Literary Language*. Bloomington: Indiana University Press, 1996.

——. *Subjects Without Selves: Transitional Texts in Modern Fiction*. Cambridge, Mass.: Harvard University Press, 1994.

——. "Words and Moods: The Transference of Literary Knowledge." *SubStance* 26, no. 3 (1997): 107–27.

Sebald, W. G. *Austerlitz*. Trans. Anthea Bell. New York: The Modern Library, 2001.

Seltzer, Mark. "Wound Culture: Trauma in the Pathological Public Sphere." *October* 80 (Spring 1997): 3–26.

Silko, Leslie Marmon. *Yellow Woman and a Beauty of the Spirit: Essays on Native American Life Today*. New York: Simon & Schuster, 1996.

Spiegelman, Art. *Maus II: A Survivor's Tale: And Here My Troubles Began*. New York: Pantheon Books, 1991.

Spivak, Gayatri Chakravorty. "Terror: A Speech After 9–11." *boundary* 2 31, no. 2 (2004): 81–111.

Thiong'o, Ngũgĩ wa. *Decolonizing the Mind: The Politics of Language in African Literature*. Oxford: James Currey Press, 1986.

——. *Detained: A Writer's Prison Diary*. Nairobi: East African Educational Publishers, 1981.

Virag, Teréz. "Children of the Holocaust and Their Children's Children: Working Through Current Trauma in the Psychotherapeutic Process." *Dynamic Psychotherapy* 2, no.1 (1984): 47–61.

Volkan, Vamik. "Traumatized Societies and Psychological Care: Expanding the Concept of Preventative Medicine." *Mind and Human Interaction* 11, no. 3 (2000): 177–94.

Volkan, Vamik, and Gabriele Ast, *Siblings in the Unconscious and Psychopathology: Womb Fantasies, Claustrophobias, Fear of Pregnancy, Murderous Rage, Animal Symbolism*. Madison, Wis.: International Universities Press, 1997.

Weigel, Sigrid. "Generation as a Symbolic Form: On the Genealogical Discourse of Memory Since 1945." *The Germanic Review* 77, no. 4 (2002): 264–77.

Weissman, Gary. *Fantasies of Witnessing: Postwar Efforts to Experience the Holocaust*. Ithaca, N.Y.: Cornell University Press, 2004.

Wensierski, Peter. "Das Leid der fruehen Jahre." In *Die Zeit*, February 9, 2006, http://www.zeit.de/2006/07/Heimkinder?page=all.

Wessells, Michael. *Child Soldiers: From Violence to Protection*. Cambridge, Mass.: Harvard University Press, 2007.

Yovell, Yoram. "From Hysteria to Posttraumatic Stress Disorder: Psychoanalysis and the Neurobiology of Traumatic Memories." *Neuro-Psychoanalysis: An Interdisciplinary Journal for Psychoanalysis and the Neurosciences* 2, no. 2 (2000): 171–81.

CPSIA information can be obtained at www.ICGtesting.com
Printed in the USA
LVOW04s0836120615

442237LV00010B/34/P